AN ABZ OF LOVE

NOTE

Eventual readers should note that this book has been written in particular for couples in their thirties and forties.

There will always be those who claim it was written for pornographical reasons.

But we feel it only fair to warn those who are looking for pornography that they will be disappointed.

Inge & Sten Hegeler

INGE & STEN HEGELER

AN ABZ OF LOVE

DRAWINGS BY EILER KRAG

TRANSLATED BY DAVID HOHNEN

*The sign of a good marital relationship is
that it can always get better — and it
goes on getting better.*

NEVILLE SPEARMAN LTD
1963

First published in Great Britain by
Neville Spearman Ltd
112 Whitfield Street London W1

Printed in Great Britain by D. R. Hillman and Sons Ltd Frome Somerset

FOREWORD

This is *not* a text-book for beginners — not an ABC. It does not deal with every aspect of love life, nor all about love from A to Z. We have merely described, in lexical form, a few aspects of sexual relationships seen from a slightly different standpoint.

Our book is meant as a personal and subjective supplement to the many outstanding scientific books on sexual enlightenment already in existence. If anybody were to read this book *only*, he — or she — would obtain a confusing impression of love between human beings. But all who are capable of reading at all already possess certain knowledge; we have, moreover, addressed ourselves in particular to people with some experience.

Naturally, we possess no infallible recipe for human happiness. We still know far too little about sexual relations, and so we are by no means able to provide a complete prescription for a happy sex life. But we do believe we have a few of the ingredients: some of them well-known, others perhaps less so.

We have tried to be straightforward and frank. This will possibly shock and offend some people. Our objective has primarily been to write a book for couples in their thirties or forties and thus also indirectly — through educationalists and parents — for the young and those who have embarked upon, or who are about to embark upon, a relationship which by rights should provide the greatest human rewards for both partners; a relationship which furthermore should preferably last as long as possible.

Laymen as well as professional people have displayed a friendly and positive interest in the preparation of the MS., and we thank them all accordingly. But as the responsibility for the book is ours alone, we feel it would be wrong to abuse anybody's authority by quoting names.

Copenhagen, September 1962

This volume is a translation of the original Danish edition. No attempt has been made to adapt the text to English or American conditions. The object has been to give an impression of sexual relationships in Scandinavia and the many problems attached thereto.

AUTHORS' NOTE

If we look through a piece of glass, irregularities and impurities may distort and discolour the impression of what we see. If we regard something through a convex lens, it appears to be upside down. But if we place a concave lens in front of the convex lens, we correct the distortion in the convex lens and things no longer appear topsy-turvy. Each one of us regards the world through his own lens, his own glasses. The effect of these glasses is that, even though we may be looking at the same thing, not all of us actually see the same thing. The lenses are ground by each individual's upbringing, disposition and other factors.

Some wear dark glasses. To others, everything looks permanently rosy. Some see nothing but foolishness, and others are encouraged by small signs of kindness.

Collectively, moreover, we all look through a common window, one that similarly distorts and discolours reality. Every society, every civilization, has made its own window. The window through which the Chinese look reveals a completely different world from what we see through our own common window. Neither of us is right.

The window also changes from time to time — our great-grandparents looked through a completely different one — for social and economical factors constantly change it in the course of an interplay at which we can only guess.

Artists and scientists strive to show us new aspects of life. This can be done in various ways.

The painter, by accentuating certain colours, can stress something which the window's discolouring property has made it difficult for us to catch sight of.

Scientists try to improve the quality of the glass so that the world we see can be a more truthful one.

This book is neither art nor science — even though it borrows ingredients from both. It is more by way of being an extra piece of glass through which we can regard a part of life. One can slip it in between one's own glasses and the window.

It is a piece of glass we have found and polished up a bit. We have looked through it and thought the world looked a bit more human. Perhaps some will think the same as we do.

Quite a lot of people have glanced over our shoulders while we were working on it. They have let us know whenever they saw something different through their glasses to that which we saw through ours. We have learned accordingly. We present this piece of glass in the full realization that not all people's glasses are the same.

i. & s.h.

A

Abdominal diseases: See Gynaecological Examination.

Abnormal: Something that is unlike what we are used to, something that departs from the accepted rules, i.e. deviates from the norm ·. If a man kisses all the pretty girls he meets we would be inclined to call him abnormal — not because he would like to do so (for there are many of us who would) but because he gives way to his desire despite the accepted rule that says this is not done.

(See Personality, Perversities, Governess, Psychopathy). *s.h.*

Abortion: Normally a pregnancy lasts 9 months + 1 week, but the child may be born prematurely and yet still thrive. This may happen right up to approx. 8 weeks before the expected date of birth. A child "born" during the course of the first 20 to 25 weeks is still insufficiently developed and will not live. Giving birth much too early in this way is called having an abortion.

An abortion may be the result of the mother falling ill, or of her having a serious accident. Some women have difficulty in carrying a child and have an abortion almost every time they become pregnant. In some cases a doctor can help prevent this happening, but we still know too little in this field.

Most women want to have children, but sometimes they become pregnant at an unfortunate moment. It may be because they are not married, are in the midst of studies, or because they have no money. In situations like these they sometimes become desperate and try to provoke an abortion: *abortus provocatus*. This can be dangerous, and Danish women are forbidden by law to attempt to provoke an abortion by intervention.

A good deal of superstition exists in this connection.

The little white speck is a human embryo 12 days after fertilization ·. Life-size.

A great number of 'methods' are talked about amongst women, various ways of producing an abortion. Many of them, such as hopping up and down, going for long walks and drinking hot toddies are naturally fairly harmless, but probably not much use either. In cases where now and again menstruation · none the less occurs, it is quite likely that it would have come anyway, i.e. without these exercises. Some of the methods recommended may result in poisonings that may prove really dangerous. Others consist in introducing some instrument or other up into the womb. This is dangerous because if performed by an unskilled person the instrument may hit the wrong place and cause a highly dangerous inflammation of the peritoneum.

Embryo, 21 days old. Life-size.

It would appear that an embryo · — or foetus · is so well protected that it is extremely difficult to dislodge by means of pills, drinks, gymnastics or the like. It demands a knowledge of anatomy, surgery and — above all — of hygiene. It is possible, for instance, to expand the neck of the womb and introduce instruments into the womb (see Sexual Organs, female). In this manner the embryo (foetus) can be loosened and the operation is usually concluded by performing a curettage ·, by means of which various remnants are removed. This is one of the methods used by doctors, and it necessitates hospitalization.

Embryo, 30 days old. Life-size.

Provoked abortion has been known for thousands of years in nearly all societies. At times it has been both legal and commonly practised, and yet at others has been punished by fines. The early Christians saw no harm in provoking an abortion, but the more an embryo gradually became endowed with an immortal soul, the greater the strictness observed.

These deliberations concerning the soul of an embryo have led the Church into adopting absurd attitudes. Thus at one point it was declared that boy embryos acquired souls long before girl embryos, and at another that it was perfectly all right to execute a woman who was pregnant and three months gone, but that a provoked abortion amounted to taking life and was therefore punishable.

Embryo, 34 days old. Life-size.

Abortus provocatus was once punishable by death in Denmark too. Nowadays greater leniency is observed — it is particularly those who assist that are punished. Recent legislature has furthermore made it possible to take into consideration particularly unfortunate factors that may justify the removal of an undesired embryo. As a rule this is arranged through *Mødrehjælpen* ·, (Mothers' Aid Centre), a maternal aid institution corresponding to the *National Council for the Unmarried Mother and Her Child* in Gt. Britain. This institution has a staff of doctors and welfare officers who are familiar with all the problems and all the possibilities of extending help that exist. It is important that application to have an abortion performed be made as early in the pregnancy as possible — preferably during the very first months — but naturally it *may* be possible to help even later.

Embryo, 1 ½ months old. Life-size.

But the law does not permit all women who want to have an abortion to have their wish fulfilled. For this reason scores of illegal abortions take place in Denmark every day — perhaps 20,000 a year. In some cases they are performed by people with inferior or no surgical training at all. People of this sort are known as quacks. Understandably enough, people are strongly warned against going to such quacks, for it can be very dangerous. On the other hand it must be admitted that it is quite astonishing in how many cases all goes well. The fact that so many thousands of abortions take place every year point to a lack of respect for the law and for the official moral code ·. It must be stressed, however, that an abortion provoked by any person not a doctor can be dangerous.

There are circles in which more than 50% of the married women have had one or several illegal abortions. It is naturally very difficult to ascertain the exact figures, but even if we make a cautious estimate we must accept the fact that more than 50% of all Danish unmarried women who become pregnant manage to have an abortion in some way or another. Such matters are seldom talked about very much, and we only hear about the cases that go wrong.

There are, however, so many physical, and in particular, psychological problems connected with these abortions that we cannot remain satisfied with the present state of affairs — which concerns us all.

If you wish to have an abortion performed it is first necessary to make sure you really are pregnant. This can be ascertained a few weeks after your menstruation period should have started. Go and see a doctor ·. (See Pregnancy tests). Thereafter apply *immediately* to *Mødrehjælpen* ·, which is there to help married as well as unmarried women. But it takes time for *Mødrehjælpen* to make its decision. An abortion is easiest to perform during the first three months — and the sooner one applies for help the easier it is.

If you are so desperate that you decide to go to a quack, bear in mind that you are running a risk. If afterwards you find yourself feeling rotten, or bleeding, or running a temperature, go and see a doctor *at once*. He is under an obligation to observe professional secrecy. In many cases it is important to have a curettage performed at a hospital.

Embryo, 2 months old. Life-size.

9

Embryo, 3 months old. Life-size.

A couple of concluding remarks obtrude at this juncture. It is so easy for us to say: "Go to *Mødrehjælpen* straight away! It's dangerous to go and see quacks!"

And yet we know that *Mødrehjælpen* only helps about 5,000 of the approximately 20,000 Danish women who have abortions every year.

Society — which means us — has a big responsibility here. We attempt to scare pregnant women away from quacks and from having illegal abortions performed — yet without being able to offer any other alternative.

All right. We have a little to offer those in the direst straits. But we fool the majority. We are furthermore pulling wool over our own eyes if we believe that this is good enough.

We give too little reliable sexual instruction ·. We keep up old taboos about sex life. We leave the young to get hold of contraceptives by themselves, because

"we don't want to start actually encouraging them to have intimate relations with one another" — as we from time to time hear irresponsible moralizers in leading positions expressing themselves.

Not until the day we have achieved ideal sexual education and ideal morals—not until then can we permit ourselves to ask: "What's the matter · with you? Why weren't you careful?"

We pat ourselves on the back, justifiably, for being able to solve the most complicated technical problems. But when it comes to fundamental human problems we are clumsier than many a so-called primitive negro tribe.   *i. & s.h.*

Foetus, 4 months old. Life-size.

Abstinence, periods of: It appears to be generally agreed that sexual intercourse · may be inadvisable during the periods just before and just after a birth.

Of course we do not know with any degree of certainty whether it is (or may be) harmful — it is merely to be on the safe side. On the other hand it is much more difficult to say exactly how long before or how long after it is inadvisable.

It depends on so many different things.

During the last couple of weeks before birth it may often be difficult for the woman, and an arduous birth may well necessitate a pause of up to six weeks after birth. In the majority of cases a woman is able to decide the matter herself. In cases of doubt it is best to consult a doctor.

It should be borne in mind that both a man and a woman can perfectly well obtain sexual satisfaction · *without* its being necessary for the man to insert his penis · into the woman's vagina · and *without* its being necessary for the man to make it difficult for the woman on account of his weight. (See Petting, Orgasm; Intercourse, sexual; and Titillation, sexual).

Many primitive peoples regard menstruation · as unclean and therefore declare sexual intercourse · to be taboo · during menstruation. This attitude is also to be met with in our society. Many women are ashamed of bleeding, and some men find it unaesthetic. It is probably connected with the fact that the details of female menstruation have always been so strongly suppressed. There are also, however, women who feel flattered that their husbands should still be interested in them "in spite of their condition". But the important point here is for each individual couple to do what it finds best. Contrary to what has been previously believed, it is neither unhealthy nor injurious.   *i. & s.h.*

Abstinence, sexual: Sexual desire is a craving felt by all people, just like hunger and thirst, and in the same way demands to be satisfied at varying intervals. We may therefore take it for granted that everybody — including those who practice sexual abstinence — obtain some form of sexual satisfaction, whether actively or passively, directly or indirectly, while asleep or awake. But a number will deny it; a few of them because it takes place to a certain extent unconsciously.

A violent artistic or other form of creative effort can partially replace and thereby reduce the sexual urge to a certain extent (see Sublimation); but any attempt at complete sexual abstinence over a long period is a rather powerful strain on a person's mind, and in the course of time very great harm has quite definitely been caused by religious and other bodies as a result of threatening and frightening young people. Increased knowledge of the nature of human sex life during recent years has reduced the amount of fanaticism displayed in these circles a good deal, but the frightening still goes on — sometimes under some form of disguise. (See also Masturbation).

Kinsey · has proved a statistical relationship between abstinence and mental disorders.

While Mohammedans have regarded it as grounds for divorce if sexual intercourse · had not taken place at least once a week, mediaeval Christianity forbade sexual intercourse on so many days of the year that in total these amounted to more than half the entire year — for forty days before Easter and forty days before Christmas, for instance. *i. & s.h.*

Adonis: Aphrodites' (Venus') lover. Term used nowadays to describe a handsome man.

Adoption: A married couple who are unable to have children themselves often take over somebody else's child and look after it as if it were their own — which is to say they adopt it.

Of course it may also take place for other reasons, for instance if a man marries a woman who already has a child. If both a child's parents die and leave the child behind, the child may be adopted by relatives.

Adoption is arranged in Denmark in particular through the offices of *Mødrehjælpen* ·. Many of the children of unmarried mothers are adopted, but there has been a decrease in the number of adoptions due to the greater degree of tolerance being shown towards unmarried mothers. There are many who would like to adopt a child, but only some 2,000 adoptions are arranged per annum in Denmark.

Adoption also naturally produces a number of practical as well as psychological problems. Unfortunately, for instance, it is common for parents not to tell children they have been adopted until they are grown up. It is understandable that adoptive parents would like to 'forget' that the child is not really their own, and that they should pretend it is their own for as long as possible. At some time, however, the child finds out — and there have been many unfortunate instances of the shock that can be produced when the discovery is made much later on. The best thing is to tell the child as soon as it is about three or four years old in conjunction with the other facts of birth (see Enlightenment, sexual). There is then the additional possibility of getting the adoptive child to enjoy the thought that it is considerably more welcome, desired and carefully 'planned' than the majority of other children. The information should be followed up to make sure it is not forgotten. If it is imparted at kindergarten age the child will take it quite as a matter of course. *i.h.*

Adultery: See Unfaithfulness.

Advertisements, matrimonial: Many people are inclined to turn up their noses at matrimonial advertisements. They should not do so. It is an excellent way of finding a life partner. Some advertisements say "advertisement serious". There are also some people who insert matrimonial advertisements for fun. In a way, matrimonial advertisements are always seriously meant, even when the advertiser declares them only to be for fun, for when it comes to the point we all want to find another person who can rescue us from our loneliness, be it in ever such a small way. If the person who inserts the advertisement is already married and has no wish to be divorced, then of course the offer of marriage is not seriously meant. But the wish to establish a permanent relationship is nearly always present. (See Homosexuals, Governess).

s.h.

Agamy: Unmarried of own free will, e.g. celibate ˙. Compare Monogamy and Bigamy.

Aggression; also restraint of: Generally speaking aggression means *attack*. An aggressor is an attacker. But the word also has a broader meaning — it implies activity and the energy to act. The term *restrained aggression* is often used in psychology, and is practically the curse of mankind, because so many people are so bound by prohibition and the need to show consideration ˙ that their aggressive spirit — in its broadest sense — becomes paralysed.

Far too many people find it difficult to get really angry when there is all reason to do so. They fail to get angry in time — which is more or less the key to the whole problem, for if an objection is made straight away it is usually more or less controlled. If one waits too long it finally comes in the form of a violent explosion, or else is deflected inwards and transformed into exaggerated love for animals, or underpants for negro children — or even in attacks resembling epileptic fits.

Pent-up aggressiveness can also result in premature ejaculation ˙ or the inability to have an erection ˙. There is no conscious connection between aggressiveness and impotence ˙, but it can naturally be used to punish or annoy somebody else. I state expressly: no conscious connection...

A woman who is angry with her husband can also punish him by not having an orgasm ˙. (See also Egoism and Consideration).

When some children display an exaggerated love for their little brothers or sisters, who (like an extra wife or an extra husband) have undeniably turned up and started to claim a share in the family's tender feelings (which previously were the prerogative of the firstborn) it may well be a form of aggressiveness that has been scolded into hiding. Because of a feeling of guilt and a bad conscience, anger is replaced by enthusiasm. But this does not mean to say that the aggressiveness has found an outlet — and pent-up aggressiveness can cleave itself a path along the strangest of channels. (See also Sexual Desire, Inhibition and Simulation).

i.h.

Aggression, inverted: The term is relatively seldom used. It is not unusual, however, for a man and a woman to decide to exchange roles — the woman assumes the active role and the man the passive. It is a game that can be called 'inverted aggression'. It is bound up with the fact that a man's pushfulness and a woman's shyness are by no means as inherent as many believe. They are

13

the roles society imposes on us — and thus it can sometimes be quite refreshing to change over. Of course there are those to whom the inverted role comes quite naturally — and those who are completely unsuited for it. Exchanging roles in this way is by no means unknown amongst animals. (See also Initiative). *s.h.*

Alcohol: The intoxicating ingredient in beer, wine and spirits. Alcohol is named as an aphrodisiac and also as a magic love potion because it is capable of breaking down self-restraint •. But a spot of self-restraint can be a useful thing to have, and alcohol is sometimes justifiably blamed for some illegitimate children and likewise for sexual crimes.

Alcohol can provide a form of substitute for a reasonably harmonious sex life.

Enjoyed in small quantitites alcohol has probably helped many a couple in situations where their self-restraint only made them shy. On the other hand too much alcohol makes most people extraordinarily unhibited and therefore permits them to nourish strong desires to indulge in various sexual pranks — but at the same time it *may* have a dilatory effect on reaching the culminating point of sexual satisfaction •, i.e. orgasm •.

Alexander VI: Pope in about the year 1500. Member of the Borgia family and especially famous on account of his having led a particularly wild life — and even managing to shock his relatively wild contemporaries. He is described as having been intelligent and strong-willed, but also ruthless and a schemer. Women found him very attractive, and he had four children with one of his mistresses, including his daughter Lucretia Borgia, with whom it was asserted that he also had sexual relationships.

Algolagnia: Pleasure resulting from pain. (See Masochism and Sadism).

Ambivalence: We all know that mothers love their children. There is nothing like maternal love. We believe that human beings can only have one feeling at a time, and we are deeply shocked and shaken if a mother calls her child 'a horrid little brat', for of course it proves she cannot love it. Of course she can. It is possible to entertain diametrically opposite feelings at one and the same time. It is possible to switch from one extreme to the other; but then they are

14

not really extremes (see Love Thermometer). A girl can be deeply and unhappily in love with a man and at the same time wish to heaven he would get himself run over — for it would solve all her problems.

A mother may feel her child to be a millstone round her neck and at the same time not want to be without it for anything in the world.

A man may love a woman passionately and at the same time hate her for the bond she thereby imposes on him.

Ambivalence is thus not indifference, but more in the nature of what is known in novels as "being the victim of conflicting emotions". Far too many people do not dare admit to both feelings in themselves because they believe that one feeling automatically cancels out the other. The result easily turns into hypocrisy. If one only permits oneself to have nice and 'acceptable' feelings, one will — against one's will — become more and more irritated.

Irritation within the sphere of sex life can result in many things — impotence ·, for instance, pseudo-frigidity (see Frigidity, pseudo) and premature ejaculation ·.

i.h.

Amenorrhoea: Non-occurence of menstruation · for one reason or another.

Amor: The Roman god of love. The Greeks called him Eros, from which the word eroticism · comes. Both peoples conceive of the god of love as a little boy with a bow-and-arrow. The French word for love is *amour*.

Amoral and **Immoral:** An *amoral* person is unconcerned with, or lacks, morals (see also Psychopathy), while the *immoral* person has morals but opposes them, or acts in defiance of them. It is a rather silly differentiation and not used very much in practice anyway.

Amulets: Objects which, according to certain religions, brought luck, protected, induced fertility or in some other way helped the wearer. A number of people still use amulets today. As a rule they like to say: "Of course I don't believe in it, but it brings me luck all the same." May be classified as one of the more harmless forms of superstition ·. (See also Phallos and Fetish).

Analcoitus, anal erotics, anal, anus: The opening at the end of the alimentary canal is called by the Latin word *anus*. That which concerns, or has to do with, the anus is called *anal*. Sexual intercourse of the form in which the penis of the male is introduced into the anus of his partner is therefore called *analcoitus*. It is practised amongst homosexual men, though not so often as generally believed.

In Britain this practice is a criminal offence carrying a maximum penalty of life imprisonment.

Anaphrodisiac: Means of reducing sexual desire ·. Hardly an attractive proposition, and no really effective method has been discovered yet — not even by surgical intervention. But it might well have its uses, especially in instances of dangerous sexual criminals ·. (See Castration).   *s.h.*

Anthropology, ethnography: Science of man — including knowledge about other peoples. There are 3,000—4,000 different peoples living in the world today, each with their own methods of upbringing, their prejudices, their moral codes, their habits; in other words, each with their own form of culture. This knowledge can teach us an extraordinary amount about what is human, natural ·, normal ·, etc., etc. We cannot experiment with people and their sex lives. Instead, therefore, we must learn from the "experiments" which have been conducted by the various societies · all over the world by the fact of their treating their members differently.

Anus: See Analcoitus.

Anxiety: A strange mechanism of the mind. In its more pronounced forms it develops into fear and even dread. Most of us have experienced varying degrees of anxiety or fear in connection with snakes, mice, spiders, open spaces, heights, authorities and so forth. They are foolish, but none the less somewhat bothersome.

Then come the more serious objects of fear from which an extraordinarily large number of people suffer dreadfully. Fear of the dark, of being alone, of being in a closed room, are all common; but this is not the place to expand on these themes.

In a way, we sometimes — unconsciously — select our own forms of anxiety. It is relatively seldom that we choose to be afraid of spiders if it so happens there are lots of them where we live. There merely has to be the risk. We talk about our fears cheerfully and by the hour. Being afraid of something is a kind of insurance policy — perhaps a bargain: "If I promise to be afraid of mice it means that in return I may do this, that, or the other thing I badly want to do but don't really dare." Naturally it is not a bargain of the conscious kind, but more in the style of the financial magnate: "If I donate 10 millions to science and the arts, then at least I have the right to be a hard and ruthless businessman." (See also Revulsion). The word 'bargain' should not be taken too literally.

Most of these forms of anxiety turn up as one grows older. The 3 or 4-year-old child starts off being afraid of the dark, later of animals or ghosts. Mice, spiders and snakes usually belong to the period of puberty — during which we do so many things our consciences (see Personality) make us uneasy about — and then along comes the diffuse kind of anxiety and selects something or other to attach itself to.

A particularly serious form of anxiety is the directly sexual fear that can make itself felt in extremely violent ways and

16

lead to large and protracted problems in life in general and sex life in particular.

The cause of our sexual anxiety is our still fairly strict moral code · which makes upbringing anti-sexual and places obstacles in the way of quiet, sensible enlightenment· on sexual questions. Any alteration in sex morals takes several generations because upbringing is of such importance to the personality · and thereby retains such a firm hold on people's minds. Psychoanalysis · may help in certain cases of sexual anxiety, but fortunately positive development often takes place in the individual who endeavours to work soberly and conscientiously with himself.

It is among women in particular that the more serious cases of sexual anxiety are encountered. It is possibly connected with the fact that women find it more difficult to derive pleasure from sexual relationships. (See Frigidity, Egoism, Consideration, Simulation).

Anxiety can cause contraction of the muscles. Experts in conscious relaxation · are often able to ease such contraction, but in such cases the anxiety itself is liberated and it may be necessary to undergo a parallel psychiatric or psycho-analytical treatment of this anxiety. The person who acknowledges his fears is in a much stronger position than the person who refuses to admit them.

Here — as in so many other respects — support from one's partner is a good as well as a necessary thing. A person who is unable to admit his sexual anxiety to his or her partner will find it much too difficult to overcome alone.   *i.h.*

Apache, apache dance: Half- or fully-fledged gangster in Paris in the old days. Also used as a name for a French pimp ·, but particularly in the connection 'apache dance', which is a brutal dance between a French pimp and his girl, often represented in ballets, etc., and often strongly romanticized. It has probably got something to do with the fact that women in our culture sometimes find a certain attraction in anything brutal, unreliable and slightly psychopathic.

Compare with the joking reference sometimes made by nice Danish ladies to their "street corner on Vesterbrogade"; in other words their innocent toying with the thought of being a prostitute ·. (See also Governess).   *i.h.*

Aphrodisiac: In the course of time many different foods, drinks, plasters and magic spells have been said to have the power to awaken sexual desires ·. These have primarily been the so-called aphrodisiacs ·, which are merely said to increase the desire (and ability) to have sexual intercourse, but also include love potions and other magical ways of making somebody fall in love with somebody else.

Agreement has not been reached concerning the extent to which spices, crushed rhinoceros horn, eggs and all the other popular things actually have any effect on sexual desires or not. Of course faith can move mountains, with the result that those who believe in pills and eggs find they work very well. The same applies to love potions. He who is convinced his beloved will become enamoured of him because of having consumed a potion or two finds himself making his subsequent approaches with greater confidence and charm — which of course increases his chances.

Alcohol · has been used for both purposes — often successfully. In such cases, however, it is not so much a question of increasing sexual desires, nor that a person has fallen in love, but rather that the various forms of restraint we normally impose upon ourselves become weakened. (See Personality). On the other hand, too much alcohol can serve to delay or prevent sexual satisfaction.   *i.h.*

The only magic formula I know is one I have mentioned under Jealousy ·. But it can only be used to win back a loved one who has cooled off — if one is lucky. (See also Frigidity, Impotence, Ejaculation).   *s.h.*

Aphrodite: The goddess of love, beauty and fertility in Greek mythology.

Appendix testis: See Epididymis.

Approach: There are many forms of sexual approach. (See also Petting). Here we are thinking especially of the husband who casually strokes his wife's cheek, breast, backside or even more intimate

"Leave me alone!"

parts and she hisses: "Can't you see I'm trying to wash up?" — "Not now! The children may be here any minute!" — "Leave me alone!" and other, even more discouraging things.

Many women probably fail to realize to how great an extent they would miss it if their husband did not let himself be tempted by them. Of course there are some women who have locked themselves up tightly with the attitude that life with a man is a cross to be borne, that husbands are tiresome animals that merely go on demanding and demanding. But even the sweetest and most affectionate women have a tendency to push their husbands away in marriage. It is all bound up with the fact that the home is her place of work and that she has no fixed working hours, but has to get the washing-up done and everything else before bedtime. It can be difficult to

relax and give oneself up to displays of tenderness. In many cases the caress is also experienced as a demand, as something which carries an obligation with it if accepted.

Perhaps Kinsey is right in believing that men are attracted at a distance, while women require a slightly more methodical, regular and tangible kind of erotic stimulation in order to let themselves be carried away — that a woman is a little more sluggish.   *i. & s.h.*

Aristophanes: Greek playwright who lived in 100 B.C. Those who are capable of reading his juicy comedies in the original express regret that we have become so prudish that it is now impossible to translate him without toning him down. His best known comedy is probably "Lysistrate", also called "The Revolt of the Women" in which all the women lock themselves in and refuse to let their men live with them until they have abolished war. Actually it is rather sad to think that denial of sexual intercourse can be used as a weapon against men. Unfortunately it is not unknown in our day either. It would be pleasanter for us girls if at least it were a double-edged sword.   *i.h.*

Art: Sex has at all times inspired artists. We have many erotic works of art from the hands of otherwise very popularly recognized and famous artists.

Apropos art: it is really quite thought-provoking to consider that the two things here in life that probably require most knowledge, experience and ability, namely the relationship between two lovers, i.e. love-life, and the relationship between parents and children, i.e. up-bringing, are both things most people reckon will 'sort themselves out some-how'.   *i.h.*

Artificial insemination: See Insemination, artificial.

Authorities: We often forget that there is no need for us to believe in authorities blindly. Whenever Professor Popkins states his opinion on the bikini, jazz, morals or youth — heavens, it seems we drink in every word every time! Despite the fact that he is actually a professor of national economy, nuclear theory, English or something else that gives him no more understanding of the subject of bikinis than Popkins the bookbinder or Popkins the manager.

We submit to some sort of notion that "seeing the professor knows so much about national economy, well.....": or that "the fellow certainly must have a sharp brain if....."

We forget each time that just because a man may be brilliant in one sphere he may be utterly hopeless in others. For that matter there are even experts, authorities and knowledgeable persons who are by no means infallible in their own fields.

If we observe the sphere of sex — which is what we are doing — the state of affairs is even worse. In many spheres of life we have to confess there is a great deal we do not know — far more than we do know. There are very few experts on the subject of sex. They know very little, and even the most scientific scientists have considerable difficulty in cleaving through the mist of antagonism, irrelevance, prejudice and hypocrisy that envelops the facts about the sex life of human beings. We, the authors of this book, are most certainly not experts in the sphere of sex life either. We have scraped together a little knowledge from theory and practice, but much more is hypothesis. Our ignorance is very great too. Let us be sceptical whenever authorities make statements about something outside their own specialized sphere. Let us be critical too, even when they appear to be on home ground.
i. & s.h.

Auto-sexuality, auto-erotism: (See Masturbation, Homosexuality, Dreams, Nocturnal Emissions).

B

Bacchus: The Roman god of wine and fertility. The Greeks called him Dionysos. At certain times he was — on account of his association with wine as well as fertility — cultivated through particularly lively feasts, which resulted in the adjective *Bacchanalian* to describe riotous parties.

Bag, scrotal: The scrotum · (see Genital Organs, male).

Ballane: A woman whose task it was in former times in Egypt and Arabia to check whether the hymen had been ruptured at weddings, especially important ones.

Barren, barrenness: See Sterility.

Bastard: If two people who are not married have a child, that child is legally known as a bastard, or illegitimate. As the word bastard has come to be used as a fairly vehement term of abuse in English nowadays, the term illegitimate is generally preferred as sounding 'nicer', being unambiguous and therefore less likely to cause offence. In Denmark (and other European countries) the word bastard is used much more straightforwardly and merely means hybrid · or cross-breed ·. In the latter sense it can also be used as a term of abuse in Danish.
s.h.

Bathing during menstruation · or pregnancy ·: Experts have been unable to agree whether this is harmful or not. Showerbaths and ordinary washing are most certainly not harmful. The discussion is concerned with having proper baths and sea- (or swimming-pool) bathing, in the course of which it is contended that water, and thus bacteria, can get into the vagina (see Genital Organs, female). But the dangers involved, particularly in former times, were very much exaggerated. Fanaticism is as a rule a bad thing, including fanatical cleanliness. It is not unthinkable that there are women whom revulsion causes to exaggerate cleanliness during this period, in other words clean and rinse so thoroughly that a risk of infection arises. (See also Irrigation). *s.h.*

Bayadere: Hindu priestess who performed as a temple dancer and practised a refined form of prostitution ·. They were recruited from the upper classes and trained by the priests.

Beards: Things found mainly on men. Like so many other things, beards also have a bearing on our sex lives. The mere fact of being able to grow a beard, as well as actually having one, is an expression of potency · and therefore a symbol of manliness.

A beard is strictly a matter of fashion: It should also be added that many men become attracted by women with a little dark shadow on their upper lip or with feminine side-whiskers. *i.h.*

Bed: The most important item of furniture in a home. Not many people realize this. It is an instrument, an arrangement or an apparatus in (or on) which to rest, make love, sleep, give birth, be ill, or die.

Mark Twain said for fun that statistics would appear to prove that it was dangerous to get into a bed — seeing that most people die there. A bed is to a very high degree a lovely thing too. The same thing applies to beds as to sexual relationships, namely that the human mind has created some pretty ingenious things. And there is no reason why we should believe that the authorized forms are the best — whether as far as beds or sexual relationships are concerned. Many beds are very badly constructed. Many people should experiment a little more with their beds as well as with their sex lives.

There are many individual wishes, and it may be hard to discover exactly what one likes best. Some like a hard bed, others a soft one. Some like a mountain of pillows to make love on, others say there is nothing like a solid bed-end. *s.h.*

Most beds can be improved. It is entirely reasonable that one should fix oneself up with, and experiment one's way towards, the form of bed both partners find most suitable to their needs. Most of us can both sleep and make love a little better if we try. *i.h.*

Bestiality: Means having sexual relations with animals.

We are familiar with the theme from countless old legends, from the Greek legend, for example, about Leda, who produced the beautiful Helen with the help of a swan. The thought that animals and human beings should be able to have children with each other has occupied many in the course of time. It is not possible. (See also Fertilization and Hybrid).

Beautiful girls have set our imaginations going when they have been carried off by gorillas in Tarzan films. They cannot have children with a gorilla either.

Kinsey · has contributed to an increased understanding of the sex life of human beings on this point too. (See also Fantasies, sexual). Jewish law originally decreed the death penalty for bestiality. This law was adopted by Christianity and extended. Intercourse between a Christian and a Jew was thus regarded as bestiality because a non-Christian was comparable to an animal. (In South Africa today it is the negroes who are the "animals" with whom it is regarded as bestiality to have intercourse). Both parties were therefore executed in the same way that both the man and the animal were execu-

Fraternization between whites and blacks in South Africa is a sexual crime on a par with bestiality.

ted in the Middle Ages. A single exception is the following story:

In 1750, Jacques Ferron was hanged for having had intercourse with a female donkey. Several respectable citizens (including the abbot of the local monastery) appeared as witnesses and declared that they had known the donkey for many years and that it had always behaved itself virtuously and as a good donkey should. The court then acquitted the donkey, declaring that it obviously must have been raped.

In Britain bestiality is a criminal offence carrying a maximum penalty of life imprisonment. *s.h.*

Betrothal: Was a formal kind of engagement in the olden days. It provided the chance of sexual relationships just like trial marriages and ordinary engagements today.

Bibliographies, erotic: In many Danish libraries there is a closed shelf. The books on this closed shelf may only be borrowed upon application to the librarian. Even more secretly guarded are the collections of so-called pornographic (see Pornography) books which public libraries in most countries keep for the pleasure of librarians and such serious scientists as concern themselves with these matters.

Erotic bibliographies are lists of the contents of these collections of forbidden books — and of books with erotic content. They may be books that have been banned by law subsequent to their publication in the normal way, but also books that have always been sold under the counter, in other words books which it has been realized beforehand could never be published through normal channels — and finally, books published in the normal way.

On the closed shelves of English libraries there are some 5,000 forbidden books.

We are always hearing from various quarters that such a large number of books of erotic content are published nowadays. This is not true at all. In the 500-year period during which books have been reasonably cheap to publish, a never-ending wave of them has appeared. A catalogue of the French erotic literature of former times contains 2,500 pages with double columns of close print. And a German catalogue is in eight volumes! These catalogues are dated 1899 and 1929 respectively. These hundreds of thousands of erotic books have never been made the subject of really systematic research. This would be able to reveal important things to us concerning our forefathers, our cultural heritage — and thus ourselves.

A small, but very interesting start has been made by the English psychologist G. R. Taylor, who in his book "Sex in History" (London: Thames & Hudson, 1953) presents some exciting theories against a background material of 250 different sources. (See also Moral Codes).

Private collections of erotic literature are far more widespread than many would imagine.   *i.h.*

Bidet: The French name for a small bath roughly the shape of a sectionized pear in which one can wash one's bottom and genitals after having been to the lavatory, before and after sexual intercourse, etc. It is a useful thing, but rare in Denmark.   *i.h.*

Bigamy, bigamist: If a married person in our society embarks upon a second marriage it is called bigamy and the person concerned a bigamist. In our society it is forbidden and punishable — according to the seriousness of the circumstances — by prison terms of up to several years. In our time it is in particular a wartime and post-war phenomenon. It is rare in Denmark, but does occur. Approximately one case is discovered per annum. In all likelihood there are more.

There are very few societies where women are permitted to have more than one husband, but they do exist — the practise is called polyandry ·. Thus the women of the Toda tribe in India as a rule marry a man's brothers as well as the man himself. Amongst the Marquesans in the Pacific it is a little different. There, it is common enough for the women to have sexual intercourse with their husband's brothers, and for men to have it with their sisters-in-law. Generally speaking the rest of the world is broader-minded and more generous towards men.

The taking of several wives and extra-marital relationships are permitted in quite a lot of societies outside our western civilization. This fact naturally kindles the imagination of many men who enjoy toying with the idea of having a harem. We must console ourselves, however, with the fact that it is expensive — and in the majority of places where polygamy is allowed it is in reality only a very small section of the upper classes that can afford to take advantage of the offer.   *s.h.*

Birgitta, Order of: A Catholic order of monks and nuns founded in the 14th century. According to its statutes, monks and nuns were obliged to live in the same monastery but without having sexual intercourse with one another. It was naturally very difficult to abide by these rules and there are thus numerous reports of transgression. (See also Castalian Order).

Birth: Here in Denmark some 70,000 children are born every year.

Approximately 9 months after fertilization · the foetus is pressed out through the woman's vagina, which expands considerably in the process. (See Genital Organs, female). A birth can be difficult and painful; it can also take place without undue difficulty.

Of recent years, Dr. Read's method "Birth Without Fear", in which the mother-to-be learns the art of relaxation from a professional instructor on the subject, has been used a good deal. It is not a completely reliable method, nor does it make a birth entirely painless, but it can help and relieve many women, particularly in view of the fact that it includes telling them beforehand exactly how a birth takes place. (See Relaxation, Gynaecologist).   *i.h.*

Birth control, means of: When a sperm cell from a man makes its way to an ovum in a woman the two fuse together; the ovum is fertilized by the sperm cell and this fertilized egg grows and in time becomes a child. (See Fertilization).

For various reasons most human beings on earth throughout the ages have wanted to decide for themselves whether the act of coition should result in fertilization or not.

Half lemons (depulped), mushrooms, crushed acacia, honey, alun, chewed grass, seaweed and many other things have been pushed up into a woman's vagina (see Genital Organs, female) in order to prevent the sperm from reaching the ovum.

It was formerly contended in fanatically religious quarters that it was an interference with nature (we might as well be told not to carry umbrellas either). But today the right to decide whether sexual intercourse shall result in birth is regarded in wide circles as a basic human liberty.

If a happy sex life is to be achieved, the fear of having unwanted children must not be too big a worry.

The Bible tells us the story of Onan, who let his seed fall upon the earth instead — and hence we have the word onanism ·, meaning masturbation, or uncompleted coition — *coitus interruptus*. This is a very common form of birth control, but must at the same time be classified as an emergency measure — for two reasons: firstly, it is not a safe method, as sperm cells may well get into the woman's vagina and womb before ejaculation · proper occurs, which means that there is a possibility of fertilization; secondly, it is distinctly unfortunate, from a mental viewpoint, if the partners withdraw from each other just at the very

moment when their emotions are most intense and common sense should no longer be required to play a part at all. It can produce a kind of insecurity that can make itself felt detrimentally throughout the act — particularly in the mind of the woman, who, after all, is the one to be literally left holding the baby if she becomes pregnant against her wish.

Another more sensible solution is the condom · This is a very thin rubber sheath which the man pulls on over his penis after pulling the foreskin well back. It fits very tightly, even round the head of the penis, but still leaves room for the sperm. A condom is much safer than *coitus interruptus* — and much more satisfying. It has, however, its disadvantages too. It may break, and many brands are quite expensive. But a really good make of condom can now be obtained at most chemists' in Denmark; it is called PLANKONDOMET and is reasonably priced. Three are sold together in a little blue-and-white cardboard carton for kr. 1.50. At the chemist's it is merely necessary to say: "I would like to have a packet of PLAN."

Those who are too shy to go to a chemist's can go to any of the many rubber goods shops in Denmark, whose assistants are accustomed to selling contraceptives all day long. In some of these shops customers can even be served, if they so choose, in a private cubicle. It is moreover possible to have contraceptives sent by giving an order by telephone or letter to any of these specialist shops — and there will be no indication on the parcel as to what it contains.

However, as we said, condoms may break, so they do not constitute the safest means of contraception. On the other hand condoms have an additional advantage, namely that they are the only contraceptive device that also affords some protection against venereal diseases. It is furthermore something used by the man. Also used is a special kind of sperm-destroying foam and sperm-destroying pills that can be pushed up into the vagina by the woman (see Genital Organs, female). These methods are not so safe, but can be used in cases where it is perhaps not vitally important to avoid a pregnancy — many young couples may be quite prepared to have a child 'some time or other' but would prefer to postpone matters a little while. (See also Vagitoria).

A brand of hormone pill has just made its appearance in Denmark under the name of *Enavid*. They are only obtainable with a doctor's prescription. The woman takes 20 pills — one a day — during the period between her menstruations and is thereby protected against becoming pregnant. Perhaps these pills are the almost ideal answer. The cost involved is some *25 kroner* a month. They have been thoroughly tested for four or five years abroad with promising results, and are at the moment being tested in Denmark too.

Then there is the Knaus Method or Rhythm Method, based on theories concerning a woman's 'safe' periods during the month. They presuppose menstruation occurring with great regularity. The Knaus Method has been explained in detail (see Menstruation chart) in spite of the degree of unreliability involved because it is a method which, if used in conjunction with other methods of birth control, can definitely diminish the likelihood of fertilization taking place. It is moreover a method which Catholics are permitted to use.

A method which has certain advantages is the use of a pessary by the woman.

A pessary is a soft rubber bowl with a solid rim. It is placed high up inside the vagina over the entrance to the womb. The rim of the pessary presses tightly against the wall of the vagina (see Genital Organs, female), thereby preventing the sperm from entering the womb and thus reaching the ovum.

A pessary has many disadvantages too, but it is generally regarded as the most reliable means of birth control. It naturally presupposes that the woman is prepared for sexual intercourse to take place — something which is often a great deal to demand in a sphere where our emotions play such a large part and are apt to take us by surprise. It furthermore necessitates a visit on the part of the woman to her doctor or other professional person in order to receive instruction in the use of the pessary. It has to be inserted in the correct manner and must be precisely the right size. But all in all there is no difficulty — any woman can learn to use a pessary.

Special ointment is rubbed into the rim of the pessary and a small amount is likewise placed inside the bowl. The woman then squats on her haunches,

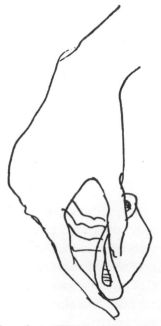

This is how the pessary should be held in order to insert. In some marriages the husband puts it in for his wife.

squeezes the pessary together between thumb and forefinger and pushes it upwards and backwards into her vagina until it disappears completely. Finally the front edge is pushed up a little further still against the pubic bone. Provided the pessary is the right size and correctly placed it cannot be felt. (See drawing).

In the morning (or 6 to 8 hours after the last coition) the pessary is removed. The vagina may be rinsed out with an irrigator before and after removal, which is done by taking hold of the pessary by the front rim between finger and thumb just behind the pubic bone and pulling it out. It should then be washed in soap and water, rinsed, dried thoroughly and powdered with talcum.

A pessary will last about a year or slightly more if looked after well and checked every now and then. This is easy to do by holding it up against the light and pulling at the rubber carefully to see whether there are any holes. Examine the rim carefully too. Oil, fat, vaseline, etc. can make the rubber brittle.

After each birth or similar major upheaval affecting the genital organs it is necessary to go and be measured for a new pessary. A pessary may be between 2 and 4 inches in diameter as it lies diagonally inside the vagina.

Where does one go in order to have measurements taken for a pessary and guidance in its use? Well, in Copenhagen, many general practitioners can be consulted. If they do not do this sort of thing themselves they will gladly recommend another doctor. Every doctor is used to being consulted about this sort of thing the whole time. There are also special clinics, and women doctors are especially ready to help.

The Danish Women Doctors' Society Club has, in conjunction with the Medical Association, chemists, midwives and several other institutions, formed a Family Planning Association, "Foreningen for Familieplanlægning". It is this association which is responsible for the above-mentioned Plan condom obtainable at most chemists ·.

The association also has a consultation clinic near Nørrebro station and the Slangerup Railway. The address is: The Clinic, Lygten 3 A, Copenhagen NV. Telephone TAGA 3705.

Anybody can apply here for help. It costs 10 *kroner* plus the price of the pessary and ointment. The clinic also has a special prescription for a particularly good and cheap ointment.

In the provinces it is a little more difficult. Only Aarhus can boast of having a special Sexual Clinic · instituted for the express purpose of providing help in sexual matters. The offices of *Mødrehjælpen* · are more concerned with women who either are or about to become mothers.

In Kolding, a sexual consultation clinic has been opened by *Dansk Kvindesamfund*.

In general, a local doctor will always help — and remember that a doctor is bound by a professional pledge of secrecy.

How old do you have to be to have a pessary?

We believe that if a girl is old enough to have children, in other words if she has begun to menstruate, then she is also old enough to have a pessary *if she wants one*. Presumably only the most sensible would apply so early anyway. But there are doctors who prefer the permission of the parents. There are also doctors who think the same way as we do and who understand that young people, even if their parents are ever so 'sensible', do not care to get the said parents mixed up in this side of their private lives. Thus a young girl may find it necessary to try several doctors.

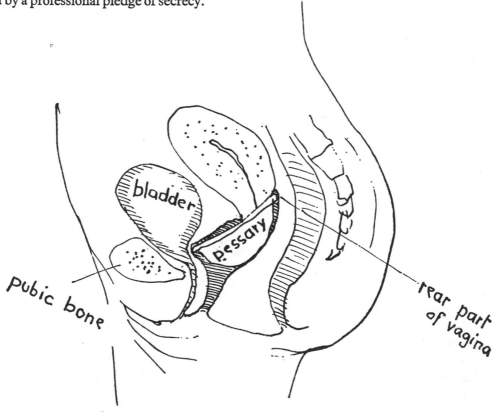

What does it cost?

All in all one should count on about 50 *kroner*. This includes having measurements taken at a doctor's, a pessary (at a chemist's . or a rubber goods shop ·) priced at about 15 *kroner*, 5 to 7 *kroner* for ointment and a check visit to the doctor afterwards. This final check visit is important so that the doctor can make sure the woman is able to insert the pessary properly by herself. Doctors report that far too many only come the first time. As guidance and instruction of this sort is not covered by national health insurance one must be prepared for the doctor to charge a normal consultation fee. In some places — at the clinic in Aarhus, for example — especially low rates are available to needy persons.

In some few instances a pessary cannot be used on account of displacement of the uterus or a similar complication. We have also known of a case of a young woman who was so hypersensitive to her pessary that she swelled up — but this was a hypersensitivity brought on for mental reasons. It transpired that the woman's mother had thoroughly scared her daughter during her childhood by urging her never to put anything up her vagina — but the hypersensitivity thus produced was none the less impractical. Anxieties of this kind are experienced by most at some time or another and may play a part in hindering or preventing the use of a pessary. A spot of sensible information in good time can prevent attitudes of this sort from arising, but it is the sort of thing that takes generations

to overcome. However, despite the practical and psychical disadvantages, there is no doubt that for the time being a pessary is the safest and most sensible form of birth control for a young couple — with the possible exception of the very initial period, when a condom is probably easier.

What actually happens at the doctor's? (See also Gynaecological examination).

After a short talk the doctor sets about taking the necessary measurements for a pessary. The woman lies on a couch with her legs bent up and spread apart and the doctor takes measurements up inside her vagina where the womb (see Genital Organs, female) begins. He then writes out a prescription which can be handed in at a chemist's, namely a prescription for a pessary and some ointment. A few days later the woman visits the doctor again, inserts her pessary so that the doctor can make sure she knows how to do it properly and that it fits as it should do. This second visit is a very useful check-up. (See also Pessary).

i. & s.h.

Birth Depression: See Wedding Depression.

Bi-sexuality: The term bi-sexuality is applied in cases where a person has male as well as female genital organs.

An old theory exists to the effect that we all go round with a certain amount of masculinity and a certain amount of feminity in us. If we look at qualities of soul and mind the theory is possibly correct. But if we use a microscope we find that every single cell in a human body is either male or female. All a man's cells are male and all a woman's cells are female. A hermaphrodite · thus only causes doubt in respect of the appearance of the genitals. It is possible to determine the sex of a hermaphrodite with certainty by observing a cell from the person concerned under a microscope.

Mental bi-sexuality is used in respect of persons who are attracted by persons of their own sex as well as those of the opposite. Figures are sometimes quoted in connection with bi-sexual and homosexual persons. For instance it is said that up to approximately $10 \, ^0/_0$ of all men are homosexual.

There is an old saying that goes: "If you haven't got what you need you must use what you've got." Normally used in ordinary, practical situations, it sounds somewhat cynical in this connection, namely as applied to sexual relationships. But it would appear to fit the bill quite well in respect of mental bi-sexuality. The experience obtained in boarding-schools, prisons, expeditions to the North Pole, in the army and in other circumstances where people have been deprived of contact with the opposite sex over protracted periods would appear to prove that once sexual needs have become sufficiently large, a person of the same sex can excite — and sexually satisfy — somebody not otherwise believed to have homosexual · tendencies. If we look at the question of mental bi-sexuality from an historical viewpoint we find it seems to have been known at all times in all societies. The best known example is probably provided by the ancient Greeks, who, though respectable husbands with wives and children, enjoyed relationships with young boys at the same time.

If we turn our attention to the animal kingdom we only need observe the male dog that cheerfully mounts any other dog it happens to meet — irrespective of sex — provided it seems willing.

If we are to derive any conclusion from this information it must be that the natural ·, ordinary thing — and likewise that most conducive to the survival of the species — is sexual relationships between persons of opposite sex. But if contact with the other sex is broken off or made difficult in some way or other, contact with the same sex is not quite so uncommon as we, thanks to the strict taboos of our civilization, have tried to make out. Generally speaking it has been found that a relationship between two persons of the same sex — one that has arisen, for instance, in a prison — would not appear to have any permanently seductive effect — the person concerned as a rule reverts to relationships with the other sex as soon as he or she is once more in a position to do so. (See also Kinsey; Homosexuality; Prostitutes, male and Heterosexuality).

s.h.

Blennorrhea: Often caused by gonorrhea (see Veneral Diseases) especially in the mucous membrane of the eyes. Was once very common amongst new-born babies, who were infected by gonorrhea in the mother during birth.

This is the reason why all babies have their eyes dripped with lunar caustic to this very day. It is specifically required by law as a preventive measure.

Boy brothels: Brothels staffed by boys prepared to place themselves at the disposal of homosexual men against payment were particularly common in the East and North Africa. They still exist.

Breast-feeding: Letting a baby suck milk from a woman's breast ·. In many cases menstruation · is delayed or prevented from taking place as long as breast-feeding is continued. Many women go on breast-feeding as long as possible with the object of avoiding becoming pregnant again; but it is wrong to assume one cannot become pregnant as long as one continues breast-feeding.

Breast, mammary glands: Women, as we all know, have breasts, and these contain mammary glands. The breasts terminate in points called nipples. Men have nipples too, but their mammary glands are not so well developed as women's. A breast consists partly of glandular tissue, partly of fat. Fat men often develop what resemble female breasts.

The mammary gland begins to develop quite early in women, in fact several years before puberty ·; but as a rule it only becomes visible between about the ages of 12 to 17.

A 'normal' breast is rather difficult to define — but let us put it this way: when a woman stands up, the fully-developed breast is not shaped like half a lemon. The upper surface is slightly concave, while the underside is convex. (See drawing). Moreover, an acute angle is formed between the underside of the breast and the skin of the actual body — in other words a fully-developed female breast hangs slightly.

Thanks to brassieres, foam rubber, corsets and other stiffeners, boys as well as men acquire some false illusions to the effect that breasts are really placed higher up, are as round as apples, enormous, and jut straight out determinedly into the air. Women themselves have even begun to believe in this myth with the result that most girls are dissatisfied with what they have got. Let us hammer one fact home with tent-pegs: breasts like these do not exist.

Many very young girls start wearing brassieres as soon as they can in order to make their breasts look bigger and higher up, etc. It is possible that a brassiere can help prevent the connective tissue from becoming strained by the weight of a too-heavy breast filled with milk — it is possible, even though it is not certain. But for a young, or even fully-developed breast it can hardly be necessary — and may even perhaps decrease the natural elasticity in the tissue.

It is furthermore a widespread superstition that breasts always hang after a birth. It is by no means always the case, but many women become somewhat fatter during and after pregnancy.

32

It is not my intention to run down brassieres. I too wish to retain some of my illusions, and there are women I certainly would not care to see without a brassiere. But I am against unnecessary brassieres. (See also Film).

Thus the female breast has come to play a large part in men's imaginations and in our sex lives. It is also named as an erogenous zone — an area that becomes sexually exciting when caressed. In the case of men it is usually true that the caressing of an otherwise forbidden area has a sexually stimulating effect — in the case of women, however, it is rarer. However, especially in the beginning, a caress anywhere, and particularly on forbidden places, is as a rule new, daring and exciting.

Many men become disappointed when they discover that some women are by no means so keen on having their breasts fondled as they had expected.

Many women dream of being able to acquire the breasts they would like by means of plastic surgery. An operation of this kind can be gone through as an out-patient i.e. there is no need to be admitted to a hospital or a clinic — and if a woman's job is not too heavy there is no reason why she should not continue working. Women who have not yet given birth can likewise have an operation of this kind performed without any detrimental effects on milk production. In Denmark the operation may cost between 1,000 and 2,000 *kroner*.

As a curiosity may be added the fact that both men and women have a so-called 'milk-line' running down either side of the stomach. It extends from the nipple down to the groin and the thigh. The breasts of most mammals develop along this line. In the case of human beings birth-marks often occur along the lines, and it is not so very rare for a woman to have more than two breasts. Henry VIII's Anne Boleyn, for instance, was said to have had too many breasts.

s.h.

Breeches: From about 1400 to 1600 it used to be the fashion in various parts of Europe for men to wear very tight breeches with a bag at the front indicating the genital organs. As we men are no less vain than women it was not uncommon to stuff a little extra something into the bag. (See also Breast, mammary glands).

s.h.

Breeding, good: What is known as 'good breeding' is, if used with discretion, a good thing. We must remember that the pattern in the carpet of human personality is woven, in a way, with a single thread. If we try too energetically to close ourselves off in a difficult, stereotyped pattern of behaviour, this tends to produce repercussions as soon as we try to find ourselves. It should be possible, as far as one's sex life is concerned, to be warm, honest, spontaneous and loving, but at the same time, within reasonable limits, an egoist. A man cannot go to bed with his wife, his fiancée, his girl friend or anybody else in a normal 'well-bred' fashion. Far too many people have cheated each other and themselves out of the loveliest experiences by

lying side by side trying to be 'well-bred' towards each other. If a woman is to spend her time thinking about being 'cultured' when lying next to a man she stands little chance of experiencing much pleasure out of it. (See also Sounds). An erotic relationship is a declaration of confidence on the part of the man towards the woman, and to an even greater degree on the part of the woman towards the man. The better this declaration of confidence is accepted, the greater the mutual pleasure to be obtained from the relationship. 'Good breeding' in the sphere of sexual relationships consists in the ability to accept one's partner's confidence in a proper, positive manner. (See also Development, Simulation, Orgasm, Sneeze).

Bridal roll: In many parts of the Far East it used to be the custom for a newly-wed couple to be given written instructions in sexual intercourse to take to bed with them on their bridal night. In Japan, for instance, it was in the form of a picture roll. In other places *pillow books* were used, these being placed under the pillow and taken out for consultation whenever doubts arose. Rather a sweet custom, really, but on the other hand it is probably preferable for both parties to be more or less informed beforehand.

i.h.

Bride, bridal gown, bridal wreath, bridal veil, 'bridal marriage': In connection with entering into a state of matrimony there have always been, in Denmark just as in the rest of the world, countless different customs and religious practices. Strictly speaking a bride is the name given to a woman from the day of her betrothal to the day of her wedding.

A bridal gown was originally white with the object of protecting the bride against evil spirits, and the bridal wreath — of myrtle — was a sign of her virginity · .

On the other hand it was also once a widespread practice for the couple to have been to bed together during the period of their betrothal — in fact it was actually the man's *right;* this was known as 'bridal marriage'. The bridal veil and the unmarried train-bearer (the bridesmaid) are likewise very old customs. The morning gift made by the bridegroom to his bride the morning after their wedding day and bridal night is likewise a relic from the days of 'marriage by purchase' as practised in olden times when the husband was obliged to recompense the bride's father for the loss of labour which his daughter represented.

Broad-mindedness: See Emancipation.

Brothel: A place employing a lot of girls with whom men can go to bed against payment. Official prostitution was abandoned in Denmark only some fifty years ago. Until then we had state-controlled, official ladies under medical supervision in official, state-authorized whorehouses, houses of ill-fame, or whatever one likes to call them.

On account of the risk of venereal diseases and criminality which often follow in the wake of illegal prostitution, it is naturally an advantage to have the sale and purchase of sexual relationships under the control of medical and state authorities. On the other hand, the notion of approving and thereby supporting an institution whereby young girls are placed at the disposal of the public with the state's blessing naturally arouses certain misgivings. Thus here in Denmark we have selected a compromise instead: prostitution is not desired, but on the other hand it cannot be dispensed with entirely either.

Other countries — Germany and Spain, for instance — have chosen to retain state-controlled prostitution and brothels. In Hamburg, Amsterdam and Brussels, for example, there are a couple of streets inhabited exclusively by such ladies. In Hamburg these streets are closed off with hoardings, and the girls recline in the windows and tempt passers-by with friendly offers.

In North Africa and South America brothels are a more established business and subject to less control. These brothels use a lot of girls, and a number of them are lured from Europe with promises of splendid jobs as mannequins, models, dancers, etc. Later on the real purpose becomes clear. It is known as 'the white slave · trade', which thus still exists, although in a heavily camouflaged form.

In the East, brothels are even more organized and varied; there are — and used to be far more — brothels specializing in boys and very young girls trained in their profession from early childhood.   *s.h.*

Buggery: See Bestiality.

36

C

Can-can: A music-hall dance popular in Paris during the Naughty Nineties. The chorus girls lifted their long, heavy skirts so high they bared their legs the whole way up. The dance aroused great indignation — and of course great interest. After all, these were the days when little boys believed women had solid bodies the whole way down to the floor — nobody was allowed to see any more than the feet of a real lady, perhaps at most an ankle if one caught a glimpse by chance. It only goes to show how everything can be made exciting — if women's faces were covered and their bodies bare from the waist down we men would doubtless think the wildest thoughts about their noses and mouths. We only need think of the veils worn by Mohammedan women.   *s.h.*

Cannibalism: The eating of human beings by human beings. It was often the victim's sexual organs that were devoured first — sometimes only — as a symbol of power, manliness, energy, aggressiveness·. Cannibalism has existed right up to our times. We are inclined to regard cannibalism as something rather revolting and repulsive· . The notion does of course come as somewhat strange. But if we civilized people in the over-cultured societies of the world had only killed those we could manage to eat, the rest of the world — i.e. the so-called primitive peoples — would possibly have felt more genuine respect for us.

Careful: "I'll be careful!" and "You must be careful!" are as a rule a man's and a woman's respective remarks to each other on the subject of birth control·.

Unfortunately being careful is not as simple as all that. Many parents have believed that when they said to their half-grown daughters: "Now then, you'll be careful, won't you?" they had done all that was necessary.

If a girl today is sensible enough to put on a pessary · before leaving home she runs the risk that her adoring boy-friend will become utterly stupefied by such forethought — in fact he may be shocked. If on the other hand the girl puts up violent opposition — the way we have decreed that nice girls should — and then finally 'gives in' — he runs the risk that she will think better of it while he is discreetly fumbling with a condom·.

It is this sort of thing — amongst others — that results in some 30,000 Danish girls becoming pregnant annually without being married to the man in question — and that at least 100,000 more women might be just as unlucky but get away with it because they do not happen to be fertile on that particular day. (See Knaus). *i. & s.h.*

Carezza: A very specialized form of intercourse. The penis · is introduced into the woman's vagina (see Sexual Organs, female) but no coital movements are undertaken and sexual satisfaction (see Orgasm) is apparently not obtained either.

The method has had and still has its supporters all over the world. They claim that this method gives them spiritual pleasure. It is not impossible (see Sublimation) but it is probably a somewhat expensive price to pay. You cannot play about with such a powerful thing as the sexual urge and get away with it. (See also Badana). *i.h.*

Casanova: 'A proper Casanova' — a term that has come to mean 'a real ladies' man'. Casanova was a Venetian who lived during the 18th century. He was first a priest — a secular abbott — later on a soldier, alchemist and adventurer. He published some frank memoirs concerning his many erotic escapades.

People were more sex-minded in those days, so this did not prevent his becoming the favourite of popes and cardinals — witty and talented as he must have been.

"A fine figure of a man," said Frederick the Great of him. In his old age he wrote industriously on all subjects from mathematical problems to poetry — apart from his autobiography.   *s.h.*

Castalian Order: An order of monks and nuns which in order to test the strength of character possessed by its members made them sleep together with no more than a crucifix between them.

Naturally enough — and fortunately — it simply did not work. The monks and the nuns 'abused' this fundamental idea — according to our source of information.

But it would be more reasonable to say the whole idea was so fantastically barbaric it is only too easy to understand why the poor creatures became completely overpowered by their sexual urges.

After all, these constitute a natural force not to be trifled with. But what a bad conscience they were given at the same time! It corresponds entirely to the terrifying propaganda of later times against masturbation ·, and the inhuman, impossible demands made — particularly from fanatically religious quarters — on young people; and older people as well. (See Birgitta Order).   *s.h.*

Castrate, castration: A boy or a man can have both testicles · removed by an operation known as castration. Those so operated are known as castrates.

There can be various reasons for castration. In the East it was necessary to have men to guard the harems ·, and as setting a fox to look after geese is seldom desirable it was felt essential to make sure these men did not perhaps take too good care of the women of the harem. Castrated men known as eunuchs were therefore used.

Until about 1825, little Italian boys used to be taken to the local barber by their mothers in order to be castrated and thereafter sold to the Turks, who paid a good price. Other advantages of castration were also discovered in Italy, for instance that the voices of castrated boys did not break upon reaching puberty and therefore stayed high and beautiful.

We are even familiar with cases of castration here in Denmark at the present day, namely in the case of men guilty of some sexual crime · or other. In a number of instances their testicles have been removed in order to destroy their sexual urges. This operation, however, is becoming rarer as it has been discovered that sexual urges by no means always disappear along with the testicles. Many scientific investigations have been published on the subject.

We men attach a great deal of importance to being sexually potent ·. A removal of the testicles and at the same time the information that all sexual urges have also been eradicated must come as something of a mental shock — a kind of trauma for most people.

It would appear that nobody's sexual urges actually increase after castration. Many retain the same sexual urges as before the operation and continue to have both erection · and ejaculation, (admittedly without spermatozoa) and the same ability to have sexual intercourse. In some, the sexual urges are decreased, and a very few report that their sexual urges disappear completely, but these latter reports are not always to be trusted. There have, for instance, been men who have been castrated in order to prevent them from committing any more sexual crimes, and their release from prison has only been authorized on condition that the operation prove entirely successful. These men have naturally had no interest in claiming they still had sexual urges.

There are, in fact, so many mental factors in this question that it seems like a jungle whenever an attempt is made to penetrate to the truth. Superstition, prejudices, myths and ignorance cause countless authors to contradict themselves on the subject.

Castration has obviously not been a sufficient guarantee that a harem-guard would keep away from the women of a harem. For this reason a eunuch was usually deprived of his penis · as well, as this provided slightly more assurance that he would not take any interest in the women as they would have little chance of satisfying him.

Of considerable importance is the age at which castration takes place, (i.e. before or after puberty ·) as castration during boyhood would appear to a very much greater extent to be accompanied by a disappearance of sexual urges. (See also Sterilization and Cryptorchism).

s.h.

Castration anxiety, castration complex: In the spheres of psychology · and psychoanalysis, the term castration anxiety is operated with, i.e. the fear of being deprived of the male sexual organs. This anxiety is fairly common amongst men, but not always in a clearly conscious form. (See also Anxiety). In women, especially little girls, similar notions are encountered such as believing they once had a penis · but that it was taken from them as a punishment. Naturally these ideas are not as concrete as described here, and are mainly found in children who have received insufficient sexual instruction.

Then comes the jealousy between brothers and sisters and the fact that mothers are often a little fonder of boys, and that men enjoy a preferential position in our society — all factors that can contribute in one way or another to such ideas. *i. & s.h.*

Catharine II of Russia: An empress who lived in the middle of the 18th century. She was famous for her insatiable appetite for sex and is said to have had official state lovers by the score. It is possible she was merely constantly unsatisfied. (See Erotomania).

Celibate: A person who abstains from sex for one reason or another. Voluntary or compulsory abstinence of this nature is practised, for instance, by the Catholic clergy, who are obliged to live in celibacy. The thought is bound up with the idea of sex life being something blasphemous and woman something unclean, but it is also a method of keeping discipline.

These unfortunate Catholic priests must have some form of sex life — even if only nocturnal ejaculations · accompanied by erotic dreams over which they have no control. Thereafter, when they get bad consciences (innocently, and without justification) concerning their 'uncleanness', their eagerness to serve their religion is intensified.

Trying to make people feel they are not as they should be seems to be the foundation upon which discipline is based in the army as well as in religion. Perhaps it is necessary — perhaps a religion that only makes reasonable demands is unable to capture people's interest. Perhaps an army collapses unless inhuman demands are made on its soldiers — but whatever the case it does not exactly further what we understand by human happiness.   *i. & s.h.*

Censorship: An estimation of some performance or other to decide whether it is permissible. It may be the prison authorities who read all letters to and from prisoners in order to decide whether they may be delivered, but it may also be the police demanding to read through and approve everything before it is published in the newspapers — or a committee of experts of one sort or another whose task it is to decide whether or not a film should be classified as unfit for children. Censorship is usually established in the holy name of morality, but history has countless examples of how censorship has been abused — either politically or artistically. In Denmark we have freedom of the press, in other words everything may be printed and published, after which the publisher must accept his responsibility accordingly. The courts may then have to decide whether whatever has been published exceeds the bounds of the permissible or not.

Freedom of the press is a good thing, but the way the law is interpreted is important too, and it is worthwhile noting that we can thank the liberal attitude manifested in our Danish courts for the fact that we are today one of the most broadminded countries as far as so-called pornography is concerned. The result is partly that a large number of suggestively erotic things are published and sold in Denmark purely with the object of making quick profits — not that it has ever been possible to prove what harm they do — and partly that it has been made possible for a number of honest and therefore artistic books to be published. This is far more important.
                                        s.h.

Charm: People with charm — whether male or female — impress others by their manner or behaviour, not their appearance. No recipe for charm can be given here — only a couple of suggestions concerning some of the ingredients. A charming person is confident — not irritatingly so, but possessed of a harmonious confidence (see Personality), and the charm makes itself particularly apparent through his or her ability to make others feel at their ease. In other words, a person with charm likes other people — is genuinely interested in them, gets them to open up, is not afraid of them, makes them feel comfortable by his (or her) humaneness and happy by his (or her) cheerful manner.

Of course there is also the superficial charm-boy who collapses like a pack of cards upon closer acquaintanceship. He is not the person described above. *s.h.*

Chastity: An attitude largely dictated by fashion. It means virginity, or abstention from sexual intercourse, and the label "pure and chaste" has often been applied to women who have refused to have anything whatsoever to do with sex. At various times religious circles have made perfectly fantastic demands upon the chastity of both men and women. (See Morals). Kinsey has drawn attention to a certain connection between fanatic abstention and the possibility of a mental disorder. (See also Sublimation).
i.h.

Chastity belts: There are countless examples of how fathers and husbands have constructed ingenious belts with the object of preventing their daughters or wives from indulging in sexual intercourse. Belts of this kind were provided with a padlock and offered for sale. The purveyor usually did good business by selling two keys — one for the husband and one for the lady. Chastity belts are bought and sold to this day.

As far as ingenuity goes I think we human beings have beaten all records with the mental belt of chastity we are given as children and which many never even realize they are wearing. Here, extra keys are of no help.

Devilishly designed apparatuses have also been constructed to prevent children from masturbating. *i.h.*

Chemists: In order to study how customers are served and what stocks are maintained, we have interviewed a number of chemists and made a number of trial purchases at different chemists all over Denmark, especially in Copenhagen. We would like to be able to write that all Denmark's chemists always have stocks of contraceptives — pessaries ·, condoms ·, pessary cream and everything else necessary to our sex lives. We would like to be able to write that everywhere we went we found unprejudiced, friendly, neutral chemists and pharmacists prepared to show the consideration due to such shy members of the public as they are inevitably confronted with from time to time.

Unfortunately we cannot. There are chemists that do not always keep a stock of everything — and there *are* shops where customers are not served as pleasantly as they might be. Of course it is not the fault of the chemists themselves. They are human beings with prejudices just like the rest of us — and their upbringing has left its mark on them just as ours has on us. In other words this is not intended as a negative criticism of shortcomings but — in the interests of consumers — a wish to draw attention to a neglected sphere.

There *are* chemists who stock everything. And the majority of them have the essentials. There are chemists where customers are treated with commendable

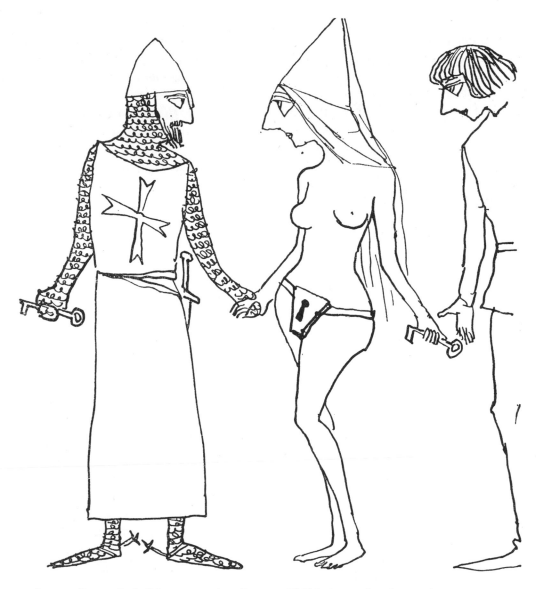

understanding, helpfulness and discretion — and in the majority of cases a customer is able to make his purchase easily and without embarrassment. Let us praise such places. But it is clear that the training of pharmacists has been neglected on this important point. It is a privilege to enjoy the confidence of the public. But it also imposes an obligation. (See also Rubber Goods Shops).

i. & s.h.

Child prostitution: (See also Prostitution). Young boys and girls have been in demand throughout the ages. In the East, for instance, small boys have been trained from their early years to provide pleasure for gentlemen whose tastes are so inclined and to get paid for it. The trade in small boys was widespread, but an even better and bigger business was to be had out of small girls. There has been a tremendous amount of child prostitution in the western world too. In our grandfathers' day — some 75 years ago — one could pick and choose between about 500 little girls whose ages ranged between 12 and 15 in Regent Street in London. This was in the Gay Nineties. (See also Virginity, Maidenhead).   *s.h.*

Child seduction, child violation: See Sexual Crimes.

Childlessness: In using this term we usually think of instances in which two people badly want to have children with one another but for some reason are unable to do so.

It was formerly believed that fertilization was dependent upon the existence of love between the parties concerned. Others have contended that an orgasm on the part of the woman is necessary to ensure fertilization.

Fertilization can of course take place perfectly well even though the parties concerned are not in love with each other and likewise even if the woman fails to obtain sexual satisfaction ˙.

Untreated venereal diseases ˙, abortions˙, and cryptorchism ˙, may, in certain cases, cause barrenness. If the Fallopian tube becomes blocked, or if the womb is, or becomes, displaced (see Genital Organs, female) the fertilization process can be impeded too. This whole question is far from having been cleared up. Childlessness, however, is a very serious problem for many people. In some cases it is possible to give assistance. (See Insemination, artificial).   *s.h.*

Children, abundance of: Found particularly amongst peoples who, either because of ignorance of birth control ˙, or for religious reasons, have more children than they can afford. Naturally everything is relative and how many children any given family can afford varies. But with the spread of enlightenment and the raising of living standards, birth rates apparently tend to drop.

Not so many years ago large families were common in Denmark — especially in the country, where of course children are able to help their parents with their work to a certain extent.   *s.h.*

Christianity and sex: As will be apparent from the many quotations and accounts spread through this book, Christian morals have varied considerably.

The representatives of Christianity — in many cases priests — have been attacked for making false translations of the Bible and misinterpretations, and for fanatical opposition to scientific demands to probe causal relations and reduce superstition. In a great number of cases it has been pointed out how inconsistent it has been of the orthodox Church to want to impose, even upon non-believers, a haphazard conception of moral behaviour as being something of eternal validity and divine instigation. The Church — Bible in hand — has in the course of time burnt nine million persons as immoral witches.

We in Denmark give little thought to such details on the Eve of St. Hans, a Midsummer's Eve celebration on which we burn dummy witches on bonfires.

44

Within the Church, too, it is the intolerant who shout loudest. Those with mild and loving hearts are not the ones who go firing off the big guns.

What we generally call a Christian attitude is more rarely met with in the wholly orthodox Church. The doctrine of respectable, pious charity, justified through its good deeds, has been rejected in favour of the doctrine of faith. Even so, it should be possible for a Christian person to find somewhere to breathe freely. The person who seeks a religion that does not preach against sin and does not regard sexual pleasure as sinful will probably be able to find, within the Christian Church, a group in favour of a non-condemnatory code of morals. For groups do exist that have a warm, positive and humane outlook on the pleasure of sexual relationships. But unfortunately, in this matter as well as in so many others, it is always the intolerant who shout loudest and insist on chivvying everybody into the same fold at any price. The mild and charitable go about their business more quietly. *i. & s.h.*

Church murals: It is a peculiar fact that there are many Christian church murals that would shock congregations were a modern painter to execute them. Now and again some of these murals are discovered — particularly in old Danish churches — and now and again they are hurriedly covered up again with a layer of whitewash.

So much is often said about the immoral, over-sexed times in which we live (see Morals), but we should bear in mind that there have been times when the public code of morals was distinctly more liberal, distinctly more 'sexy' — and even had the Church's blessing. What applies to an even greater extent to other religions is that love, both in and out of the service of procreation, has been warmly accepted. *s.h.*

This fellow was not considered offensive when he was painted in about 1500 — in a Danish Church near Skanderborg. Now whitewashed over.

Cinema and motion-pictures: In connection with the business of going to the cinema we come up against a psychological mechanism that is of interest in other spheres of activity as well. If a friend says to us: "You must go and see "*French Without Tears*" — it's terribly funny, fantastically well acted and extremely exciting!" — and then we duly go and see it, his praising of it to the skies often results in our saying, afterwards: "Well — I suppose it was quite amusing, really." In other words, considerably milder praise. Conversely, if he says: ""*The Red Horses*" — what utter trash! Amateurishly acted, and as for the plot......!" — then there is a very great chance of our saying, after having seen it: "Well, I don't know — it wasn't all *that* bad, you know."

Our expectations often influence the kind of experience we have. (See Wedding Depression and Love Thermometer).

i.h.

Circumcision: An operation performed on the foreskin · of the penis ·. The foreskin is pulled forward and the part extending beyond the tip of the actual penis is cut off.

This is how the foreskin is folded round the glans, or head of the penis ·.

The foreskin is pulled forward and cut off.

The two circular edges are sewn together.

Result : the foreskin has become shorter.

As the foreskin is double (because it turns back on itself and ends up being attached firmly behind the glans, or head of the penis) the two severed edges are then sewn together the whole way round. When these edges have grown together again the result is a foreskin as before, only shorter.

It is a religious practice amongst Jews, and it is among them we are most familiar with it; but it is a · very widespread custom throughout the world and in many other peoples too.

Circumcision has two distinct advantages i. e. the problem of difficulty in pulling back the foreskin is obviated, and the penis itself is easier to keep clean and less sensitive. However, it is superstition to think that circumcision serves to protract intercourse on account of reduced sensitivity. But if faith can move mountains, then superstition · may as well be able to protract sexual intercourse. *s.h.*

Civil marriage, civil wedding: In former times in Denmark the Church alone was authorized to marry people. But nowadays marriages performed by a registrar, a mayor, parish executive officer or chairman of a parish council, in other words by civil authorities, are accepted on an equal basis with those performed by the Church. Just as in the case of confirmation, however, there is still a fairly strong leaning towards the church ceremony — ("You're not properly married unless you have been married in church") — without this necessarily having so very much to do with actual religious sentiments. From a common sense viewpoint one might assert that it makes little odds — or even point out that as far as non-believers are concerned a civil marriage would be a little more honest. Many people have their children christened, "to be on the safe side", too. But then common sense never has been a strong point amongst human beings. *i.h.*

Clap: Gonorrhea, see Venereal Diseases.

Climacterium: The second sexual crisis in a woman's life. The first is puberty ·, when menstruation begins; during the climacterium it gradually ceases.

During a woman's climacteric period, which may last a couple of years, her chances of having children are greatly reduced and afterwards practically non-existent. This second sexual crisis as a rule takes place during a woman's forties — in many instances at about the same time as her children are involved in puberty, which can cause a lot of trouble as both are out of balance.

A woman notices the arrival of her climacterium through irregular bleedings and hot periods and waves of heat passing through her. It was formerly believed that this meant a woman's leave-taking from sexual pleasures. This is entirely wrong. On the contrary, there are instances of women who, once they no longer have to be 'careful', blossom forth and get more out of their sex lives than before. At any rate a characteristic of the woman is that her sexual urges, unlike those of the man, do not decrease. (See Kinsey).

Men have nothing corresponding to the climacterium. A man retains his ability to beget children up to an advanced age — and his sexual urges too.

A man may, however, find himself at about the same time — during his forties — in a bit of a mental transition period involving a few minor crises. Suddenly it dawns on him he can never manage to do all the things he dreamed about doing when he was young. Suddenly he has to realize that his life has culminated, that his future path is rigidly marked out for him and that there is nothing he can do about it. *i. & s.h.*

Clitoral orgasm: Every orgasm a woman has is a clitoral orgasm — as a rule fairly directly, in rarer instances indirectly.

In order to understand the true nature of an orgasm it is necessary to understand this line of thought. An orgasm is felt through almost the whole body, including the muscles, and including the vaginal walls, which contract during an orgasm. But an orgasm does not occur as a result of any physical influence up inside the vagina, nor as a result of touching the womb, as many believe.

It is the pleasurable physical influence on the clitoris, indirectly or (as a rule) directly, that culminates in an orgasm.

It was once believed that a 'vaginal' orgasm was more refined than a clitoral orgasm, but this is a misunderstanding.

Vaginal orgasms do not exist. What people sometimes think is a vaginal orgasm is an indirect influence on the clitoris through the muscle fibres and nerve endings at the entrance to the vagina. This and other forms of indirect clitoral orgasm are rare compared to orgasms caused by direct external influence on the clitoris, which is the most common type.

(See also Petting, Satisfaction, Masturbation, Egoism, Consideration, Frigidity).
s.h.

Clitoris: A little bud-shaped organ in the woman corresponding to the tip of the penis · in the man. A clitoris may be large, may be small. Here are a few

Normal clitoris in three different women, all shown life-size. The size of a clitoris can also vary in the individual woman as sexual excitation causes it to fill with blood and swell up — an erection corresponding precisely to that of a man's penis.

examples drawn natural size but not filled with blood. The clitoris is situated about an inch above the mouth of the urethra.

The clitoris is the focal point of a woman's feelings of sexual pleasure just as the head of the penis in the man. Just like a penis, a clitoris can become filled with blood and bigger, and two 'muscles', corresponding to the shaft of the penis in a man, can raise the clitoris into a state of erection ·.

The clitoris is the sensitive switch, which, when subjected to constant external influence, turns on an orgasm ·. This influence is very intense and marked by a sense of pleasure. This spreads gradually over increasingly large areas and culminates in an almost painful sensation of pleasure that surges through most of the body and thus produces sexual satisfaction, i.e. an orgasm.

The word clitoris is derived from the Greek word for "key" — the old Greeks having the correct notion that this organ is the key to feminine sexuality.

(See Genital Organs, female; Orgasm, Petting, Satisfaction, Consideration, Egoism, Masturbation, Frigidity, Clitoral orgasm; Differences, sexual; and Titillation, sexual). *s.h.*

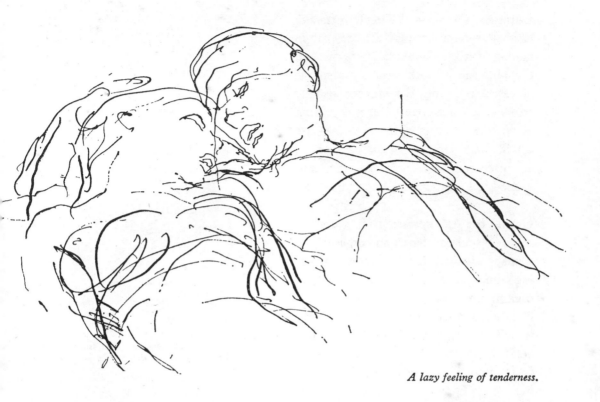

A lazy feeling of tenderness.

Code, moral: See Morals.

Coition: Means the act of sexual intercourse.

Coitus: Means sexual intercourse, copulation. There is a well-known Latin saying to the effect that everybody feels in a bad humour after sexual intercourse. Fortunately this is not correct, but many have been disappointed because they had expected everything to be so wonderful afterwards. (See also Cinema and Wedding Depression). A number of people, especially women, have found that a man, once he has 'got his way' becomes fairly listless and disinterested. This may seem somewhat crude to a woman, especially if she herself has not been satisfied. But if both parties have been satisfied there is no reason for them to be sad. Once both have had their needs fulfilled, a relaxed, satisfied, peaceful mood is only natural. A kind of lazy tenderness is about the most one can manage — and certainly not the intense concentration felt before or during intercourse.

i. & s.h.

Coitus interruptus: See Birth Control.

Colours: The Animal Kingdom teaches us that colours can play a large part in mating dances. Monkeys' bottoms and the plumage of cock birds are a couple of cases in point. We humans also lay stress on colours. A little lipstick, a spot of powder, shading of the eyelids — we call it 'war paint' for fun, because we are prepared to let ourselves be conquered ·. Lighting is of importance too.

Rolled-up condom with extra reservoir for sperm.

Come, to: An expression often used to mean ejaculate, have an orgasm, be sexually satisfied. It can be very disturbing (and have a delaying effect on orgasm) to a man as well as to a woman if either partner says, whilst intercourse is still in progress: "Haven't you come yet?" or in any other way gives vent to irritation or impatience. (See also Breeding, good; Egoism, Consideration, Simulation). *i.h.*

Rolled-up, ordinary condom. This is the way it looks before being unrolled over the erected penis.

Conception: Means fertilization. Contraception · thus means the prevention of fertilization. (See Birth Control).

Concubine: Means a mistress, as a rule in the higher social spheres, the regular mistress of a king or prince. (See Courtesan).

Condom: A very thin bag of rubber to draw on to the penis with the object of preventing the sperm cells from being flung out inside the woman's vagina (see Genital Organs, female). It is a method of birth control ·, of preventing fertilization ·. In Denmark condoms can be bought at chemists · and at rubber goods shops ·. They can also be obtained at a number of barber's shops and at a few tobacconists. More than 10 million condoms are sold in Denmark annually. Condoms range in price from 50 øre each (such as the Plan condom on sale at chemists) up to 3 or 4 *kroner* apiece.

Condoms are obtainable either with or without a little extra reservoir for the sperm (see diagram), but there is no need to use a condom with a reservoir; it is possibly not quite as durable because it may result in rubber rubbing against rubber.

50

Instructions for use:

An ordinary condom (without a reservoir) is rolled on to the (erected) penis after the foreskin has been pulled back as far as possible. Be careful not to tear the rubber with your nails. The condom should then fit smoothly and tightly all over the penis in its erected state. (See Erection). If the head of the penis is very sensitive it may help if a specially lubricated condom is used, or if some vegetable ointment can be smeared on, but preferably externally only, otherwise the condom may slide off. External use of such jelly or ointment is used particularly in cases when the woman's vagina is dry to start with — which is by no means unusual or abnormal as some men believe. Vegetable ointment or jelly is better than grease, vaseline, cream or spit — which, however, can all be used.

— — —

After the man has had his orgasm ·, erection · ceases. His penis · becomes softer, floppier and smaller. In other words the penis no longer fills out the condom, which in turn means that the latter is no longer so firmly held in place. It is therefore important that the man, when he withdraws his penis, takes care not to let the condom slide off and stay inside the woman's vagina and thereby allow the sperm to flow out.

Condoms can also be ordered by telephone or by letter.

Condoms may be said to provide fairly good protection. The chances of pregnancy resulting from sexual intercourse without the use of any form of contraceptive have been calculated as being 1 in 35. As far as it is possible to estimate, a good condom, correctly used, should only break in one case out of two hundred.

But statistics are dangerous things to use. There is no consolation in the chances of fertilization being small if one happens to hit the thirty-fifth time with the one condom out of the two hundred that breaks.

But statistics tell us that it must take quite a lot of sexual intercourse, quite a lot of bad luck and (presumably in particular) quite a lot of ignorance to create the many thousands of children conceived in Denmark every year without their parents' being married.

The condom is quite definitely to be recommended to young people at the commencement of sexual relationships between them — and in cases where the girl is very shy.

A condom furthermore affords protection against venereal disease ·. Just after birth and in the case of certain displacements of the womb a condom is best too. Finally, a condom has the advantage that it is possible to check immediately after use whether the protection sought has been effective.

Those who are very nervous about having a baby can combine the use of a condom with the Knaus Method, in other words select the last 10 days prior to the next menstruation for having intercourse · — and avoid the days round the fifteenth day before the next menstruation. Using both a condom and the Knaus Method, the chances of fertilization should be very, very small. (See Menstruation Chart). Another kind of contraceptive that can be used in conjunction with the condom in order to be even more on the safe side is a special sperm-destroying cream, or foam tablets — but these can only be obtained with a doctor's prescription. And naturally a condom can be combined with the use of a pessary ·.

s.h.

Connection: It may be appropriate to stress the importance of the connection which naturally exists between sex life and the rest of life, between sex and society ·, between the practice of cohabitation and society.

Not only is sex an important part of any civilization, but it is moreover closely bound up with all the other parts of the civilization in question. We cannot alter the attitude held towards the sexual side of life without at the same time being obliged to alter the entire society in question in many other important respects — and vice versa. A relationship between two persons can be regarded as a Lilliputian society, as a small-scale model of the society in which they live.

Seeing that sex has occupied a special position for so many years and has been something whose presence was denied in respectable company, there is no use our saying today, in *surprised* tones:

"Heavens, is that you? (dear sex) — why on earth haven't you come over and joined the rest of us ages ago?"

i. & s.h.

Conscience: All the built-in moral ideas we have about what we should do and what we should not. These ideas are built into our minds in the course of our upbringing, partly by our parents, who in turn have taken over such ideas from their own parents. But others share in building up our consciences. (See also "One"). Conscience is thus a part of the super ego (see Personality). There is no questioning the fact that we ought to have a conscience, i.e. certain moral ideas as to what is right and wrong. The question is merely whether the particular ideas we and our society implant in our children's minds are the most right in all respects.

If we regard history and accounts of other peoples with an open mind and try to put aside all our prejudices for a few moments, we see that such peoples manage to get by with an entirely different kind of morality — that their conscience is a different one on many points. And these different peoples also manage to live together. Added to which is the fact that a very large number of people in our society suffer from highly neurotic symptoms that ruin their lives for them. This is the bill we have to pay for having a moral code — and thereby a conscience that does not suit all people in all spheres.

It is obvious that freedom — complete freedom — would create even greater neuroses. But then that is yet another extreme.

Nor will we ever reach the point when all people will be able to live without any conflicts with their consciences. But we know of societies in which a greater part of their members would appear to be more harmonious than we are. So we have a goal to strive for. Fortunately, nice things are happening the whole time. Only a few years ago, masturbation produced bad consciences that became nightmares for large sections of humanity. Young people — and old people too — fought the bloodiest and most tragic fights with their sexual urges — and lost the battle — with the result that their consciences gave them the most dreadful guilt complexes. At least we have obtained slightly milder, friendlier and more humane consciences on this score.

i. & s.h.

Consideration: (See also Egoism, Simulation; and Breeding, good).

A couple of generations ago it suddenly became modern to deny that a woman could have sexual feelings or interests. We are always fairly obedient to the dictates of both fashion and moral codes, with the result that many women suppressed their feelings. (See also Frigidity). A few girls had stronger feelings than they knew how to suppress and therefore became hysterical ·. And a number naturally had sexual feelings which were permitted to find some sort of unrestricted outlet anyway. They probably felt themselves a little immoral and abnormal, but nature · got her way.

During the past few decades women have once more been permitted to have sex lives. In the process the pendulum swung rather much to the opposite side, and it became the fashion to cultivate a woman's sex life and help it along in every possible way. It is an understandable reaction, and

right enough in its way too, but consideration is something which cuts both ways.

Van de Velde, the Dutch author and doctor, did a great deal to help couples with their love life. But by overstressing the responsibility and part played by the man he managed to do women a disservice at the same time. It became a man's duty to insist upon his wife's having an orgasm .

Consideration can become a demand.

Men's vanity · is no less than that of women, merely of a slightly different kind. And causing a woman's sex life to blossom forth can become a man's pride. But it is not a plant that can be hauled up out of the ground in order to make it grow — it needs handling with tact, patience and the offer of a possibility of development — not with a demand. A woman's orgasm should not be a scalp in a man's belt, but something from which she first and foremost derives pleasure.

The same thing applies to all interhuman relationships, namely that misplaced consideration can be a serious thing to fool around with. Far too many couples do things they both believe the other person wants to do.

Jack Sprat could eat no fat,
His wife could eat no lean.
Between them both they managed
To lick the platter clean.

But unfortunately there are marriages in which the husband has forced himself to eat the fat for 25 years because he believes his wife likes the lean, and during the same period she has laboriously chewed her way through the lean because she thought he wanted the fat.

Couples like this will hardly ever be able to face discovering the truth. (See also Defeat, Giving).

Many couples who discuss, for instance, going to the cinema, know how one of them may say: "Well darling, what would you like to do?" To which the other may reply: "All right, let's go . . ." — in the belief that the one who asked in the first place really wanted to go. It would be much better if one of them said: "I actually want to go to the pictures tonight — how do you feel?" And then the other could frankly admit to inclination or disinclination. In this way each is able to take stock of how much or how little the other wants to go to the pictures.

Perhaps she will reply: "I don't feel like going at all!" And then he can say: "All right, I'm not that madly keen — let's stay at home." Or she can say: "I'm not particularly keen, but I don't mind going at all." And then he can say: "I would really like to very much — come on, let's go!" Sometimes one forms the impression that each is afraid of accepting the responsibility for the action in question because it may turn out to be a fiasco, afraid that the other person may say afterwards: "It's all your fault, you were the one who wanted to!" — no matter whether it was stay at home or go to the pictures.

Naturally consideration is connected with the problem that many people have a hard time finding out what it is they want anyway. (See Picnicking). This applies particularly to sexual relationships. It may take years of work to find out what one really wants most — what one dares to want, and what gives one most pleasure. Exaggerated consideration can delay this work. For there is no point in the person who knows what he or she wants always giving in to the person who never manages to find out — or the other way round. Just like Tigger in the Winnie-the-Pooh stories, before we manage to find out what it is we like best we sometimes have to taste a number of things which may turn out to be the kind "Tiggers don't like".

Men know comparatively little about the incompleted, semi-orgasms · that are much worse than being cheated out of a sneeze·. Women do, and fear them.

This is not meant as an encouragement to show blatant lack of consideration. The young, inexperienced girl in particular — in view of the upbringing she has had — has every right to demand romance ·, tenderness, carefulness and patience. (See also Petting). *i.h.*

Continence: Temperance, especially sexual. (See Abstinence, Chastity).

Contraception, contraceptives: See Birth Control.

Conquer: It is said that the man is the conquerer and the girl the conquered. This is something of an illusion. Even those of us who are not the kind to get snapped up will none the less time and

54

The dream of conquering· and being conquered is humourously illustrated here by this drawing of an apache couple. But it is not such an exaggeration of many people's fantasies· and ideas as one might think.

again be confronted with the fact that the girls we suddenly discover and begin to court have already had their eye on us for a long time and are impatiently waiting for us to take steps.

For many married men and not so very few married women, the thought that marriage deprives them of the pleasure of conquering — or being conquered — is unbearable.

This is a serious problem and one that is not easy to solve. After 10 or 20 years of marriage it is only a real artist that can brace himself to attempt the conquest of his wife.

She too needs to be something of an artist at living in order to feel herself conquered — in fact to join in the fun at all. (See also Don Juan, Courtship and Unfaithfulness). *s.h.*

Coprography: The writing of forbidden words (see also Erotographomania and Naughty Words).

Coprolalia, erotolalia: The increasing of sexual excitement by saying, or hearing, sexual words. It is often called a perversity ·, but like so many other perversities so widespread there is no cause whatsoever for classifying it as abnormal ·. (See Norms, also Naughty Words and Jokes).

Any number of men in the kingdom of Denmark use a few matter-of-fact expressions by way of introduction to sexual intercourse, expressions it would be impossible to print without shocking lots of people. Jaunty words of this kind stimulate men a little — consciously or unconsciously — and sometimes their wives too.

We have met women who have told us they liked hearing words of this sort, but that their husbands thought they were perverse. There are also women who are indifferent, and others who get worked up in a different way — namely revolted. All three groups are to be found within the framework of normal sexual relationships.

The fact that words can have this effect is connected with the artificial barrier erected by our public code of morals around the subject of sexual urges . and sexual relationships ·. The result is that a few extra spices are sometimes needed to whet an appetite that is often there all right but not given a proper chance of manifesting itself. (See also Personality and Erotographomania).   *i. & s.h.*

In the original Danish edition—and in the Swedish and Norwegian—this space carried a piece of text. Although it is permissible to print this in Scandinavia legal opinion has warned us against its inclusion in the English edition. We apologise to all readers. *The Editors.*

Corset: An apparatus designed to give the female body a different shape (see also Breast). At certain times the corset has been almost as painful an instrument as the tightly laced shoes · of Chinese women.

Cosmetics: Everything which, like lipstick, powder, perfume, corsets, plastic · operations, etc., etc., serves to alter existing features, i.e. the real appearance of a person.

It is understandable that we should want to try and help nature and get as close as possible to the current ideal of beauty. In the majority of cases it is probably painless, but fashion can be a rigorous task-master. (See Film). And we have many examples of the way fashion has inflicted damage on the human body — Chinese girls' feet, high-heeled 'winkle-picker' shoes ·, the bodices of olden times (see Corset) etc.

There is also the danger that a man may start to believe that a film star's breasts · stick out into the air, firmly and horizontally, even when naked, and therefore

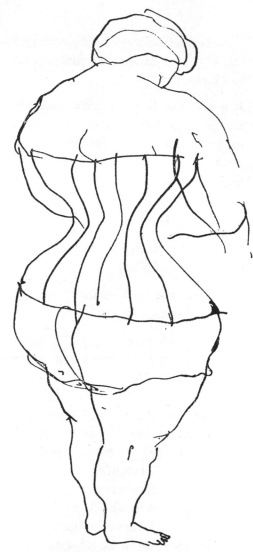

Instruments of torture like this have been used in order "to support the weak human body". Professional people have recommended its use, but it is a whim of fashion, not a prescription for health. In societies · where fat women are regarded as the most beautiful, the lady would never have hit upon this brainwave.

The converse sort of thing applies to the ladies: Bing Crosby and Charles Boyer wear a wig in the films. There are undoubtedly a number of male film stars who suffer from sweaty feet. Marlon Brando is said to have been somewhat demonstrative about letting his wind go free. We are sorry if we are being on the crude side and shattering anybody's illusions. But as long as there are still people who think they are abnormal and alone with these problems it will go on being necessary to throw a little light on such matters. Reality is only tactless to those to screw up their eyes against the light.   *i. & s.h.*

Court, courting, courtship: To pay court to a woman, to woo, lay siege too, admire, etc., etc., are all exciting things for most men as long as they form part of a planned conquest ·. Women as a rule enjoy this sort of thing too — and they like it if men continue even after having made their conquest. The majority of women like a little old-fashioned gallantry because it makes them feel more attractive and feminine ·.

Many men neglect the art of courtship or any display of gallantry towards their girl, fiancée or wife. It should form part of the spirit of inventiveness which should constitute a duty in any relationship.

Not a tiresome duty, but a pleasurable sport — an expression of all the things one means but forgets to say. It may be a bunch of violets for no particular reason, a helping hand getting off a bus or tram (not always in Denmark the matter of course it often is in other countries), a little box of chocolates to

become dissatisfied with his own girl whom he knows at closer, more revealing quarters.

And if he believes in the lie that nine out of ten film stars never go to the lavatory things are getting dangerous, for it will make him inhuman in his general attitude and in his demands.

Even though a couple may have been married for many years, this sort of thing should not be an insuperable symbol of love and solicitude.

cheer one up at menstruation time — and many other things.

But unfortunately it must also be noted that there are women who deny their feminity and cannot accept these things in the same generous spirit. After all, the whole play in the relationship between two persons is more complicated — and if *he* has squandered his week's wages on drink, *she* will not be touched by a penn'orth of boiled sweets.

But it is a neglected sphere.

Gallantry can be a cover-up for contempt for a woman — but I still feel feminists could permit themselves to be feminine.

i.h.

Courtesan: A *distinguished* prostitute — this of course immediately makes people less indignant.

It is told how Bernard Shaw once asked his dining partner whether she would go to bed with a man for five hundred pounds.

The lady smiled at the old rascal and said roguishly: "Well, it would depend on how good-looking he was ..."

"Would you do it for ten bob?" continued Bernard Shaw.

"What do you take me for?" burst out the lady indignantly.

"We've already settled that question" said Shaw drily. "All we are discussing now is the price." *i.h.*

Couvade: A rather amusing and quite widespread custom amongst many peoples. The husband retires to bed either before or after his child's birth and allows himself to be comforted, waited on and congratulated as though he had the child himself. Today, many women in our western civilization would be able to name similar examples of the so-called stronger sex's ability to accept the kudos instead of the hard work — birth. (See also Sissy).

Crab-louse: A flat little creature who likes to stay amongst the hairs round the genital organs, but can also spread to other hairy regions including the eyebrows and beard, but not the hair on the top of the head. Crab-lice spread from one person to the next in the course of intimate relationships, sexual intercourse in particular. In other words one can 'catch' crab-lice (*Phthirius pubis*) just like a venereal disease ·. They reproduce themselves very rapidly. They lay eggs down along the stiff hairs, under the skin, where they produce a violent, pricking itch. Crab-lice and their eggs can be very easily killed with the help of various medicaments. Any doctor · can help. And every doctor is naturally honour bound to keep whatever his patients confide to him to himself. It is also possible to buy *Liquor penticidi* at any chemist's. (It can also be used against fleas). *s.h.*

Cremaster reflex: Muscle fibres enclose each testicle · in the scrotum · rather like a basket-ball net. If the inner side of the thigh is scratched very gently and painlessly, the testicle on that side will be slowly lifted by the 'net'. This reflex is tested to check whether the nerve paths in this section are in order — just as an electrician checks whether the current is reaching a certain point. *s.h.*

Crime, sexual: Sexual behaviour forbidden by law. Incest ·, for example, is forbidden; so are certain instances of seduction ·, procuring ·, prostitution without having some lawful occupation at the same time, the spreading of venereal diseases ·, rape ·, *abortus provocatus*, certain forms of exhibitionism when it is not permitted, and other crimes against public decency.

By sexual crimes we think particularly, however, about sexual acts and attacks against children. As a rule it is a case of the person in question showing his genital organs. It is not uncommon for the person to fondle the child, fondle the child's genital organs, or encourage the child to touch his. In very rare cases there is a question of actual attempts at intercourse with the child. In such cases it is obvious that there may be a question of physical harm, i.e. of the child's body suffering damage.

The mental harm produced by these sexual acts towards children depends to a certain extent on the sexual upbringing the child has had (see Enlightenment, sexual; and Education, sexual) and the enlightenment the child has been given.

A child that has been scared beforehand, and whose relationships with sex are full of prohibitions and anxieties, will naturally be particularly prone to suffer mental harm too.

The child who has a calmer, more natural, less fearful attitude to sex can experience quite a lot without this necessarily causing mental damage. Quite a large number of women can remember having had sexual approaches made to them by men when they were children — in about half the cases by friends or relations in their own homes.

Little girls are so often spoken of as being innocent little things. But innocent little things can also have a desire for phsycial contact and for being fondled.

Whether we choose to call such desires sexual desires, or call sexual desires desires to be fondled, is immaterial.

seduction to masturbation is forbidden by law. Kinsey · showed in his report how one American in three had thus broken the law with another person.

There are countries where sexual crimes against children are unknown, and there are societies · whose population can hardly get married at all because their rules for incest are so complicated and comprehensive they are all much too closely related to one another.

i. & s.h.

Cross-breed: The word is used to describe children of parents of different races, e.g. negro and white. The Danish word for cross-breed (*bastard·*) is also sometimes used as a term of abuse. This is bound up with the fact of the existence of certain racial theories that culminated in the worship of pure Germanic, or Aryan blood, by the Nazis of Germany up until the end of World War II. In brief, crude terms, these theories are based on the contention that certain individual human races are superior to others. It was furthermore contended that any intermingling of races resulted in children inheriting the worst character traits from both races.

Nowadays we tend to express contempt for the way the Nazis declared their hate for Jews, likewise for the negro problems existing in the USA and South Africa.

On the other hand we ought not to forget that a certain degree of anti-semitism still has its supporters here in Denmark — and that it even exists in people who believe themselves to be unprejudiced.

Grown women are allowed to do all sorts af things to small boys without anybody as much as raising an eyebrow.

Added to which, children are warned and told so much about bad men and naughty men that the very thought easily becomes exciting.

Very small boys are not so often subjected to sexual approaches — or at any rate they seldom experience them as such.

There are things that are punished severely as sexual crimes in one country but not at all in another. In South Africa, blacks and whites are not allowed to have sexual intercourse with one another (see also Bestiality). In certain states in the USA,

60

Nor should we forget that we Danes have done some pretty dreadful things in our big colony, Greenland, of the kind the colonizers and *Herrenfolk* of former times are usually accused of. The racial theories we officially reject and which we classify as Nazi in spirit can likewise be met with elsewhere: in American films, for instance, where negroes are largely represented playing the roles of servants or buffoons; in Danish children's books, where a particularly large number of villains are represented as being racial mixtures; and in ourselves the day our brother or father (but especially our sister or mother) wants to marry a negro.

s.h.

Cryptorchism, cryptorchidism: The term used when both testicles · have not descended into the scrotum ·. The testicles are formed in the abdominal cavity — the place corresponding to where the female sexual glands, or ovaries (see Genital Organs, female) are situated in the woman.

But just before birth (or shortly after) the male testicles slide down into the scrotum through a hole in the abdominal cavity. (As a rule the hole closes again, but sometimes a portion of the intestines can press its way out through it causing what is known as hernia). However, it is by no means rare that one or both testicles fail to glide down into the scrotum. This can prove destructive to the sperm-producing tissue of the testicle and it is therefore important that parents immediately consult a doctor if their new-born son's testicles have not descended into the scrotum.

If a man only has one testicle he will still as a rule be able to have children. If both are missing it is more doubtful. However, quite a lot can be achieved by hormone treatment and the like. It is important to consult a doctor as soon as possible. An intensified form of castration anxiety can also occur in connection with cryptorchism.

A false form of cryptorchism can arise by one of the testicles slipping up into the inguinal canal now and again, especially when the scrotum is subjected to pressure. As a rule it is rather unpleasant, but not dangerous provided it can be gently pressed down again. (See Sterility, Testicles).

s.h.

61

In the original Danish edition, as well as in the Swedish and Norwegian, this space carried an illustration. Although it was allowed in Scandinavia legal opinion has warned us against its inclusion. We apologise to all readers for this omission and recognise that no intelligent adult would have regarded this particular illustration as being offensive.

The Editors.

Culture, cultured: See Breeding, good; and Anthropology.

Cunnilingus; cunnilinctus (cunnilinctio): A special form of sexual intercourse in which the man tickles the woman's clitoris · (see Sexual Organs, female) with his tongue. As a result of the violent taboos we impose on our sex lives in our western civilization, this is something one does not talk about. (See Anilinctio).

Kinsey, however, mentions that up to 50% of more experienced persons have practised intercourse of this sort. (See also Fellatio).

It must moreover be stressed that it is one of the forms of intercourse in which the woman is satisfied entirely without making demands on a man's erection or other form of staying power, in other words independently of the man's potency ·. There are furthermore many women for whom it is the most reliable way of obtaining sexual satisfaction.

i. & s.h.

Curettage, curetting: When effecting a curettage, a start is made by expanding the very narrow canal that leads from the vagina · up through the neck of the womb and into the cavity of the womb (see Genital Organs, female). The mucous membrane is then scraped off the walls of the cavity of the womb — either the entire mucous membrane or parts of it. Curettage is performed after an abortion · in order to be certain that all the pregnant tissue has been removed. A curettage can also be carried out in the case of irregular menstruation ·, inflammations and other disorders. *i.h.*

D

Deep orgasm: See Clitoral Orgasm.

Defeat: Fiascos and defeats occur in all people's lives. But there is a special kind of defeat that is connected with sex life, namely the defeat many women feel when they are sexually satisfied, i.e. when they have an orgasm ·.

Many women refuse to give their husbands the triumph. They feel that he conquers them, beats them down, takes something from them and condescendingly gives them something. (See also Superiority, struggle for). It sounds illogical and confused, but then emotions are not always sensible. It is bound up with the poor custom that it is up to the man to satisfy the woman but that the lord of creation satisfies himself — that we talk about a woman's giving herself to a man, submitting to him.

This is nonsense, but one cannot eradicate the misunderstanding from one night to the next. One can merely draw attention to the fact that a woman is responsible for her own sexual satisfaction. She should use a man for her own ends, sexually. He is the means she should employ to achieve them.

It is utterly wrong that something so lovely should be experienced as a defeat instead of the victory it really is for both parties. (See Consideration, Simulation).

i. & s.h.

Defloration: Deflowering — rupture of hymen ·. (See Maidenhead).

Defloration-right; jus primae noctis, jus cunni; marchette, cazzagio: These all mean the right to have sexual intercourse with a bride or virgin before her husband. This custom, which we today regard as barbaric, was common amongst many different peoples and all over Europe during the Middle Ages. As a rule it formed part of a religious defence mechanism designed to ensure the fertility of the union in question by diverting the interest of the gods from the couple. (See also Joseph's Night). Naturally it was not nearly as barbaric as we imagine for the simple reason that it was an accepted custom, just as it has been an accepted custom for the chiefs of certain negro tribes to break the maidenheads of all the virgins in the tribe — including those of their own daughters. There are examples of priests and monks having held — and exercised — this right to deflower a bride in the presence of witnesses. Those who wished they lived in the 'good old days' with the chance to exercise this right — this duty — should bear in mind that it is unlikely all the girls were equally luscious, and furthermore that it had nowhere near the same interest then as it would have now. *s.h.*

Deformity Fetishism: There are men and women who experience particular sensual pleasure from going to bed with somebody who has some physical defect or deformity. A hunch back, a wooden leg or extreme ugliness may all well cause their particular excitement. A black patch over one eye can create a very manly effect too — it was featured in a smart American shirt advertisement some years ago. A squint is also said to have its charms.

If we feel the need of applying some general label to feelings of this sort we may call them *deformity fetishism* — but we must remember that even though in individual cases this may develop into a peculiarity — an abnormity·, or perversity, some might say — it is really, just as in the case of sadism, masochism, exhibitionism · and a few other isms, something we all have a little of in our own characters. Unfortunately a certain strength of character is required in order to face up to facts — especially facts concerning ourselves — in our society, where so many normal things are hushed up and denied. "Yes, but we don't have to wallow in such things, do we?" some will ask. Let us answer with an example. Let us imagine to ourselves a family which refuses to accept one of its members. They overlook him, deny his existence at family reunions and forget his name a moment after he has been introduced to them. The person who has been doing the introducing of this unwanted member of the family finally becomes annoyed and makes the said member stand up on a table, whereupon he claps his hands and shouts out:

"Hullo, everybody! This is your own flesh and blood, your cousin Joe Soap, a member of your family!"

This violent introduction would never have been necessary if the other members of the family had not endeavoured, by their attitude, to neglect and ignore his existence. It would have been understandable if the individual concerned had gone out into the garden and heaved a brick in through the window at his fine family.

It is the same thing with the feelings and urges we refuse to own up to. Most mental disturbances can be traced back to things like this, things we dared not face up to, and which create havoc in other ways instead.   *i. & s.h.*

Degeneration: Means a gradual decrease in physical or mental abilities. All are agreed, for instance, that an arm that is never used degenerates — withers away. But many believe, quite illogically, that the sexual organs can be overburdened, or that a man can only manage to have a limited number of ejaculations ·.

Many men thus go round with a completely unfounded fear that one day they will have used up all their ammunition. It would be the same thing as saying we should save our strength for fear of using it all up. Or that we should refrain from burdening our brains by going to school and instead 'save up' for being especially bright when grown-up.

Degeneration is a word frequently abused and which should be used more carefully. (See also Exaggeration).   *i. & s.h.*

Demands for sexual satisfaction: See Simulation, Consideration and Vanity.

Demeter: Greek goddess of fertility. She was worshipped at somewhat lively feasts, and women used to bake sacrificial cakes for her in the shape of the male sexual organ (see Phallos).

Demimonde: Literally means 'half world'. A more respectable word for prostitute.

Demivierge: Means half virgin. See Virgin, technical. See also Petting.

Depilation: Means removal of hair. The plucking of eyebrows is common in our western civilization, and women remove hair from their armpits and their legs. Certain religions require the removal (wholly or partially) of head hair, but there are also primitive peoples that remove the hair round their sexual organs. Films are a good barometer of our tastes. It is refreshing to see that of recent years there have been films in which both the hero and the heroine have dared to admit they have hair under their armpits. If we all had one eye in the middle of our forehead we would think two eyes ugly. Beauty treatment is an excellent thing, but it can be overdone and thereby give us false illusions. Ten out of ten delightful film stars pick their noses. (See also Film). If we are unable to face up to this truth life becomes unbearable for our wives and sweethearts — who will find it impossible to live up to our ideals.   *i. & s.h.*

Depression: See Wedding Depression.

Derailment, sexual: See Perversity.

Dermatology: The science of treating the skin, especially skin diseases.

Descensus test: Descent of the testicles ·. These are formed in a boy prior to birth up in the abdominal cavity corresponding to where a woman's ovaries · are situated, but descend just before birth into the scrotum ·, or bag, designed to hold them. (See also Cryptorchism).

Descensus uteri: Descent of the womb. (See Genital Organs, female).

Descensus vagina: Descent of the vagina. (See Genital Organs, female).

Desire: See Sexual need.

Detumescens: Relaxation of the sexual organs after having been filled with blood and erected. (See Erection).

Development: Erotic development proceeds slowly. The process of adjustment between a man and a woman takes time.

It is in particular the woman's adjustment to the man that takes time, and irremediable damage has been done because girl-friends have untruthfully confided to each other how wonderful 'it' was from the first moment, and thereby screwed up the expectations of the inexperienced to unreasonable heights with corresponding disappointment as a result. (See Wedding Depression).

It is very, very seldom that a couple's erotic relationships can be described as anywhere near good from the start, nor do they improve within a couple of days, weeks, or months. Not until 6 months or so have passed is it sometimes possible to look back and say: "Do you remember in the beginning?" and smile at one another ... for by then things are possibly getting better.

Naturally we have drawn things a bit diagrammatically here, but there are good reasons for warning against unhealthy optimism and old wives' tales. A reasonably satisfactory sex life requires a serious effort and great patience on the part of both parties. Nobody can be said to have the ideal, perfect sex life, but a number are on the road towards it — and the road is by no means boring. Another

thing about erotic development is that it often moves by jumps. We would like our erotic development to be like this:

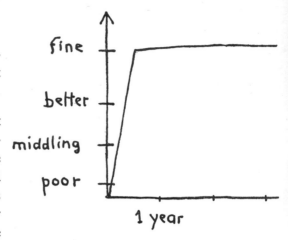

i.e. that we very rapidly and regularly become cleverer and cleverer. And at any rate we imagine it goes something like this:

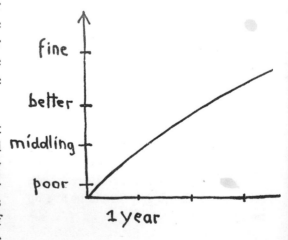

a steady, even improvement in one's achievements.

But this is not the way things go at all. Erotic development may very well be like this:

after swinging around a certain point for a time, very small swings to and from in either direction, a sudden drop with the resultant feeling of hopelessness: "It's all going b----- well wrong..." and then suddenly a jump: "It's much better than it was!" — once more pendulation around one point for a time, then a drop, then that hopeless feeling, improvement again, etc., etc., without ever reaching the absolute ideal. Disappointments · and depressions are necessary features of any process of learning, any development.

Kinsey · has proved that the more school education women have had, the greater sexual harmony they achieve. Sexual harmony is defined here as satisfying technique · in sexual intercourse. It might seem to indicate that greater intelligence or increased knowledge rendered women more willing to experiment ·, and that experimentation is the road to greater benefits for the woman.

But time favours good development too.
i. & s.h.

Diaphragm: A pessary (see Birth Control).

Dippoldismus: Another example of one of these words used to label some type of action. It means the desire to beat children with the object of becoming sexually excited, in other words a kind of sadism ·.
It is only mentioned here because this desire is somewhat commoner than one might think.

There is no doubt that in former times schoolmasters and schoolmistresses with unsatisfactory sex lives took pleasure in administering corporal punishment. It is obvious that pleasures of this sort must have had unfortunate effects on the children who suffered from them.

Of course one may strike one's child in self-defence. It is calculated, pleasure-giving cruelty that is dangerous.

(See also Upbringing, Governess, Sadism, Masochism). *s.h.*

Dirty words: See Words, naughty.

Dirty jokes: See Jokes.

Disappointment: It would be leaning too much towards romanticism if we did not stress the fact that human love life can contain a lot of disappointments — particularly as regards relationships between women and men. Homosexual relationships naturally have different, sometimes bigger problems, but as a rule greater equality or greater experience is involved. Above all, they do not

A dot · after a word refers to an article under this heading.   67

hold out all the hypocritical expectations ·
we make on heterosexual relationships.

There is not the same demand on
potency on the part of the man, and the
chances of orgasm are easier for the
woman because homosexual intercourse
is more varied than the ordinary,
patented form of heterosexual intercourse
we have been told to stick to.

No matter how difficult it may be, let
us for a moment try to peer over the
rims of the glasses which distort our
everyday world. Let us try to ignore the
prejudices we keep up in respect of
homosexuality ·.

In a homosexual relationship there is no
risk of having children. The risk of
catching a venereal disease · is possibly
less. The chances of both partners
obtaining sexual satisfaction is considerably greater because it is a question
of two persons of the same sex who are
better aware of the feelings involved.

Our conclusion from this unprejudiced
little tabulation must be that the attraction between the two sexes, (i.e. heterosexual attraction) — must, despite all the
difficulties, be far stronger than the
attraction between persons of the same
sex. In order to reassure pessimists even
further it may be added that even amongst
peoples who may choose freely between
heterosexual and homosexual satisfaction,
in fact even amongst those who practice
the ceremony of having all the boys of
the tribe initiated into homosexual acts
upon reaching puberty — even there, the
majority prefer the other sex.

If we compare heterosexual sex life with
masturbation ·, we obtain almost the
same result: fewer disappointments, easier
orgasms. So even though one is aware of
the disappointments of sex — heterosexual sex life — it will still not scare
anybody out of trying anyway. It will
not cause anybody to give up.

But the expectations concerning "the
wonderful thing that is going to happen
now" have embittered the years of learning (see also Practice) for many young,
heterosexual couples who have believed
that they were abnormal ·, warped ·,
impotent · or frigid ·.

Many married couples have drifted away
from each other and have believed that
their sex life was a total failure.

i. & s.h.

Discharge: The secretions which can
come from the woman's vagina (see
Genital Organs, female) outside the period
of her menstruation. Most women have
experienced this at certain periods. It can
be the symptoms of an inflammation
of the abdomen of one sort or another
so it is best to consult a doctor. In order
to enable the doctor to examine the
nature of the trouble the woman should
not have a vaginal douche before going
to see him, but merely wash herself
externally. (See also Gynaecological
Examination). i.h.

Disinclination: In the same way that
one can feel less active and energetic in
other spheres at times, it is naturally
also possible to be off form sexually.

All development · — including that of a sexual relationship — moves by jumps, with periods of progress interspersed by setbacks and standstills.

If a person never feels any desire, or if a considerable time passes without his or her feeling any desire, it may of course be a serious symptom, the root of which may be difficult to get at. On the other hand it is extremely rare that disinclination has physical reasons. Disinclination nearly always has mental reasons.

Disinclination may be due to inhibitions·, anxiety ·, acquired revulsion · and many other things. Women in particular are often brought up to be afraid of sexual relations. Disinclination may also be a restrained wish to experiment ·. Many women actually impede their husband's desire to play in a very intolerant · fashion. But men are not so very much better, for in their vanity · they often demand that a woman should enjoy precisely what they happen to regard as normal ·.

The conservatism of the woman is a little more understandable. (See Understanding). As a rule she has greater difficulty in obtaining sexual satisfaction ·. If a couple has developed a way of making love that provides the woman with a certain guarantee of having an orgasm ·, it is not so surprising if she is a little unwilling to embark on dubious experimentation. But experiments do not necessarily hold pleasure for the man only. Experiments have opened up new worlds for many women. Here too, one should talk matters over frankly and try to reach a more stimulating compromise.

A man as a rule has received a freer upbringing. He should lead the way, and, via gentle pressure, attempt to get round any too great a display of reserve. But it must be done patiently and with the proper kind of consideration. Far too many men and women adopt the attitude that if they fail to reap the full benefits of the ordinary, standardized, common system of love-making "then we're on the way to perversity and sin — and then there's just no point in the whole business at all."

This unfortunate attitude is wrong. Nature · is far more bountiful and tolerant. The strict conception of sin is something invented by pessimistic moralists. They have patented a kind of Nature for which no possible creator would ever accept responsibility. These strictly prejudiced people believe the whole world will come to an end if human beings are allowed to be human beings.   *i. & s.h.*

Divorce: Is, as a rule, a regrettable solution to marital problems. On the other hand it is perhaps even worse to stay together. Marriage in one form or another is known amongst all peoples, and the majority of those who marry probably regard marriage as a task to be completed together.

A divorce is a declaration of defeat, an incompleted task. Even those who flit from one relationship to the next (see Promiscuity) have a desire to settle down with 'the one and only'. She — or he — is dissatisfied with endlessly incompleted tasks too.

(Incidentally, a psychological mechanism exists that causes problems unsolved to remain in our minds and nag at us. Things that succeed, tasks with whose solution we are satisfied, are more easily forgotten).

Here in Denmark we have a very high divorce rate (six to seven thousand divorces a year) and other countries chide us for it. It does not necessarily mean that we have more unhappy marriages than other countries. It may merely mean that it is not against our moral · code to break off an unhappy marriage.

Many hundred thousands of people in Denmark have tried being divorced.

No matter how we try to interpret the many divorces, they still prove that human beings cannot always discover how to get on tolerably with one another.

The part played by sex in marital shipwrecks has often been discussed. This is an offshoot of the special position sexual matters have been allocated — in other spheres too.

It is an entirely wrong way of regarding the problem, because non-sexual problems in the course of living together will result in sexual problems — and sexual problems in the course of living together will result in problems in other spheres.

Life together for two people is a carpet woven with a single thread. The sexual side of this relationship is one of the patterns in this carpet, a pattern that is interwoven with all the other patterns.

It is an interplay between all the aspects of living, but we cannot say anything at all about sexual problems having been the cause of so-and-so many marital shipwrecks.

We know that masturbation · in marriage can be a problem. We know that the question of orgasm ·, frequency of sexual intercourse, the importance of potency · and many other things are tangible problems in many relationships. What is normal, and what is abnormal?

If people believe their sex life together is unsatisfactory because they set up ideal demands which nobody else can meet — well, we are in a poor way.

Far too many husbands believe that all girls with the exception of their own wife are more passionate and 'better at it'. Far too many women believe that they themselves are hopeless, but that if only the right man would come along (who somehow never has) he would be able to arouse them just like the Prince and the Sleeping Beauty. (See Passion and Inferiority).

Far too many possibilities are neglected within the wide limits available. In young people and young couples a frank desire to achieve understanding exists. But it can sometimes be too late, in which case there is nothing for it but to part. If one knows a little about what to expect of the other party, and realizes the difficulties everybody has had, or will have — then there should be a chance of overcoming them together too. (See also Disappointment).

In other spheres we realize how knowledge renders problems smaller. In the sphere of sex there not only exists a colossal amount of ignorance but also a great amount of opposition to enlightenment. It takes time to build up a life together with somebody — and the sexual side of it is by no means the least. It requires patience and mutual confidence, but not too much modesty · and not too much vanity · and misplaced consideration ·. The recipe is by no means easy and our object here is not that of 'forcing' any couple to stay together.

But much dissatisfaction could be turned into a will to cooperate, and to optimism, if we knew a little more about each other and about ourselves.   *i. & s.h.*

Doctors: All doctors are naturally bound by a professional pledge of secrecy, i.e. to keep everything their patients tell them to themselves.

In the course of time most doctors experience most sides of human nature and develop a great degree of tolerance ·. They become very understanding and helpful. It would be nice to be able to say that all doctors were equally understanding and helpful.

Unfortunately this is not possible. Doctors can differ just like all other kinds of people, and some of them demonstrate a rather strict and condemnatory attitude. This applies to doctors, psychologists ·, nurses and others whose task in life it is to help others — they too may have their prejudices ·. Now it so happens that doctors enjoy particularly great confidence. We approach them with frankness and in the expectation of meeting under-

standing and helpfulness — and therefore any eventual condemnatory attitude on their part is felt even more keenly. A slightly unfriendly word, a slightly questioning eyebrow — and we sometimes feel as though we had been socked in the eye with a wet rag.

The best thing to do is try another doctor — perhaps a psychiatrist ·, or a woman doctor, or a gynaecologist. Let us mention here that in Denmark, of recent years, some women doctors in particular have taken this question up.

Unfortunately none but the very youngest of doctors nowadays has ever learnt anything about human sex life during the course of his, or her, studies. This applies to doctors, psychologists and others. This important field is still neglected. This is a result of our still-slightly-too-strict code of morals·.

Kinsey · was originally a professor of zoology, but discovered how little we know about man. His investigations ought to have been carried out long ago — and considerable information still needs collecting.   *i. & s.h.*

Domina: Means mistress in the dominating sense of the word. Used particularly in connection with masochistic men (see Masochism and Governess).

Don Juan: Just as Casanova ·, an historic person as well as an everyday term. He lived in the 14th century and has been immortalized in a number of plays. The term 'a Don Juan' has always implied a lady's man, skirt-chaser, seducer of women, and has now passed into psychological terminology, i.e. 'a Don Juan complex', by which is understood what most of we married men probably have experienced, namely a desire, by means of new conquests·, to find out whether we are still capable of enchanting the girls. As far as men are concerned the crux of the matter is whether the girl will go to bed with them.

Women have their 'Don Juan complex' too, but it is satisfied much more easily — merely by enjoying the ardent glances of the men as they go for a stroll through the streets.   *s.h.*

Don Juan, the conqueror.

Douche, vaginal: The term used for rinsing out the vagina (see Genital Organs, female) with the help of an irrigator or vaginal syringe. Normally speaking it should not be necessary, because a woman's vagina is self-cleansing. When using a pessary · as a contraceptive one may, however, rinse out the vagina with lukewarm water to which half a tablespoonful of kitchen salt has been added — before removing the pessary.   *i.h.*

Dreams: Play a part in our sex lives in various ways. For one thing, dreams of a directly sexual nature are quite frequently the cause of orgasms · in both women and men. In men they may result in ejaculation ·, in other words a directly visible result of the dream.

In women an orgasm in the course of a dream is more easily forgotten, more easily suppressed ·. (See also Fantasies, sexual).

Sexual desires can furthermore manifest themselves in disguise — in the form of symbols — in a number of dreams. (See also Psychoanalysis, Freud, Orgasm; and Emissions, nocturnal).

Dreams, interpretation of: See Freud and Psychoanalysis.

Dysmennorrhea: Irregular or painful menstruation ·.

E

Education, sexual: By this, two things may be meant:

1) The part of upbringing · which in particular has a bearing on a person's subsequent sex life.
2) A narrower sense: direct sexual enlightenment ·.

We realize today that upbringing as a whole is of importance to an adult's sex life (see also Relationship) because a person's sex life is a very important and considerable part of life as a whole.

Now and again we have an opportunity of seeing clearly how certain factors in a person's upbringing later influence certain factors in his or her sex life (see Governess).

It is obvious that indirect sexual upbringing is far more important than the direct form — in other words that upbringing as a whole plays a far larger part than the conscious, direct form of sexual enlightenment.

So when we talk about being open-minded and natural, we must face the fact that none of us can ever acquire an open mind or be capable of behaving entirely as in nature ·. The most we can develop is a slightly more open mind, freed from the worst of the injunctions received during a strict upbringing. We can become slightly more tolerant (see Intolerance) — partly towards ourselves, partly towards others, and partly towards the society in which we live. (See also Emancipation).

To achieve the right balance between freedom and responsibility is probably the greatest objective a person can set himself — far more important and also far more difficult than landing monkeys on Mars. We can establish this much, namely that within historic time we have on occasions been much farther from the ideal balance, but that at other times we have been somewhat nearer.

So there is no reason to stand up and say: "Never before have we human beings had such opportunities of growing up in harmony with our own demands and those of society." There is plenty of work ahead.   *i.h.*

Egg tube, egg duct: See Genital Organs, female.

Egoism, egoist: Self-interest, self-interested person. Normally egoism is regarded as something negative and undesirable. We do not agree here. On the contrary, we would like to speak up for the principle of healthy egoism. A person who has his or her reasonable needs fulfilled also can afford to pass on any surplus to others. Perhaps there is something to be said for the realistic observation that if I make this, that or the other contribution, I will receive something else in return — there must be a certain balance in life. The person who merely gives and gives soon produces a deficit — and what is more, creates egoists around him.

It is in the very sphere of our love lives that a certain degree of egoism is necessary, and where misplaced consideration · can be disastrous. There are many couples where the woman is only concerned with satisfying the man, and the man only thinks of satisfying the woman. Each believes he or she is showing consideration, but in reality they are making unhealthy, egoistic demands on the other person instead of using the other person to a somewhat greater degree as a means of satisfying themselves, which after all is just as important.

These thoughts can very easily be misunderstood. We are not suggesting that the man should merely satisfy himself as quickly as possible and take no further notice of the woman. But in his attempts to satisfy her, he should not forget himself and his own satisfaction ·. He should, rather, offer her an opportunity of satisfying herself — whether she cares to take advantage of it, or is able to do so, is her lookout and concerns her alone.

Here she should try to be the healthy egoist who says: "Try this, that or the other way, it's nicer" — without too much modesty. (See also Initiative).

We should be affectionate towards ourselves, be able to be fond of ourselves, accept ourselves. Far too many people's lives are spoiled because as time goes on they no longer have any idea what they want — because they dare not face up to facts. This is not something we are born with, but acquired during our upbringing. The baby that howls when it wants food or wants to be picked up, is a pure egoist who gives nothing and demands everything. Gradually the child learns that the rest of us have a right to be here too. It learns to give in order to receive — and things become more balanced.   *i. & s.h.*

Ejaculation: When a man's sexual excitement reaches a sufficiently pronounced degree he experiences intense pleasure that culminates in ejaculation, i.e. a number of rhythmical contractions of the bladder in which the sperm is stored, and in the passage leading out to the tip of the penis (see Genital Organs, male), by means of which the sperm is squirted out in a number of small portions. The penis does not necessarily have to be hard, or erected (see Erection) in order for ejaculation to take place, but is as a rule. Thus we see that ejaculation of sperm is dependent upon a man's feeling of sexual pleasure. Very few men have any problems in connection with the ejaculation of their sperm with one exception: it happens too soon!

This premature ejaculation is bound up with many different things. (See also Orgasm). In many cases a long time may have passed since he last obtained sexual satisfaction, with the result that his nerves are on edge and expectations great — and he finds himself ejaculating almost before he has started.

74

It may also be a kind of revenge. Many will object and say: "But I don't *want* to ejaculate so quickly!" which is of course true too. On the other hand it may be that misplaced consideration · (see Egoism) succeeds in taking revenge unconsciously — without one's realizing it. If a man is exaggeratedly considerate and attaches far too much importance to satisfying a woman, a certain amount of irritation may arise about her taking "so long about it". And this irritation may well result in uncontrollably quick ejaculation. It may help — if circumstances are reasonably good and there is no hurry — if an agreement is reached beforehand: "I'll just have an ejaculation first to relieve the worst tension without your needing to take part very much — and then later on we can both try together peacefully." This is an example of healthy and sensible egoism which in the long run can be of benefit to both partners — instead of working up to something great and wonderful and then being sadly disappointed. For, once the girl is lying there on her back, unsatisfied and deeply disappointed, everything seems to go wrong and everything seems impossible. All too many wives know just what it means when their husbands insist on their having an orgasm — and how it makes them more 'tied up' than ever. Finally they pretend to have had one — for the sake of peace and so as not to wound his vanity — for it is this which demands satisfaction. In exactly the same way, a demand from the woman for staying power on the part of the man can have the opposite effect — he has an ejaculation sooner than ever.

Premature ejaculation can have many causes, but by far the majority of them are mental. There may be some anxiety · or other, moral scruples, revulsion ·, shame, and many other things that may be very difficult to sort out on account of their not being isolated factors but bound up with the entire personality of the person concerned. (See also Breeding, good). Psychoanalysis · will often prove the best and profoundest answer, but it is a lengthy, arduous and expensive business because it is impossible to attack the problem directly. If it is possible to help by means of small short cuts and a kind of treatment of the symptoms, it may in many cases prove sufficient, because this particular problem is a sort of fence that has to be got over.

If a successful jump at it is made somehow or other, the mere fact of doing so increases self-confidence, and the chances of cure are thus likewise increased automatically — a good start has been made.

Conversely, a single accident can have a paralysing effect and thereby start things moving in completely the wrong direction — which can be equally difficult to remedy. Retarded ejaculation — despite erection and desire — is rarer, but many will find themselves experiencing it in periods. This too will often have a complicated mental cause. In a number of cases it is because the man — consciously or otherwise — wants a change.

It may be that he would like to try a different position — or another girl. The latter is the more serious problem and not so easy to solve. The sex life of the couple in question may have got into a backwater — small pinpricks can become almost unhealable wounds — and such problems may become almost impossible to solve. Abstinence over a period can help — talking it over frankly together too, likewise honesty and tact. All of which can be very difficult in practice.

The couple can also choose a technique that makes them independent of the man's sexual potency.

Caressing of the clitoris with the fingers before ·actual intercourse takes place, likewise during actual intercourse, is often effective and is common in the course of a normal sex life.

(See also Aggression, Ambivalence, Impotency, Potency, Titillation, sexual; Orgasm and Satisfaction).   *s.h.*

Emancipated: Being emancipated is perhaps regarded as slightly ridiculous today, while broad-mindedness has acquired a certain degree of respect — even though this too has met with disapproval. The words emancipated and broad-minded have both been 'fashionable', which can be detrimental even to the best of causes. Nowadays one can read short stories in which the author lets an upperclass lady confide to the gentleman at her side at dinner that "...

I'm just crazy about broad-mindedness, you know..."

But emancipation and broad-mindedness should be taken seriously, even though both are more the expression of a wish than a reality. For no matter how much

we resist we can never entirely liberate ourselves from the upbringing we have received — from our background, which leaves its mark on us for life.

Even the most expensive and painstaking psychoanalysis cannot wipe the blackboard of the soul entirely clean, but it may at least help us to read and understand what is written on it. Even the best and most honest desire in the world cannot liberate our mind from every prejudice ·. It may be a little bitter and heart-breaking to realize we have to drag at any rate a little of our past with us, but there is no reason for this to make us despair of any improvement at all.

If we decide quite clearly in our minds just what our prejudices are, and that our attitudes may be influenced by the wrong authorities · (see also Morals) much is already won. The woman who, by way of a start, acknowledges her exaggerated modesty · and admits she perhaps is a little too prudish, is on the way to emancipating herself. And the man who realizes that his wish to satisfy his loved one is perhaps dictated to a greater extent by masculine vanity · and less by consideration is on his way towards broader-mindedness too. Let us go on being a little crazy about emancipation and broad-mindedness. At least it produces results. We have come far during recent decades. Let us console ourselves with the fact that the completely emancipated and broad-minded human being would be utterly unfitted to live in any human society at all.   *i. & s.h.*

Emancipation: Used particularly in connection with female emancipation, by which we understand the fight to liberate woman from her dependence upon man, a dependence which, in Denmark — and many other countries — manifests itself in her taking her husband's name upon marriage, not being permitted to submit separate income tax returns, receiving lower wages for the same work, and many other things, both large and small.

Naturally she has advantages from her state of dependence too: fewer economic problems, fewer economic responsibilities, the pleasure of greater gallantry being displayed towards her.

We sometimes speak of 'emancipated women' in slightly disparaging tones, the inference being that their independence has made them less feminine. This is a pity — for presumably there is no need for us to deny our sex in the course of our anxiety to acquire the same status as men.

This whole question becomes no less complicated on account of the fact that many women — even the so-called feminists — themselves betray the fight for emancipation.

Those who champion the 'liberation of women' are still obliged to be demonstrative about it, which shows we have not come very far. Of course we do not get put in prison for it any more, but we are still regarded with a certain measure of superiority, are made fun of, and some of our own number are often worse than men.   *i.h.*

Emissions, nocturnal: The name given to involuntary ejaculations of sperm in the man. (See also Ejaculation). When boys reach the age of 14—15 their testicles (see Genital Organs, male) start producing sperm cells.

This production happens entirely independently of external factors. Every second, hundreds and thousands of sperm cells are produced — and stored in special depots. When these depots are full, and sperm cells continue to be produced, space has to be made for them — and this is done by letting some of the sperm be ejaculated through the penis. (See Genital Organs, male; Masturbation, Orgasm, Fertilization).

The ejaculation of sperm usually takes place in conjunction with an intense feeling of erotic pleasure. As a rule ejaculation takes place by means of masturbation · — i.e. by means of a conscious, intentional effort to bring forth this pleasurable sensation and the corresponding emptying of the sperm depots.

But if they are not emptied in this fashion — and if the depots, as stated, become filled to capacity — the pressure of the sperm in combination with the increasing sexual needs can produce erotic dreams of such an intensely titillating kind that the result is an orgasm · during sleep. As such nightly emissions usually come instead of — and later than — masturbation or possible sexual intercourse, the satisfaction obtained is as a rule more intense and even more pleasurable — in the same way that food tastes best when one is very hungry.

Many boys in the course of time have been frightened by these emissions — but there is no cause for this.

Nocturnal emissions are an entirely normal way of emptying the sperm depots — just as normal as masturbation and sexual intercourse. In former times nocturnal emissions were also regarded as sinful — in the same way so many other pleasurable things have been regarded as sinful. (See also Epicurean).

Monks who had nocturnal emissions were made to do severe penances — yet another sad example of a negative attitude towards the utterly natural features of sexual development.

It is not rare for a boy's first ejaculation to take place in the form of an emission during sleep. A few orgasms *without* ejaculation of sperm may also take place — a kind of painful, erotic, pleasurable sensation — because the need for orgasm and the need for ejaculation of sperm are not always the same — even though they collaborate.

Thus in a way it is neither the dreams, masturbation nor sexual intercourse that bring on the orgasm and the ejaculation of sperm, but the increasing sexual needs, i.e. the increasing sexual urge *and* the filled sperm depots that bring on the desire to dream erotically, masturbate or have sexual intercourse.

These above-mentioned first orgasms can be brought on by sliding down a banister, climbing a rope and many other ways involving the pressing, squeezing or rubbing of the penis. But the point is that they do not come *because* one slides — they only come when the sexual need has manifested itself.

Nocturnal emissions do not take place in women, but their sexual needs increase in the same way as those of men and can be satisfied, i.e. result in orgasm, through nocturnal erotic dreams, masturbation, and sexual intercourse.

In the same way that a little mucus, with no sperm content, can be secreted from the man's penis when sexually stimulated, glandular secretions can also take place in the woman inside and at the entrance to the vagina, e.g. from the glands in the larger vaginal lips. (See Genital Organs, female). *i. & s.h.*

Engagement: See Betrothal.

Enlightenment, sexual: It is of importance that children be given honest answers to the questions they quite naturally pose, because it is exciting to learn where we all come from; much more exciting and personal than where bricks come from.

A logical result of the democratic attitude is that we should try to bring our children up in a straightforward atmosphere without hypocrisy. The same applies to young people.

The entire unconscious, indirect form of sexual upbringing ·, however, is much more important. Sexual enlightenment is not a patent medicine or a recipe for happiness that solves all difficulties. It is only a very tiny part of something important.

In so saying it must be stressed that we who are now grown-up are products of our own upbringing, i.e. of all the fortunate and less fortunate influences we have received during our period of growing up — in just the same way as our parents were products of the conditions and influences governing their upbringing.

We can pass the blame on backwards as far as we like and say that it is neither our fault, nor that of our parents, nor anybody else's that society and our moral code are the way they are today. We cannot do so very much to alter the existing state of affairs and we cannot put it right at all. We can patch it up a little here and there. We can fight for a small change here, a bigger one there, but the total result will only amount to small scratches on the surface. Nevertheless, we can be optimistic and observe, in many small things, that the world is actually making progress. A lot of very welcome things have happened during the course of the past 25 years. We can try to cling on to these, defend them, and continue working along the same lines.

It is not so many years ago that botany was regarded, in wide circles, as being too indecent a subject to teach children.

Thus we probably have to appeal in particular to the young, and to young couples, who still have the injustices fresh in their minds and are still willing to fight a little. Once we have settled into our thirties or forties we acquire a certain mildness and lamblike piousness and declare that "it's p-p-probably a little exaggerated — w-w-we have n-never actually s-s-suffered on account of the upbringing we were given." And it is both a good thing and a bad thing that we should have adapted ourselves and toed the line as well as we have.

It is a good thing because both we and society are best served by a spot of adaption — we *must* adapt ourselves.

But it is a little sad that such love should make us blind.   *s.h.*

Environment, social: See Upbringing.

Epicurean: One who attaches great importance to pleasures. This is regarded as being slightly sinful, a case of the psychological mechanism once summed up effectively in a remark made at a ladies' lunch party: "What a shame all the things that are lovely are either sinful or fattening!"

It is not uncommon to fear the envy of the gods. We are a little afraid of the things that are nice. We say "Touch wood!" (and say it is only for fun — but it is a curiously persistent sort of joke). We believe that warm, fresh white bread is unhealthy, though it is only unhealthy for those who have trouble with their digestions — and even for them it is merely a little heavy to digest. We believe that brown iodine is better than the red kind, merely because the brown kind stings and the red does not. We smoke filter cigarettes as a token of our subservience to the god of cancer — even though we know it is of no help.

There are many examples of the fact that we modern people are full of this sort of superstition ·.

This is also the psychological explanation why a great number of unpleasantly drastic remedies really can help, especially in the case of psychic difficulties. Cold showerbaths, early morning gymnastics and other forms of self-torture are examples of things we impose upon ourselves in order to be allowed to enjoy life in other ways. (See also Anxiety and Joseph's Night).

There is no need to deprive anybody of their beliefs, or to advise against the drastic remedies. They work — and many of us need some form of self-discipline or other — unfortunately. We are probably brought up not to be able to tolerate enjoying ourselves too much — it gives us a feeling of insecurity and a slightly bad conscience ·. (See also Celibate).   *i. & s.h.*

Epididymis, or appendix testis: Behind the testicles (see Genital Organs, male) are a number of small, oblong, soft tubules. The testicles themselves can be felt inside the scrotum like two plums, but the epididymis consists of a tube some 20 feet in length in which the sperm is stored. It is possible that the sperm cells undergo a kind of ripening process while stored here.

Epididymitis: Is an inflammation that may be caused by gonorrhea (see Venereal Diseases) or tuberculosis. The epididymis swells up and becomes taut and sore. The inflammation may result in sterility · if not treated by a doctor without delay.

If a man becomes violently sexually excited without being able to ejaculate · the epididymis may also swell up a little and be sore for a few minutes or hours, but this has nothing to do with any inflammation. It is not pleasant, but it is not dangerous.   *s.h.*

Erection: In sexual connections the term is used principally to describe the state of the penis ·, or male sexual organ, when it becomes harder, firmer, bigger and longer by reason of blood streaming into it and filling the tissue, and when, at the same time, special muscles lift this hard penis from its normal, downward-hanging position and make it point away from the body and slightly upwards — that is, when the man is standing up. Erection goes together with the desire for sexual satisfaction. Erection is — as all men know — entirely uncontrollable. It is impossible to decide to have an erection and have one — or the reverse. (See also Ejaculation, Potency, Intercourse). Erection occurs in the woman as a result of sexual desire too, here its being a question of the

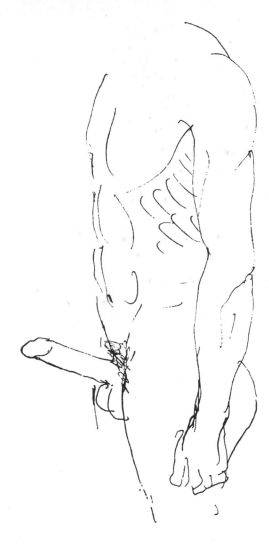

Many young women have been given a serious fright simply because of being unprepared to see a man like this.

clitoris · (see Genital Organs, female) a small organ corresponding to the very tip of the penis on a man, and which in the same way becomes larger when filled with blood. A woman also has special muscles that raise the clitoris.

The opposite of erection — a state of relaxation which takes place when the blood flows away and the muscles themselves relax — is called detumescens.

Erection in the woman provides increased excitation in an already sensitive organ. In the man it enables him to press his penis into a woman's vagina (see Genital Organs, female). This fact, namely that erection is necessary to ordinary sexual intercourse, has resulted in its being very much influenced by mental factors in the man. Anxiety · and other forms of uncertainty can thus result in erection disappearing at highly inconvenient moments. Many in the course of time have believed, for instance, that particular virility was required to break through a woman's hymen (see Maidenhead); they have become afraid, and the state of erection has decreased or vanished entirely because of this very anxiety. (See also Aggression). On the other hand erection is not necessary. A man can easily be sexually satisfied and have ejaculation without.

Many have formerly believed that erection on the man's part was necessary in order for a woman to be satisfied. It has been believed — quite erroneously — that orgasm · in the woman was brought about by sensations inside the vagina ·. (See Clitoral and Vaginal Orgasm). This naturally has made many men nervous, and such nervousness may be sufficient to prevent erection or to bring about very rapid ejaculation ·. But the point is that erection is not necessary in order to satisfy a woman. (See Petting).

i. & s.h.

Erogenous zones: Areas of the body said to be particularly capable of arousing sexual passions and desires. Many authors of books of sexual instruction include detailed descriptions of these areas. By a comparison of their directives we find that *everything*, with the possible exception of the shinbone and the forearm, is classified as an erogenous zone in the woman — for it is the woman in particular in whom we are interested. Common to all of them are the sexual organs, breasts and mouth; but the ears, the hairline on the forehead and the inside of the thighs are frequently mentioned too.

These areas need not all be taken too literally. A woman can become sexually excited from being caressed anywhere on the body at all, but naturally more so on the forbidden areas. On the other hand there are women who do not experience any particular sensations when caressed. Then again, there are women who feel such caressing so intensely they become frightened and behave as though they were downright revolted by it.

There are also women who are disgusted and who deny its having any inspiring effect on them whatsoever. (See also Revulsion). This is another subject on which it is best to talk matters over.

We must also remember that when a young couple have just got to know one another, everything is exciting and sexually stirring. It is only later on that one gradually finds out what one likes and what one's partner likes. It may take years — and some never find out at all. (See also Inclination).

It is furthermore possible that Kinsey is right when he says that men in general can become excited by what they think and imagine, while women in the maj-

ority of cases become sexually aroused by kisses and caresses. If this sexual difference does actually exist, whether by nature or acquired, it would explain something of the activity of the man as opposed to the passivity of the woman. (See Initiative).

Finally we must bear in mind that erogenous areas can be cultivated. (See Pavlov). If a man, for instance, always begins by patting his loved one on the tip of her nose by way of leading up to further caresses and their whole sex life — and that such sex life, of course, is a matter of pleasure to her — this pat on the nose will soon become a signal, a sign that something good is on its way — and it will thus become an erogenous zone in the person concerned.

i. & s.h.

Eros: Also known as Amor, or Cupid. The god of love, armed with a bow-and-arrow.

Erotics: Anything and everything connected with sexual love.

A typical public lavatory drawing.

82

Erotographomania: The desire to write about, or draw, sexual subjects.

Drawings and inscriptions made on the doors and walls of public lavatories can be said to be the outcome of such desires.

When it comes to the point, we all quite enjoy busying ourselves with these subjects. It is the manner in which we do so that varies in its acceptability. Some ways are ingenious, others less so.

The person who makes rude drawings, writes rude words, sends letters containing crude remarks or proposals, or anything of this nature, is not necessarily so very unhinged or abnormal. It is merely not a particularly ingenious way of giving vent to these desires.

We have given vent to our erotographomania — in one way — by writing this book. Some will feel this way is not particularly ingenious either. Others will perhaps write indignant letters to say that books like this should be forbidden. This is a more ingenious way.

All of us manage to satisfy our need to occupy ourselves with sex.

There are, incidentally, scholastic, scientific works on the lavatory drawings and inscriptions of the world — for example *Krauss : Antropophyteia,* printed privately, Leipzig.

A thesis on the subject is being prepared in Denmark by Leo Weissberg, B. A., *Epigraphica obscaena hauniensis.*

Clumsy, symbolic · drawings like this are found all over the world. In civilized societies they are relegated to the walls and doors of public lavatories.

Kinsey · too, in his report on the sex life of American women, presents some interesting analyses on p. 673 ff.

i. & s.h.

Erotomaniac, erotomania: Pursuing an exaggeratedly active sex life is classified as erotomania and a person who indulges in an exaggerated amount of sexual activity as an erotomaniac. There is even a special term for male erotomania, namely satyriasis, and one for female, nymphomania. In the course of time both terms have been considerably abused.

Vigorous men and women have been called erotomaniacs because it is not the done thing to reveal one's desires. It has also been used as the name of a disease:

"He is suffering from erotomania" — quite erroneously, for after all it is not a disease, but possibly the *symptom* of one. Furthermore, what is often simply the case is not increased sexual urges, but unsatisfied sexual urges that have for this reason mounted and mounted without being able to find an outlet.

In the course of time many women have had the label erotomaniac pinned on to them because they have anxiously sought a man with whom they could satisfy their sexual desires. It would be more correct to say of them that their will to obtain sexual satisfaction has been stronger than normal, and that their ability to obtain it has possibly been less.

Precisely the same thing can occur in men — although it is much less frequent.

What naturally has a distinct bearing on the matter is that women are seldom able to permit themselves many liberties before being called erotomaniacs. A man can go much further without being similarly classified.

Men find it easier to obtain physical satisfaction, but some psychic derangement can prevent mental satisfaction. It is not uncommon for men to find they simply must go to bed with many girls, a new one each time, in order to convince themselves about their masculinity. (See Don Juan). There is thus here no question of an increase in sexual urges either, but of something which renders sexual satisfaction in the more usual way difficult.

There are many other things we classify as erotomania without justification. It is possible that persons do exist with exaggerated sexual urges, even though it sounds a little illogical. Of course we know of people who eat too much and become fat; but once they are absolutely stuffed at least they stop. We do not say of such persons that they are suffering from exaggeratedly increased hunger, but merely say their appetites are somewhat out of balance. Percentually speaking it is, after all, only a matter of small divergencies — a few calories a day.

In certain cases of mental deficiency and mental disorders we observe an apparent increase in sexual desires, but whether this is really so is open to doubt. It is more likely their inhibitions that are lacking or have disappeared, and/or an unsatisfied sex life, that will prove to be the cause of the condition.

It would probably be wiser of us to exercise more care before accusing anybody of erotomania as long as we observers are so unreliable on account of our own prejudices · and as long as we are unable to measure the strength of sexual urges and therefore have no knowledge as to what is normal and what is not. We get so easily shocked by those who have more fun than we do — or who do what we dare not do (See Indignation). And we have a tendency to regard whatever happens to be lovely as unhealthy and sinful (see Epicurean).

i. & s.h.

Ethnography: See Anthropology.

Eunuch: See Castration.

Excess: In nearly all works both large and small on the subject of sexual instruction — up to and including those of our day — one can read that "sex is not harmful provided it is not practised to excess." Let it suffice to quote a very widely sold medical sex-manual which helped to form our grandparents' and parents' attitude towards sex — and thus, unfortunately, ours too:

"Satisfaction of the sexual urges before sexual maturity has been fully reached during approximately the twentieth year is harmful, particularly when achieved by unnatural means such as masturbation and bestiality ·. At a sexually mature age a moderate measure of sexual satisfaction has as a rule no harmful influence on the health ...."

People have thus been filled with such nonsense as this — and still are to a more or less camouflaged degree.

Several books could be filled with quotations of this kind. "It is now realized that masturbation is not harmful provided it is not practised to excess" is another example of an inaccurate, negative attitude.

Let us clear up one or two misunderstandings once and for all. Masturbation, sexual satisfaction and other forms of sexual activity are not practised to excess.

Of course a thing *can* be practised to excess. We *can* eat so much that our stomachs burst — but it is very seldom.

We can run and run and run until we fall down dead — but that is very seldom too. In by far the majority of cases we regulate ourselves excellently. (See also Erotomania and Degeneration).

As long as we have no idea when sex can be said to be practised to excess, no sensible purpose is served by warning against excesses.

We cannot say that three acts of sexual intercourse a week is the most healthy thing when we know that certain native tribes practice intercourse several times every night. We cannot say it is wrong to masturbate every day when we know that many people do so several times a day without detrimental effect.

Kinsey mentions a woman who had approximately 70 orgasms a week.

Naturally a person should be able to control his desires. We do not permit ourselves to steal food from a shop just because we have no money on us.

Far too many young people have tortured themselves in the course of time with the cruellest forms of self-reproach on account of these irresponsible forms of mental terrorism. "As long as I don't do it too much!" — "I mustn't practise it to excess" they have groaned to themselves with the blackest of consciences — while men and women (who should have been able to remember their own youth better) have stood up and self-righteously preached: "He who overcomes himself ..." Basically it is probably a question of believing in man as he is — or not. (See also Superstition).

After all, we find no cause to go round wagging an admonitory forefinger and warning: "The passing of water is harmless — provided it is not practised to excess." *i. & s.h.*

Excitation, sexual: See Titillation, sexual.

Exhibitionism: The desire to show one-self. Used particularly of men who derive satisfaction from undoing their flybuttons and showing their genital organs to passers-by, especially women and children. Such men are called exhibitionists.

Exhibitionism naturally does not exist in countries where nakedness is accepted. (See Perversity and Deformity Fetishism).

Many grown-ups receive a bad fright if they meet an exhibitionist. The sight of one may look a little frightening, but to the best of our knowledge there has never been any instance of an exhibitionist who also attacked the person or persons to whom he bared himself. So apart from the visual shock he is a fairly harmless fellow. (See also Understanding and Peeping Tom).

While small children usually take this sort of experience very calmly, larger children are often badly frightened. But it is not until one has learnt that it is 'naughty' that one can become frightened by nakedness or exhibitionism. (See Nudism).

Within the sphere of psychology, the word exhibitionism is used in a much broader sense as it includes all desire to perform, draw attention to oneself, be the centre of interest, show off — when it becomes a pleasure and moreover one which we all recognize in ourselves. It is very nice to give a lecture, stand up and sing a song, be able to tell funny stories, appear on a stage, and so on — and many people suffer a great deal from having strong desires to perform show off but either being unable to do so or

not daring. (See also Vanity, Shyness, Slave Trade).

In the course of a normal sex life, exhibitionism, in the narrow as well as the broad sense of the word, plays a large part too. Most people like to show themselves naked to their partner and be accepted and admired.

In the original Danish edition, as well as in the Swedish and Norwegian, this space carried an illustration. Although it was allowed in Scandinavia legal opinion has warned us against its inclusion. We apologise to all readers for this omission and recognise that no intelligent adult would have regarded this particular illustration as being offensive.

The Editors.

Women have many legal possibilities of practising exhibitionism. Tight sweaters, decolleté or short dresses, and so forth. The cotton wool padding (see also Breeches) men have on their shoulders is a form of exhibitionism too. (See also Fetishism and the drawing next to the article on Modesty).   *i. & s.h.*

Expectations: See Cinema and Wedding Depression.

Experience: It can be quite useful to differentiate between the experienced world and the physical.

In the physical world we can determine, soberly and precisely, that things are like this or like that. A colour, for instance, can be measured and described in terms of wave-lengths. A note of music can be described in oscillations — in the physical world.

But every person experiences things in his own way. A scared person believes that unpleasant things must be hiding in a dark corridor that — physically — is entirely empty.

A colour-blind person may find it hard to see a red flag against a pale green background because red and green merge into one in his eyes. An audile person — who understands things he hears best — will get more out of a lecture than a visile person, who understands things he reads or sees better. Even though physically speaking the lecture is the same in both cases.

Nor is there any use in a doctor's saying: "There's nothing the matter with you!" just because he is unable, physically, to measure any deviation from normal. We may none the less be feeling awful — and we may be right.

We are obliged to accept — and respect — the fact that another person can experience a thing in an entirely different manner from the way we experience it

ourselves. This applies to matters of love and sex too.

We each have our individual mental and physical equipment — which determine to a great extent what we experience and how we experience it. *i. & s.h.*

A more acceptable way of showing off.

87

Experiment, to: The idea of trying something new has, within the sphere of sex, become synonymous with changing one's partner.

Far too many are afraid of trying something new *together*. They believe that unless they enjoy a perfect sex life they might just as well change partners. Young animals often experiment with their sex lives. We know of many human societies · in which it is fully accepted practice for children and young people to play — with themselves, with others of the same sex and with others of the opposite sex.

When they play at 'Mothers and Fathers' they give their imaginations full rein.

We, in our society, have elected to forbid all experimentation. Whether it is right of us is open to discussion, but we cannot change matters from one day to the next.

We can, however, accept the consequences of having been placed under restraint. We can accept the fact that a great deal of experimentation, of trial and error and training, is necessary.

We are not born with the ability to pursue happy sex lives. Even if we removed all our prejudices · and all our bungling it does not mean we would be all ready to have a marvellous time.

We first have to go through a period of seeking, testing, practice ·. Nothing is quite so difficult as knowing exactly what one wants. We are permitted to develop prowess in many other fields by going through a period of clumsy playing first.

It is therefore of great importance for two people who want to build up a happy sex life together to realize they must be prepared to experiment and practise. And this experimentation never stops.

In time many couples probably find the form that provides most satisfaction for both, but there is no reason to believe that perfection has thereby been obtained.

Sexual relations can go on becoming nicer than ever, and a certain amount of variation is entirely reasonable.

Women in particular often find it difficult to accept this playing — the experimental side of sex. Women seldom play at other things the way men can.

But after all, the experimentation has mutual pleasure as its object.

It is not certain that the ordinary form of sexual intercourse is the one to provide the greatest satisfaction. Why accept the bed supplied by the furniture and mattress manufacturers as being the perfect form of bower?

We can learn — from masturbation techniques, homosexual intercourse techniques and petting, that the ordinary form of sexual intercourse is not necessarily the position that provides the greatest advantages. We can, moreover, with the help of pillows, bed-ends and other devices, experiment until we find the form of love life that gives us the pleasantest sensations.

Other people's sex lives are not so tame and unimaginative as one might think by seeing them and hearing them speak.

They are well-guarded secrets. But the human imagination does not permit itself to be cowed.   *i. & s.h.*

F

Facts, facing up to: Many people have a very poor knowledge of themselves — they are very loath to face up to facts. Seeing that so many perfectly normal things are hushed into silence, it is hardly surprising that a great many people go round believing themselves to be the only people in the world to have this or that particular problem.

Others believe we can all become better people if we suppress and deny the things that must be regarded as common to all mankind. It was once modern to refuse to admit that a normal woman had sexual desires. If a lady felt such urges she could go and see her doctor · and get a sedative.

If Kinsey · had interviewed women in those days, a great number of nice, self-respecting ladies would have firmly insisted they never had any sexual desires at all.   *s.h.*

Faithfulness: To be boundlessly faithful to each other is the objective many couples set themselves. In our society we demand that a woman should not carry on a sexual relationship with more than one man at a time.

We are slightly more generous when it comes to men "because they are more polygamous · by nature". To start with this is probably untrue. Amongst peoples whose women are permitted to have sexual relationships outside their marriages we see them avail themselves of the chance just as eagerly as men. Perhaps the boundless faithfulness we go in for is a somewhat irksome fetter few can tolerate for ever. Kinsey's · figures would indicate this. A particularly large number of men and quite a number of women have sexual relationships outside their marriages.

But many social, economic and religious factors render it not quite so easy for us to adopt the same liberal customs as those practised by the Polynesians, for instance.

They most certainly are not permitted to have sexual relationships with 'anybody' — there are very precise rules as to who is allowed to have them with whom. We, on the other hand, have chosen unconditional faithfulness as the goal and ideal, and therefore have to try to live up to that ideal. But we must at least concede the other person's right to feel attracted sexually by others, likewise the right to let their imaginations play with the thought of others. (See Fantasies, sexual, and Unfaithfulness).

And we should not regard it as an irreparable disaster if the other party should happen to be tempted beyond his or her powers of control.

The above should not be interpreted by anyone as an encouragement to practice uninhibited unfaithfulness. With the rules we have, unfaithfulness is a heavy burden. *i. & s.h.*

Fallopian tube: The egg duct (see Genital Organs, female).

Family planning: Another way of saying birth control ·, the idea being to emphasize the bearing on the interests of society as a whole. Thus there is a Family Planning Association with a clinic in Copenhagen which also sees to it that the chemists of the country stock good, cheap contraceptives, etc.

Anybody can apply to this clinic and have a talk with an understanding woman doctor ·. Unmarried as well as married women can have themselves measured for a pessary ·, get a prescription for a pessary and ointment, and receive instruction in using them. For address and opening hours see Birth Control.

s. h.

Family way, to put in the: Make pregnant, get with child. The expression conveys an undertone of its having been against the girl's will. *i. h.*

Fantasies, sexual: It is very common for sexual excitement to be accompanied by erotic mental images. It is a well-known fact that a man's nocturnal emissions may be accompanied by daring erotic dreams · and that women can likewise have erotic dreams that end with an orgasm ·. But the majority of people also give their imagination free

The family planning clinic in Copenhagen is near the Slangerup Railway.

rein in the mental images or fantasies that may accompany, for example, masturbation or actual intercourse. These are daydreams which we more or less consciously choose ourselves, mental images that have a sexually exciting effect.

These are not always of equal clarity. Some people see very clear images just as on a cinema screen. To others the scenery is hazier, and the performers possibly have no faces. It is not necessarily a question of visual experiences — they may well be sensory experiences, muscle sensations, or experiences connected with sounds, tastes or smells; they may be very complicated and they may be very simple.

90

Kinsey · is of the opinion that women in particular tend to choose to think about something they have tried, i.e. recall former experiences. Men are said to be able to dream to a greater extent about things they have never tried. There are also researchers who are of the opinion that sexual fantasies are somewhat less frequent in women.

Some women, however, are able to have orgasms in rare instances solely with the help of their imaginations. This is less frequent in men. (But see Emissions, nocturnal).

It is very difficult to get to the bottom of the matter. We do not think there are such very great differences between men and women on this point. But in our society women are not allowed to tell anybody about their fantasies. Many normal women, however, are able to tell that they let their imaginations wander on 'experiences' at which they have never been present. Completely normal and healthy women can tell how they have found themselves imagining scenes featuring incest ·, prostitution ·, rape ·, homosexuality ·, exhibitionism ·, masochism ·, sadism · and many other isms. In such scenes they may themselves have been playing the chief part, a secondary part, or they may merely have been a spectator.

None of these mental images or fantasies need cause anybody any concern.

It is very common for women and men to indulge in this sort of thing when masturbating and particularly in the course of sexual intercourse. Such mental images may well occur during the transition period just before sleep, or as proper dreams.

Most people's erotic fantasies are bolder than this.

In much the same way, a man can fall into a daydream in which he is riding through a murderous shower of arrows from hostile Red Indians with the object of relieving the fort single-handed. But were the job offered to him in reality he would probably decline with thanks.

Just because we toy with a thought does not necessarily mean we intend to realize it as well. On the contrary, here is an instance where we can use the somewhat overworked phrase 'working off steam' — for this is all we are doing.

In other words there is nothing whatsoever perverse about it — this sort of thing is merely one of the many safety valves of a normal, healthy mind. *i. & s.h.*

Fashion: We may smile at women's fashion whims and at the fact that they bow to the tyranny of fashion dictators. But we men do the same. We may be a little slow about it, but we find that long skirts or short skirts, in turn, are delightful, that stockings should be seamless or that breasts · should stick out into the air horizontally in defiance of the law of gravity. We ourselves wear waistcoats, ties, turn-ups on our trousers, lapels on our jackets and shoes any native would yell at if he were made to press his 'underdeveloped' feet into them. Fashion is merely part of the demand society makes on us to conform.

Admittedly a somewhat unimportant and pointless part — which is perhaps why we are able to realize it. *s.h.*

Father fixation: See Mother fixation and Oedipus Complex.

Feet: See Shoes.

Fellatio, fellation: A special form of sexual intercourse (corresponding to cunnilinctio ·) in which the woman touches the man's penis · with her lips and tongue. It was a big shock to the Americans when Kinsey's · report showed that variations of this sort were quite common. In the USA, where sexual taboos · are even stricter than in Europe and the laws far more prudish and inhuman, it transpired that approximately 90% of all Americans had performed sexual actions for which they could have been imprisoned if they had been brought to the notice of a court of law.

A strict moral code is powerful because it allies itself with our bad consciences ·.

By means of hushings-up, lies and suppressions of the truth, it endeavours to force science and humaneness into obedience. The self-appointed guardians of public morals do not even content themselves with saying: "You are not as good as you ought to be "— for that is an opinion to which they are entitled if they so choose. — Oh no, they say to each single one of the 90%: "*You* are not as good as *all* the others" — which of course is not true. *s.h.*

Fertilization: The common form of fertilization consists in two single cells, one male and one female, coming into contact with one another, whereupon they fuse, become one cell, which in turn then begins to grow by dividing itself and becoming 2, 4, 8, 16 . . . . . . cells.

The contention is furthermore that the female cell is fertilized by the male cell, which is regarded as the active partner that as a rule seeks out the expectant, more passive partner, namely the female cell. (See furthermore Sexual Intercourse, Genital Organs, Pregnancy, Menstruation, etc.).

Generally speaking a woman is able to have children when she is between the ages of 14 and 45, in other words from the time of her first menstruation at the commencement of puberty until that of her menopause ·, which is when menstruation ceases, usually during the forties. Throughout these approximately 30 years one egg, a female cell, matures in and is loosened from one of her ovaries every month; this is called ovulation. When the egg is mature it can be fertilized by coming into contact with a male cell, a sperm cell from a man.

The man in question must also be sexually mature, in other words be producing sperm cells, and this starts as a rule at about the age of 14 and continues throughout the rest of life. Each ejaculation · by the man contains several hundred million sperm cells, in other words a fantastically abundant quantity considering that only one is required for fertilization. If every single sperm cell became a child, a single man would be able to populate the whole world by means of a single ejaculation. It may provide some idea of the tremendous quantity of sperm cells involved if it is borne in mind that a sexually mature man fabricates thousands of sperm cells every second of his life, day and night.

When two cells meet, the sperm cell forces its way into the egg cell and at the same time discards the long tail which helped it on its way. When the two cells fuse, the egg cell furthermore becomes impenetrable to all other cells. Fertilization can presumably only take place during the period of approximately 24 hours, which is the time the mature egg cell takes to complete its journey from the ovary to the womb via the oviduct. It is believed that fertilization can take place during the first 72 hours after the sperm cell has entered the vagina.

While the egg cell is on its way to the womb, the lining, e.g. the mucosa of the womb, prepares itself to receive a fertilized egg. If the egg cell has become fertilized on its way to the womb, it will lodge itself in the mucosa and start growing there as an embryo that will become a child nine months later.

If the egg cell has not been fertilized when it reaches the womb, the uterine mucosa which was there in readiness is ejected. In the process, several small veinlets are ruptured, which results in a certain amount of bleeding (see Menstruation). The blood from this bleeding is in reality very little, but as it becomes mixed with several other liquids, and because blood is a very strong dye in itself, it appears to be much more.   *s.h.*

That bit about a man being able to fertilize all the women of the world by means of a single ejaculation just shows how terribly conceited men can be! By way of retaliation we might mention that some time in the future we women will be able to populate the world without using men. It is already possible today to fertilize a female rabbit's egg cells without the use of sperm cells (see Insemination, artificial) and thus produce the sweetest little she-rabbits.   *i.h.*

Fertilization, days conducive to: It is believed that the chances of fertilization · taking place are greatest on the days round about the 15th day before *the next* menstruation. It is thus these days which should be chosen for intercourse by those anxious to have children, and avoided by those who are not. (See Birth Control and Menstruation Chart).   *s.h.*

Feticide: Criminal abortion.

Fetish: Something or other said to be imbued with mystical powers in the same fashion as amulettes, relics and talismans.

Fetishism: Like so many other isms (see also Deformity Fetishism), this is to be encountered in normal sex life. In the case of exhibitionism · masochism · and sadism · for example, these can occur and be a source of mutual pleasure in any sexual relationship between human beings. It is not until it becomes the only way of obtaining sexual satisfaction, or if it involves encroachment on others, that these isms can be said to become obnoxious. Fetishism is what we call it, for instance, when a man becomes sexually excited by female underclothes (minus the girl inside) and by her shoes, stockings, etc. There is also hair fetishism and pregnancy fetishism, in which a woman's hair, or her stomach — respectively — act as sexual stimulants. These are all sensations any normal man will recognize, particularly during puberty. (See also Colours).

But such things do not become aberrant, and perhaps unfortunate, until a man's whole sex life begins to consist in cuddling a detached brassiere, or in cutting off girl's pigtails, for then it means his normal, versatile sex life has become inhibited and obstructed, and he may start encroaching upon others, which naturally cannot be tolerated, no matter how much psychological explanation and sympathy for the poor man we may be able to produce.

We have spoken of fetishism particularly in connection with men. Fetishism exists amongst normal women too, for instance in the hoarding of old love-letters; but it is rarer.

Catholicism, for example, involves the worship of things, i.e. relics.   *i. & s.h.*

Film: Sex interests us all, and so films likewise employ eroticism to a very great extent with the object of attracting audiences. As Poul Henningsen contends in "Eroticism for the Millions" (Thaning & Appel, 1957) the feature film that endeavours to arouse the greatest possible interest and the least amount of indignation is a good yardstick of the prevailing official code of morals. Artistic films, on the other hand, try to reveal to us the untruthfulness and hypocrisy of our times and are therefore ahead of their day.

94

The heroes and heroines of films are to a great extent creators of fashion and help determine ideals. A very small detail can illustrate this: formerly, heroines shaved their eyebrows and armpits and the chests of heroes were bare and pink. Nowadays heroines have almost been allowed to keep their eyebrows, even though they are often slightly adjusted — and a few have been permitted to show us they have hair in their armpits just like other women. Men are allowed to have hair on their chests now, too. It may not sound so very much, but it is nevertheless a symptom of a tendency towards truth and realism, something that permits these heroes to come down to the level of ordinary mortals. (See also Breast and Depilation).

Apart from films with erotic content there are also secret, pornographic · films that are shown privately to those particularly interested. *i. & s.h.*

Flagellant, flagellation: One who whips himself; the practice of so doing. A religious custom particularly widespread during the 300-year period from 1200 to 1500; hordes of fanatics with priests and banners at their head used to go from town to town, praying and whipping. There are furthermore instances, both before and after this period, of individual flagellants who were elevated to sainthood.

We have many examples of how severely restrained sexual urges can result in two typical forms of activity:

a) A violently 'moral' · attitude, in which the person concerned places himself on a pedestal and persecutes and punishes, energetically and imaginatively, all those who think differently to himself.

b) Self-abasement. A desire in a person to bring the scorn of others down upon himself, inflict torture, flagellation, etc., etc., all on account of a violent guilt complex ·. (See also Masochism).

Flux: See Discharge.

Foetus: From the end of the third month after the ovum is fertilized · until birth takes place, an unborn child is called a foetus. (See also Abortion).

Foreplay, pre-coital: See Love-play.

Foreskin: (See also Genital Organs, male). The part of the skin of the penis · that can be drawn out over the head of this organ. The foreskin is often too tight, with the result that it cannot be pulled back from the tip of the penis, or at any rate only with difficulty. Jews have their foreskins removed by circumcision, which can be quite a practical step. In time a foreskin may become less tight, but it is also possible to go to a doctor and be operated. It may be of help to mention here that the foreskin is not particularly sensitive, it is the uncovered tip of the penis that can be as sensitive as an eyeball. (See Circumcision).

Tightness of the foreskin is also known as phimosis, and when a foreskin cannot be pulled forward again it is called paraphimosis. Phimosis can result in an inflammation (balanitis) because bacteriae may collect; but this is something one should see a doctor about.   *s.h.*

Form, to be off: Being off form sexually, being disinclined · to have sexual intercourse for varying lengths of time, can have many and complicated causes. Some of the commoner ones are mentioned here in simplified terms. Several of these may of course be combined in varying intensity. The most understandable, natural and reasonable cause for being sexually off form is naturally that the person in question already happens to be satisfied ·, already have had his or her sexual fill. (See also Disinclination).

The possibility of being used as a means of satisfying the other person is, to a far greater extent, a question of working out the most suitable technique for one's sexual intercourse.

There is a kind of disinterest in which the urge is there but is not acknowledged, or not experienced ·. It is like needing food without having an appetite. (See also Refusal to eat).

It may be anxiety about becoming pregnant, ordinary anxiety about sex life in general, or fear of not being satisfied.

The fear of pregnancy can possibly be alleviated by combining various forms and methods of contraception (see Birth Control). If one wanted to set about things with a vengeance it would of course be possible to select non-fertile days according to the Knaus · method, a sperm-destroying cream or vagitorium ·, a pessary, a condom · and finish off with a vaginal douche ·. It would naturally involve a spot of bother, but even a combination of a few of these methods would reduce the chances of pregnancy considerably.

An anxiety about sexual relations as a whole is something implanted in us during our upbringing — perhaps not so much in men as in women. But a woman who had no sexual anxiety whatsoever would very easily be able to activate it in most men.

Such anxiety can, in the majority of cases, be overcome by affection, patience and a gentle, mild pressure on the part of the other person. But it is not as easy as it may sound. Time will also help a little, but satisfying experiences are what count most when it is a question of reducing sexual anxiety.

And here we come to the very question of fear of not being satisfied. If a woman, time and time again, experiences the greatest pleasure and desire when having sexual intercourse, this would naturally constitute the best argument for getting rid of the anxiety. (But anxiety can also render such experiences difficult to obtain). Conversely, the consciousness of not going to be satisfied, of going to be "cheated out of one's orgasm ·'" will be able to produce the anxiety or increase an already existing anxiety. Both parties must be prepared to experiment ·, practise ·, until they find the right technique or techniques, i.e. the forms of sexual intercourse which provide both of them with the greatest guarantee of securing orgasm for both. (See also Titillation, sexual; and Petting).

It all sounds very matter-of-fact and not very romantic ·, but an unsatisfied person derives little pleasure from observing the bloom of innocence on the delicate wings of his or her soul. It is a form of delicacy and modesty · that is often pursued into the tragically paradoxical. The fact that both partners know they have, together, developed a form of sexual relationship that assures them satisfaction is a better foundation upon which to be romantic.

Disinterest, being off form, can also be due to irritation or anger. It can be something in an entirely different sphere of their relationship — or it can be something that has nothing to do with their relationship whatsoever. (See also Connection).

Here, a factor of importance is likewise that sexual relationships in our society are used by women to a great extent for the purpose of rewarding or punishing.

(This is perhaps biologically determined. In many species of animals the offer of intercourse is used as a sign of submission with which to appease an aggressive male). (But see also Defeat).

Irritation or anger on some small or large point can also put a man off in the same way.

Very great preoccupation or absorption in something may also steal some of the energy. A pending examination or similar task that absorbs all a person's powers can take away a certain amount of sexual energy. (See also Sublimation).

It is important to realize that the causes of most of the forms of false disinclination can be particularly complicated and difficult to sort out.

The falsely disinclined woman will thus not feel her factual sexual urges, but on the other hand will experience · clearly her disinclination and possibly also actual dislike and revulsion ·. The man will similarly find it hard to understand why his wife does not interest him.

Only a very positive and honest spot of analysis will be able to disentangle all the threads. *i. & s.h.*

French letter: A contraceptive sheath. (See Condom, Birth Control).

Freud, Sigmund (1856—1939): An Austrian doctor who started to take an interest in nervous disorders. He experimented with hypnotism, but discovered that a great many long conversations in which the doctor remained fairly passive, yet at the same time positive and interested, had a curative effect in themselves. From this he developed psychoanalysis ·, an impressive achievement for a single man, in which he builds up a number of penetrating theories and hypotheses concerning the things that take place in the human mind. By far the greater part of these thoughts have proved extraordinarily fruitful and useful in the treatment of nervous disorders. In a brilliant fashion he has therefore succeeded in making his mark, not only on the sciences of psychology · and psychiatry ·, but also on a considerable part of our western culture.

His interpretation of dreams is probably the best known side to his activity — and the most misunderstood because he operates so much with sexual symbols ·.

But for a start he did not take things nearly so literally as many of his later interpreters have done, and secondly, sexual wishes often disguise themselves in symbols for the simple reason that sexual wishes are forbidden — taboo — in our cultural sphere.

If we become very hungry or thirsty during our sleep it is not uncommon, and quite logical, for us to dream we are eating or drinking. On the other hand if a moral person covets his neighbour's wife he cannot always permit himself to dream about it. Perhaps in his dreams he shows her the Eiffel Tower, or they go up or down in a lift together, or do something else peculiar that serves to camouflage a more or less conscious wish.

Furthermore we must bear in mind that even during our waking hours we make use of an extraordinary number of symbols and circumlocution when we want to talk about things that are taboo.

A lady does not piddle or even pee. She visits the bathroom, spends a penny or merely powders her nose. At the other end of the scale exist expressions of considerable juiciness. And there are any number of expressions meaning to have sexual intercourse, most of them unmentionable in polite society or in print, but in some strange fashion known to most of us anyway.

Freud not only interpreted the meaning of dreams — including the utterly confused and apparently meaningless ones — but likewise concerned himself with the mental life we all have but which we do not always want to admit we have, or face up to ·, and with the forces active there. One of the many things to his credit is that he proved the existence of a form of sexual feeling in all children — something to which a blind eye had been turned until then. (Many still do today).

Of particular interest is naturally his pointing to the fact that repressed sexual desires can cause nervous disorders (see

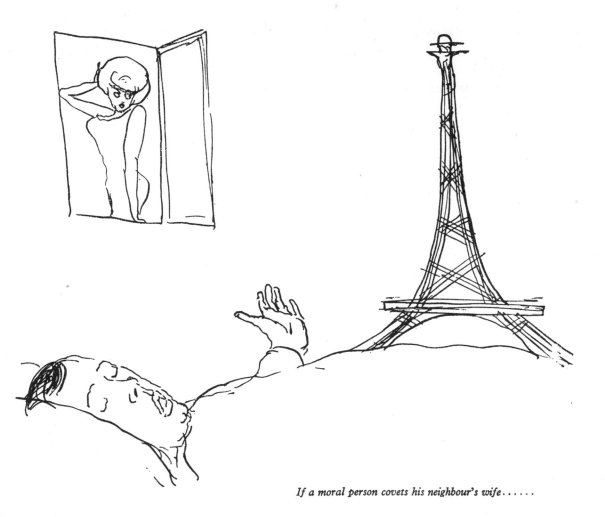

If a moral person covets his neighbour's wife......

also Personality). Many were astonished that Freud stressed sexual desires, but it is bound up with the fact that of all strong desires, it is the sexual ones in particular that we are forced to repress.

Nobody forbids us to be hungry or thirsty. Nobody feels obliged to deny that they themselves now and again can feel hungry and thirsty too.

But from childhood onward sexual needs are something we are made to feel ashamed of. They have been placed in a special light by the same people who now say: "Why must there be so much talk about sex — why can't it be left alone to form a 'natural' part of our lives?" (See also Deformity Fetishism and Connection). Freud — and psychoanalysis — have often likewise been accused of wanting to do away with conscience; the feeling of guilt: This is an understandable misunderstanding — but no more correct for all that. Psychoanalysis is a means amongst other things, of attempting to give the patient a reasonable sense of responsibility ·, one which can put him in a position to live in a community. It is the unconscious, entirely unreasonable guilt complexes that can give rise to compulsive actions, etc., which analysis tries to unravel. *s.h.*

Frigid, frigidity: Literally mean *cold*. The words are applied to women and imply that they possess no sexual feelings or interests whatsoever. The terms have been used a good deal, and many husbands will be willing to swear their wives are frigid, that they are completely disinterested in everything connected with sex. Doctors · have used the terms too, but of recent years slightly more caution has been observed in declaring a person to be entirely devoid of sexual feelings.

Nowadays it is realized that mental mechanisms such as inhibitions and repressions (see Personality) can fool the doctor as well as the patient.

We also know of periods in history during which the official code of morals simply refused to admit that women could experience pleasure in sexual activity at all, and when — the opposite of present-day practice — the professing of interest in sex was regarded as an ailment suffered by a limited number of women. When one considers how it was possible to pull the wool over the eyes of whole societies in this way there is every reason to be suspicious of all attempts to deny women sexual feelings.

If we regard the sexual urge (see Sexual need) as a need comparable to the need to eat and drink (and there is no reason why we should not do so) it is most unlikely that any person should be born without the urge to reproduce his or her kind — or whatever one may choose to call it.

If we imagined to ourselves that we were sitting on another planet and observing this earth down through the ages we would have to admit that powerful forces must certainly be at play. The sexual urge must be a remarkably persistent thing. So many attempts have been made in the course of time to deny, suppress, convert, or eradicate the sexual forces that only a need of the same kind as hunger-and-thirst would have been able to survive the attacks.

Many women have been pushed out into a false (but none the less tragic) state of frigidity because they themselves and their husbands have been given wrong information concerning orgasm · (see also Clitoral Orgasm).

In all the cases in which contended frigidity has been carefully examined it has been found that the woman in question certainly did have sexual feelings.

Kinsey ·, too, puts a large question-mark after the diagnosis 'frigid'. False frigidity, pseudo-frigidity, is on the other hand not so very rare. A strict moral code can make us deny facts and forget the things we "wish" to forget, so the conclusion we must draw is that it sounds unlikely — perhaps impossible — that even a small number of women should be devoid of sexual feelings. (See also Desire).
i. & s.h.

G

Gallantry: In some cases a superficial mannerism, but it may also — as it should — be an expression of respect for a fellow human, which is what a woman is, and for affectionate care. The latter is naturally of greater value than the former, but both should be regarded in the light of the norms and accepted rules for behaviour in the society in question. American men often seem 'gallant' to Danish girls, merely because American habits of behaviour are more gallant than Danish habits. A person measures his or her own worth amongst other things by the amount of consideration · others show him — or her.   *i.h.*

Geisha: The name given to a Japanese girl versed in the arts of singing and dancing after many years of training in the art of entertaining. A very large amount of prostitution · exists in Japan too, but the task of a geisha would not appear to be that of a prostitute. Japanese prostitutes, however, are also very carefully trained in the art of entertaining, so it is perhaps understandable that we Europeans should make mistakes, especially as the brothels · and tea-houses with geisha girls were often in the same district. Many European chorus-girls know what it is like, i.e. that 'being a chorus-girl obviously means you will go to bed with any and everybody who is willing to pay.'

Genital Organs, female: The female genital organs are located between the navel, the thighs and the groin. (See diagram 3). Externally we can see the 'mount of Venus', which is the little triangular hillock covered with hair. We can just discern the crevice between the larger vaginal lips (*labia majora*) and in some instances we can just discern a little of the edge of the smaller vaginal lips (*labia minora*) within too.

101

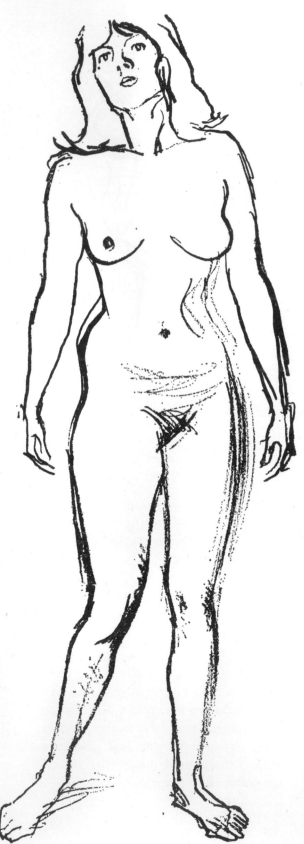

It is not until the legs are spread apart that more of the genital organs can be seen from the outside. (See diagram 4). The large lips then open up and we can see the next set of small lips. These small lips join in a tip at the top, and here there is a small thing called the clitoris ⋅. This is a very sensitive organ indeed and corresponds to the tip of a man's penis. As a rule it is not very big, but just like a man's penis it can become filled with blood and likewise erect and become bigger (see Erection). It is by means of rhythmical pressure or tickling or by indirect stimulation of the many nerves in this organ that a woman experiences the pleasant sensations that culminate in an orgasm ⋅ — also known as sexual satisfaction ⋅.

Beneath and behind the clitoris is the mouth of the urine pipe (the urethra) that comes down from the bladder located behind the mount of Venus and the bone which can be felt here, known as the pubis, or pubic bone.

Beneath the mouth of the urine pipe, but still between the small lips is the entrance to the vagina, which is a tube leading diagonally upwards inside the woman's body. It is the vagina into which the man inserts his penis when he has sexual intercourse with a woman. And it is inside the vagina that his sperm squirts out when he ejaculates ⋅.

As stated, the vagina is a tube, and the end of this we can see from outside is more or less closed on all women by a piece of membranous tissue known as

Figure 3.

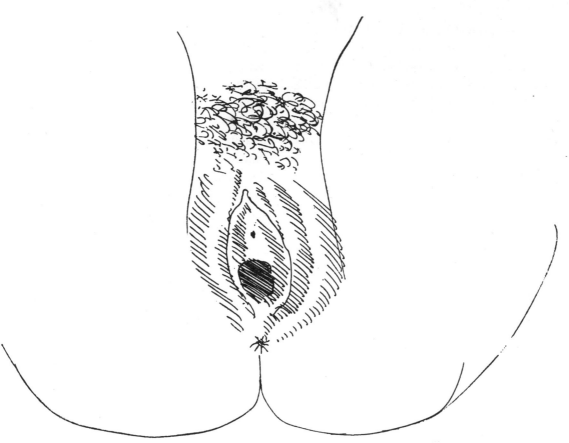

Figure 4. The outer genital organs of a woman seen from below.

the hymen or maidenhead. This is to be found on all the females of the human race. It may get broken as a result of washing, masturbation or in some other way, but failing this it will as a rule break the first time the woman has sexual intercourse by reason of the pressure of the man's penis entering the vagina.

It is very seldom that the hymen completely closes the entrance to the vagina — after all, it is from this outlet a woman's monthly bleeding (see Menstruation) takes place. (If it were completely closed the menstrual blood would not be able to get out, in which case a doctor has to open it; but this is not particularly difficult, nor particularly painful. As already stated, it is very seldom necessary anyway).

Below the entrance to the vagina the small lips meet again. Below them, between the thighs and down to the mouth of the anus, is a flat little area known as the *perineum*. The large lips do not join completely but flatten out at the point where the thighs, the bottom and the *perineum* meet. This is all that can be seen from the outside, partly when a woman is standing normally, and partly when her legs are spread out.

A woman's internal genital organs.
If we imagine to ourselves an ordinary large pear and a cardboard tube some four inches in length and about an inch in diameter it will make it easier to follow the genital organs further on. The cardboard tube represents the vaginal tube, and we can now place the end of the pear with the stalk in it (which represents the neck of the womb, or the cervix) into the top end of the cardboard tube.

But the womb, or *uterus*, is hollow. Let us imagine that we have pulled the stalk out of the pear and carefully scraped out the core through the little hole left — then we would have a very narrow passage (the cervical canal) leading into a cavity. If we were now to glue the pear tightly into the cardboard tube all round the edge, our model would correspond to the female womb and the vaginal canal.

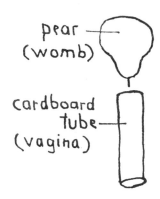

This is how the womb, or uterus, is joined to the vaginal canal, which extends upwards and backwards at an angle. At the point where the stalk is attached to the pear is a small kind of mucous 'plug' which receives eventual male sperm cells.

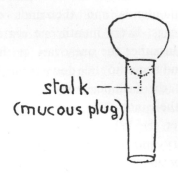

The vagina is thus *completely* closed at one end because the womb is fastened into the end of the canal like a cork — there is no joint that can come 'unstuck' for the simple reason that it is formed by continuous, unbroken flesh. All there is in the way of an opening is the very narrow little passage up through the middle of the 'plug' — corresponding to the hole after the removal of the stalk — which leads on into the cavity of the womb, i.e. corresponding to the cavity inside the pear which we made by carefully scraping out the core. In other words, *nothing can disappear* up a woman's vagina.

A man's penis only reaches as far as the mucous 'plug' at the entrance to the womb. The passage is so small that only a very thin stick — no bigger than a matchstick — could possibly pass from the vagina up through the cervical canal and into the cavity of the womb. It is inside this cavity of the womb that a fertilized egg, or ovum, becomes lodged and here that the foetus grows until birth. (See Fertilization). The inside walls of the womb are of mucous membrane, rather like the inside walls of the mouth.

Every month, the mucous lining of the wombs prepares to receive a fertilized egg — in an adult woman, that is — and if the egg reaches the womb *without* being fertilized, the womb sheds its mucous membrane. When this membrane is shed, a couple of small blood vessels break, and it bleeds a little, but not nearly as much as it might seem. Most of the 'blood' from menstruation is mucus and mucous membrane brightly dyed by blood. A single drop of blood is enough to dye half a glass of water. No more than couple more drops are necessary before the water will turn dark red.

But where does this egg come from? How do we get any further on from the cavity of the womb? Here we must use our model again, our cardboard tube and our pear. Let us stick a drinking-straw into the pear from either side — one from the right and one from the left, right into the cavity where we hollowed out the core. These are known as the Fallopian tubes, egg ducts or oviducts, because they conduct the egg, or ovum, down into the cavity of the womb. If we then stick a plum on to the other end of each straw, our model of the internal sexual organs of a woman will be complete.

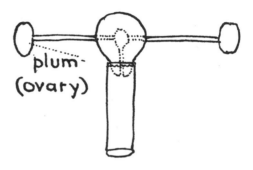

plum- (ovary)

The two plums correspond to the ovaries, which produce an egg every month. (See Fertilization). The ovaries (which in our model are the plums) contain thousands and thousands of potential eggs. Every month one egg is ready — in either the one ovary or the other — and begins to slide down through the straw (the Fallopian tube) into the cavity of the womb. The egg may come from either the left hand or the right hand ovary and is set in motion by special hormones that undergo complicated processes.

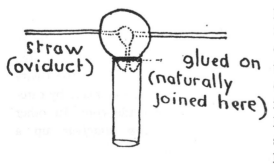

straw (oviduct)   glued on (naturally joined here)

If the egg, on its way through the Fallopian tube, meets a sperm cell that has been squirted into the vagina from the man's penis and has found its way up through the mucous 'plug' in the narrow passage located at the bottom of the pear-shaped womb, and thereafter swum up through the cervical canal into the cavity of the womb, and from here moved on up into one of the Fallopian tubes — then, fertilization may occur by virtue of the fact that the egg cell and the sperm cell fuse into one.

(If the egg is *not* fertilized by the time it comes into the cavity of the womb the womb sheds its lining of mucous membrane as explained above, and the unfertilized egg is expelled together with the mucous membrane and blood in the course of the menstruation process.)

On the other hand the fertilized egg — the one which became fused together with a sperm cell that had swum up into the Fallopian tube (the drinking-straw in our model) — becomes firmly lodged in the mucous membrane in the cavity of the womb, which, as we mentioned before, prepares itself to receive a fertilized egg (in adult women) every month.

The fertilized egg that is now lodged in the mucous membrane on the inside walls of the cavity of the womb (where we hollowed out the core of our pear) grows on to the blood vessels there and becomes an embryo which in turn receives blood from the woman and is thereby enabled to go on growing. A membrane (known as the amnion) containing a kind of water (known as amniotic fluid) is then formed about the embryo, and the womb starts growing too. The cavity inside the womb becomes bigger and bigger, and some nine months later the foetus is ready to be born — to become a child.

In order that the child may be able to come out of the womb through the cervical canal — which is no bigger than a matchstick — the canal itself has to grow a great deal too. The child then passes through it at birth down into the vaginal tube (which has also in the meantime become larger and can expand elastically) and finally glides out through the bottom end of the vaginal tube, out into the world.

The genital organs of the woman are thus all the organs used in the course of sexual intercourse, fertilization and birth.

To clarify the above description we have used a very simple model. As a model it is accurate enough, but of course like most models it has been very much simplified. Those who are interested in more detailed information can examine diagram No. 5, where we have tried to illustrate the actual anatomical construction. In addition, practically every book of sexual guidance has more detailed and accurate descriptions which will be found easy to understand after studying the model utilized above. (See also Genital Organs, their appearance and size). *i. & s.h.*

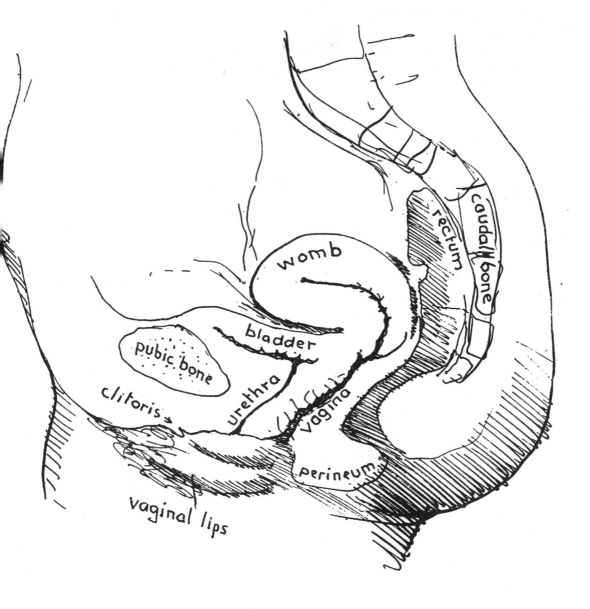

Figure 5.

On this sectionized lady can be seen, from the left (front) the pubic bone, and behind it the empty bladder, from which the urethra descends. To the left of the mouth of the urethra can just be seen the clitoris · below the middle of the pubic bone. To the right of the mouth of the urethra is the vagina, which, its wall in folds, extends right up to the womb, which curves forwards. To the right of the womb, i.e. behind it, is the rectum, and behind that the end of the spine, the caudal bone.

Genital Organs, male: We found the female genital organs located round the abdomen. A man's genital organs are more concentrated in the crutch. Just as in a woman we find hair, but in a man it continues up to the navel in a point.

A man's penis is located at the point corresponding to the little cushion of flesh known as the mount of Venus on a woman. Penis is the Latin word for prick, prong, John Thomas, or whatever terms the individual happens to favour but which, thanks to our strict code of morals, are not supposed to appear in print no matter how wide and utterly commonplace their daily use is amongst millions of people. But to avoid offending those who would otherwise be certain to declare themselves offended we shall stick to the more formal medical term and write *penis*. (See also Words, naughty).

The penis — or primary male sexual organ — is thus located just in front of the bone known as the pubic bone.

Normally, a man's penis hangs limply downwards — see the first drawing, which shows a man and his external genital organs the way girls normally see their fathers or brothers in their homes.

When a man's sexual needs reach a certain degree of intensity, some chance circumstance can release a mechanism that fills his penis with blood. This causes it to become quite a lot larger and firmer (see drawing accompanying article on Erection). If we want to use a comparison with another kind of need we could say that it corresponds to the fact that when our appetite — our hunger urge — has reached a certain intensity, our mouths begin to water at the mere thought of food or as soon as we are reminded of food.

An erection is not a reaction a man can control. It happens quite independently of the brain or the will.

Below and behind the penis we find the scrotum, a skin bag containing the testicles, or balls, two hard glands which produce spermatozoa — sperm cells.

The testicles are actually formed up in the abdominal cavity, approximately in the same place as the ovaries in a woman.

But at about the time of birth they slide out of the abdominal cavity and down into the scrotum together with the pipes leading from the gland to the urine pipe (the urethra). (See also Cryptorchism and Hermaphrodite).

Behind the scrotum and between his thighs, his backside and his anus · a man also has a flat area called the perineum. Just as in the woman, the urine bladder is behind the pubic bone, and from the bladder the urine pipe goes down under the pubic bone, where it joins the pipe coming from the testicles. These two united pipes continue as one pipe through the centre of the penis and out to its tip. Around the pipe is a certain amount of spongey tissue which thus becomes filled with blood during an erection ·. At the end of the penis the pipe passes through a harder, bulb-like tip known as the head of the penis, or glans.

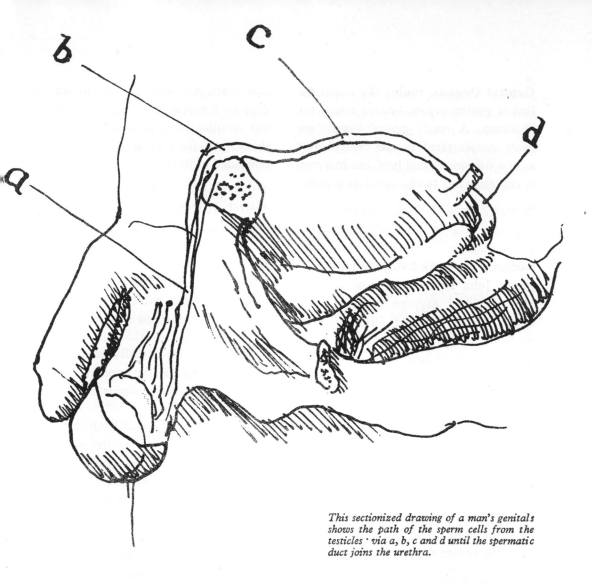

This sectionized drawing of a man's genitals shows the path of the sperm cells from the testicles · via a, b, c and d until the spermatic duct joins the urethra.

Around the whole penis there is soft skin that normally is in folds or wrinkled, but becomes thin and taut in the course of an erection. The outermost part of the skin round the head of the penis is bent inwards and is attached just behind the head of the penis.

The head of the penis is very sensitive, as there are many nerves, and when erection takes place the outermost, turned-in part of the skin — known as the foreskin — slides back and lays bare the sensitive surface of the head of the penis.

A man's sexual pleasure is principally aroused by a rhythmical rubbing or pressure on the tip of the penis. This pleasant sensation finally results in orgasm · — sexual satisfaction. This climax is nearly always accompanied by ejaculation of spérm. The sperm, which come from the testicles, is stored in the sperm bladder. When the orgasm reaches culmination, the sperm is emptied from the sperm bladder through the pipe in the penis and pumped by muscles out through the tip of the penis in small squirts. *i. & s.h.*

109

Genital Organs, their appearance and size: Many people are worried about whether their genital organs look the same as other people's. Well, it so happens that we all look fairly different in the face, and the same applies to the other end.

Some have large noses, others small.

Some have large mouths, others small.

Even so, most of us manage to find somebody who enjoys kissing us. And being kissed by us. When we are very young we worry a lot about our appearances. Later on we realize it is not nearly so important in the long run. The same thing applies to the genital organs. It is very seldom that size and appearance play any importance in any lasting relationship during which two people are to build up a pleasurable sex life together. Far too much superstition has made people unhappy.

Women have believed that a man with a larger penis would help them to become satisfied more easily. Or that a narrower vagina would mean greater pleasure for both parties.

This is all due to the belief that nature only intended human beings to practice one single form of sexual intercourse, and that this form would immediately make all parties satisfied. Men with a penis no larger than a babe's finger have been able to satisfy women with exceptionally large vaginas — and have been satisfied themselves. Men with quite large penises have been unable to satisfy girls with rather small vaginas quite simply because they have assumed that these factors would be sufficient *in themselves*. Imagination and cooperation, mutual frankness and confidence are far more important if good results are to be obtained — likewise patience and practice ·. In by far the majority of cases appearance and size play no part at all.

Uncertainty, inhibitions ·, shyness, anxiety are all far more disturbing factors.

The vagina of the woman is very elastic; at the moment of birth it can permit the passage of an entire child. There is thus no reason to believe that any penis will ever prove too big for a vagina, nor that any vagina will ever prove too narrow.

The elasticity of the vagina makes it possible for it to adapt itself to all sizes of penis. It is anxiety · and muscular tension (see Relaxation) that can cause pain. It is a lack of muscle consciousness that can cause a woman to find her vagina too limp or a penis too small for her.

Of course people are born from time to time whose genital organs are completely deformed (see Hermaphrodites) just the same way as people are born with harelips or other forms of facial irregularity.

But they too can become happy and satisfied, and others can become happy and satisfied with *them*.

It is best to go and see your doctor · if you think there is something wrong at either one end or the other. In the majority of cases he will be able to pacify us and tell us it is nothing unusual or particularly unfortunate. In the few instances where it really is unfortunate he will usually be able to help. The sooner one goes to see him the easier it will be. With the strict moral code and sex taboos which we still uphold, it is far more often mental problems rather than physical conflicts that prevent us from having a satisfactory sex life. This is not meant as a form of consolation, for many physical problems would be quicker, cheaper and easier to solve. The mental causes are more difficult and obstinate to eradicate. This is merely an attempt to put things — and problems — in their right place.

If anybody is interested in knowing the average measurements of a penis, a clitoris or a vagina, here they are: in its erected state the male penis is some $5\frac{1}{2}$ to 6 inches along its upper side. A clitoris, in a state of erection, may be between $\frac{3}{8}''$ to $1\frac{1}{2}''$ in length, and the vagina only some 3 or 4 inches deep. This is sufficient, for the penis does not penetrate right up to its root.   *i. & s.h.*

Genital Organs, their hygiene: The genital organs of both men and women can naturally be washed with ordinary soap and warm water. Remains of urine soon begin to smell strongly.

Women have a number of crooks and crannies in which remains of urine, glandular secretions and so forth may easily gather.

In the case of a man it is particularly beneath and inside the foreskin that various remains may collect and which may be difficult to get rid of, particularly if the foreskin is hard to pull back.

Once upon a time, it was not uncommon to stuff a little extra something into the bag . . .
(See Breeches)

The skin on the genital organs is very thin and sensitive. Many have wanted to make themselves more attractive with a few drops of perfume or similar product containing spirits. Those who have done so usually regret it, for it smarts abominably, even though it passes off in due course.   *s.h.*

Gigolo: The word is used in particular of men who dance with women and get paid for it, i.e. a kind of male geisha ·; but also of male prostitutes.

Giving: It is only women who 'give themselves' to a man, bestow their favours, or their bodies or their love or whatever it may be. Men do not 'give themselves'. There is possibly a biological background — something similar has been observed in some monkeys. But it is also a relic of the days when women were not acknowledged to have any sexual feelings. It is an attitude that can be unfortunate, because a woman may be tempted to use her own, or the man's satisfaction as a weapon. (See Simulation, Vanity, Submission, Aggression, Love, Defeat).   *i.h.*

Glans: Latin word meaning acorn and used to describe the tip of a man's penis and a woman's clitoris.

Gonorrhoea: A venereal disease · caused by bacteriae called gonococci. Dangerous if not treated quickly.

Governess: A Danish slang expression for a woman who is willing to whip or chastise men who actually want this stern sort of treatment in order to become sexually excited. (See Masochism).

Many prostitutes can report having had customers who ask to be hit and punished and humiliated because they derive special pleasure from it. We have had an opportunity of talking to two Danish ladies about it, two ladies who have an intimate knowledge of this side of sex life. As a result of their information we established contact with almost 100 men and were enabled to hear about their experiences and special wishes. These were men from all walks of life — well-known artists, university men, office-workers and labourers — and they described refined methods of torture which were essential to their sexual excitement and satisfaction. Certain common traits kept on reappearing — traits which, from a psychological viewpoint, are interesting because they can tell us something about the origins of these feelings. Here are a few of the statements made by these men:

".... I often long back to the days of my childhood .... to those years of upbringing when I was given sound instruction in the meaning of obedience..."

".... I keep looking for a domineering woman...."

".... I'm very fond of children, but I don't care too much for these modern methods of upbringing...."

".... I dream about meeting a domineering woman before whom I can fall on my knees and whose humble slave I can become...."

".....ever since my beloved childhood governess, I have longed to meet an authoritative woman......"

".....I would so like to meet a woman who would educate me and make me her obedient pupil......"

"As a boy I was brought up by an aunt. She stuck to the principle that one must punish those whom one loves. I was scared stiff of her, and in those days I was none too enthusiastic when, dressed up in my cousin Betty's clothes from top to toe — my flogging suit, as she used to call it — I was caned several times for the same offence.

"Today of course I can see it was wrong to bring a boy up that way. But the strange thing is that today, now that I am grown up and don't have to answer to anybody for anything, I often long back to my aunt and her cane, or for an authoritative lady who goes in for the same methods of upbringing. It's abnormal, I know, but I can't help dreaming about a girl of the domineering type, and the refined way she'd have of punishing me. Of course it would hurt when she hit me ......and I would lie there and beg for mercy, terrified, waiting for the next blow — but I wouldn't dare defend myself for fear of her breaking off our relationship......"

The latter case was a 25-year old man. It is easy to see how his remarks contain exactly the same basic features as those of the other six (and also transvestism ·). These men do not know each other. Like many, many others of the same mentality, they live spread all over Denmark. They have the same dreams, the same fantasies, apparently inspired by vivid experiences during childhood.

Masochistic · fantasies · are by no means rare and are thus not abnormal whether in men or women. But in the above case there is a question of a fairly pronounced degree of masochism and of a desire to see the fantasies put into practice.

It forms a clear example of how experiences early on in life can influence a person's sex life.

In our patriarchal society it is easier for a woman with masochistic leanings of one degree or another to find herself a partner — all she need do is irritate her husband a little more than usual and incite him to resort to the punishments which she, whether consciously (or not entirely so) desires. It is more difficult for men.

It would be very difficult to cure all these people — even though it can be done. It is presumably in the interests of all that those with unusual interests find each other, i.e. that people with slightly more sadistic tendencies than normally the case should have the opportunity of finding persons with slightly more masochistic tastes than usual — rather than let people who feel differently about such matters suffer.

There is therefore good reason for drawing attention to the fact that these people with "special interests" or who are "interested in old-fashioned methods of upbringing" — people who describe themselves as obedient or authoritative and who are looking for people who are domineering or humble — that these people have found their way to another circle of human beings who feel differently, namely the homosexuals ·. This should not be interpreted to mean that there are circles here in Denmark who have got together for the purpose of indulging in all sorts of sexual perversions together.

No, it is us — the nice, ordinary, prudish, prejudiced members of society who force these people to go where there is greater understanding and where the chances of finding a partner are therefore greater too. From the viewpoint of society itself it is perhaps unfortunate that there should be so many people whose sex lives are so divergent — but it is something we must accept.

In magazines for homosexuals · — homophiles — those having such interests have been able to seek and find contact with each other through the classified advertisement columns. This is rather a fortunate trend — fortunate for society, fortunate for those of us who feel differently — and for those who feel differently. Let us be proud of the fact that we in Denmark are a little more tolerant than is the case in many other countries. *i. & s.h.*

Gratitude: May claim a word or two of mention. We are thinking here in particular of the gratitude parents expect from their children. Young people often likewise have bad consciences about not having been more grateful to their parents.

Can the idea really be that we parents are supposed to have the lot back again? Are children really supposed to return everything their parents have showered upon them — care, tenderness, consideration?

We parents also got a lot of that sort of thing from our parents. Have we returned it? Our children will have children too one day — would it not be better if they passed on whatever surplus they have by then to those children? That would straighten the account. But in a marriage the balance probably needs to be a little more direct. Both partners should give each other the same amount — and the same thing applies to friendships and other interhuman relationships. We ought to give and receive equally. The accounts should balance.

Income and expenditure should tally. *i. & s.h.*

Groin: The transitional part of the body between the front of the thigh and the bottom of the abdomen and the genitals. The groin forms a furrow when we sit down or bend over.

Guilt, guilt complex: The very embarrassing kind of bad conscience · with which far too many people go round.

Guilt and guilt complex are things which at worst can be mental · disorders that can lead to suicide · or to human tragedy in some other form. The responsibility which society takes upon itself in burdening so many of its members with an entirely unjustified guilt complex is a very heavy one indeed. (See Flagellant).

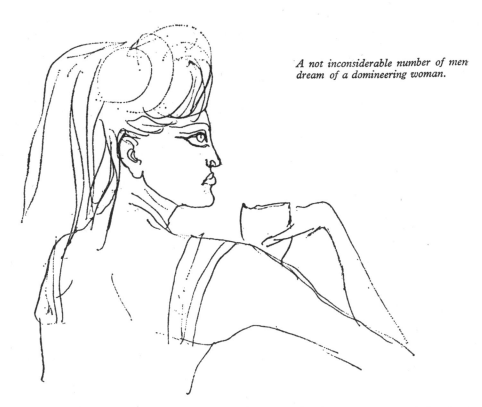

A not inconsiderable number of men dream of a domineering woman.

It is quite encouraging to see that psychological experiments would appear to prove quite clearly that scare propaganda, threats, and guilt-producing argumentation have a poorer and weaker effect than calm, sober enlightenment.

i.h.

Gynaecology, gynaecologist, gynaecological examination: A gynaecologist is a doctor who is a specialist in gynaecology, in other words in diseases and complaints of the female genital organs. As a rule this includes assistance at births, but not venereal diseases ·. Ordinary G.P.s (national health scheme doctors) conduct examinations of the abdomen if menstruation · is irregular, in cases of pregnancy, and if measurements are to be taken for a pessary ·. (See also Birth Control).

What actually happens at an abdominal examination?

We will try to answer this question and describe the situation a little. Naturally one should have washed oneself both back and front beforehand, but irrigation · should not be performed as it can alter the internal state of the vagina (see Genital Organs, female) and wash away things that might be able to give the doctor valuable information. As a rule the doctor asks the woman to remove her knickers and suspender belt. This is done behind a curtain or screen. Some doctors leave the room. Having undressed the woman lies on a high couch on a clean sheet with her legs spread out and her knees resting in a couple of supports. For some this may seem a somewhat unpleasant, defenceless position to be in,

but it is necessary if the doctor is to be able to do his work. In order to perform the examination he will often use a couple of instruments which make it easier to see up inside the vagina. These instruments may feel rather unpleasant to some people, (especially if the woman tenses the muscles of her abdomen from nervousness) but no greater expansion of the vagina is effected than in the case of normal sexual intercourse ·.

When taking measurements for a pessary a few soft rings of varying sizes may be inserted to try.

The doctor wears rubber or plastic gloves when conducting the examination. Having looked up inside the vagina he inserts his forefinger and middle finger and feels. In order to cause as little inconvenience as possible he uses a cream. He may feel first with one hand and then with the other in order to form an impression of both sides. At the same time he places one hand on the abdomen of the person he is examining and presses. In some cases it is necessary to feel with one finger inside the vagina and one in the rectum at the same time in order to obtain better information concerning the state of the abdomen. *i.h.*

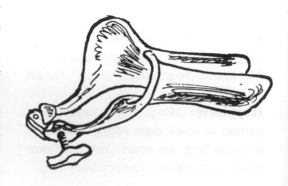

116

H

Hair: Men as a rule have more hair than women as they have hair on their face and more hair all over their bodies, especially on the chest. Hair plays a part in our sex lives. Many women talk about a manly moustache or give sweet little gasps at the sight of a hairy wrist or a manly chest. In corresponding fashion there are men who love long hair on women, a little dark shadow along the upper lip, side-whiskers, hairy legs, long eyelashes, etc., etc. Tastes fortunately differ. If we regard the question historically and ethnographically (which can be instructive) we see that hair-styles, hair-growth, hair-colour, etc., change from country to country and from one period to another. In ancient Greece all hair was removed with the exception of that on the head. The ancient Egyptians, on the other hand, favoured the clean-shaven pate.

Fetishism · in respect of female hair is also encountered in extreme forms, such as that manifested by the lopping off of pigtails dangling from the heads of completely strange women. Gentlemen also exist who hang on to collections of curly locks cut from pubic hair, i.e. hair round the genitals ·.   *i.h.*

Happiness: Many people expect their partner to make them happy. Happiness is something we must create for ourselves — *together* with somebody else.

Harem: A collection of wives belonging to an Eastern gentleman is called a harem. Literally a harem means the part of the house where the wife or wives live.

Polygamy has been practised among many peoples, including the earliest Protestant sects, which in certain instances — just as in that of Luther himself — permitted a man to be married to several women at the same time. (See also Bigamy, Morals and Castrate).

Head (of the penis): See Genital Organs, male.

Heat, to be on: Used to describe the period during which animals want to mate with one another. It corresponds to sexual desires in human beings, but in animals is usually confined to specific periods, as a rule when there is a possibility of fertilization ·. It is thus when a female is on heat that the male's desire to mate is aroused. In the majority of mammals these periods are restricted in the female to once or twice a year, but many domestic animals — e.g. the mare, the sow, the cow, the goat and the ewe — get on heat at very short intervals and can thus be fertilized just as often.

Cats and bitches get on heat as a rule twice a year. A bitch only has sexual interests during these periods and at the same time gives off a special smell which acts as a sexual stimulant on male dogs.

Male dogs can thus get stimulated by any bitches of any breed provided they are on heat, but can apparently derive satisfaction from another male if the latter proves willing. It has been believed that males have greater sexual interests than females and for this reason more capable in this respect than females — within the animal kingdom. However, it would appear that the majority of females when on heat are able to exhaust several males. These things are naturally of interest in connection with human relationships, and the possibility has therefore also been investigated whether a woman by any chance should have a particular period between her menstruations during which she is more sexually interested than at other times. The logical assumption would be approximately 15 days before the next menstruation, seeing that the chance of fertilization is greatest at this time. However, the contrary would appear to be the case. The women asked in the course of the investigation referred to said they felt most inclined to sexual relationships just before and just after their menstruation. The explanation may be that many couples abstain from sexual intercourse as long as menstruation is in process, partly for practical reasons (sheet-soiling) and partly because of ancient taboos · and notions concerning a woman's 'uncleanness' during her menstruation. (See Abstinence, periods of). The fact that one accepts these days of abstinence possibly stimulates both parties to increased activity in just the same way that any short period of abstinence can have a stimulating effect.

i.h.

Hermaphrodite, hermaphroditism:
The name is derived from a son of Hermes and Aphrodite. According to the legend, the son of these two Greek gods was half man and half woman, especially in regard to the sexual organs ·. Many types of hermaphroditism exist. Naturally there are also less marked degrees — some women, for instance, have an exceptionally large clitoris · (see Genital Organs, female). Hermaphroditism can naturally result in problems and unhappiness for those concerned, but there are nevertheless countless examples of hermaphrodites who have elected to live as men or women in happy marriages.

Hermaphroditism is always used in connection with the anatomy of the genital organs. As shown on the diagram there can be intermediary forms which may be difficult to determine. But under the microscope it is possible to state precisely whether a person is a man or woman.

Every single cell in a woman's body is female and every single cell in a man's body is male. From a cellular viewpoint there is no such thing as a hermaphrodite.

(Complicated chromosome relationships exist in very special cases, but this is another matter). This sounds complicated and it is, because there are three sides to the question to be taken into consideration: 1) The cellular condition, by means of which it is possible to determine conclusively under a microscope whether a person is of one sex or another. 2) The anatomical form of the genital organs, both internally and externally — in this case it is more difficult because there are indeterminate transitional forms.

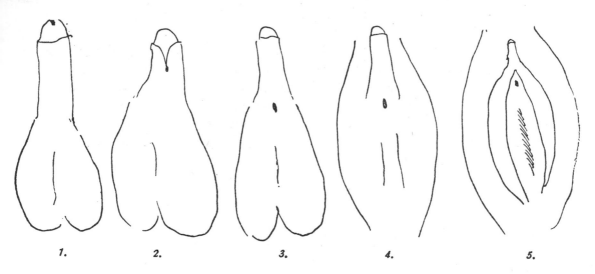

Three examples of irregular development.

These drawings show, very schematically, how the urethra can terminate at various points. No. 1 shows the hole at the tip of the penis · and normal testicles · as is the case with the majority of men.

No. 5 shows normal genital organs in a woman : outermost, the large lips (labia majora) ; within these, the small lips (labia minora) converge upwards in the clitoris · ; just beneath the clitoris can be seen the end of the urethra, and beneath this in turn the entrance to the vagina.

It is not unusual for the urethra to terminate just below the tip as shown in No. 2. This need not necessarily affect the sex life of the person concerned, nor his passing of water, nor his procreative powers. In No. 3 the urethra terminates right down at the root of the penis, which in turn is smaller, and the testicles are not so pronounced. No. 4 is more of a transitional form, anatomically speaking. The urethra ends beneath the penis, which is considerably smaller, and there is a suggestion of the large and small lips instead of testicles ; but there is no vaginal opening. No. 4 may be said to be a hermaphrodite.

And 3):

Which sex the person concerned actually feels himself or herself to be. This may sometimes be the most complicated side of all because it may be in opposition to both the anatomy of the genital organs and the cells.

Sometimes the person who decides a child's sex at birth may choose wrong on account of hermaphroditism, and when the child is grown-up it discovers that it feels as if it rightly belongs to the other sex. Thus there exists the possibility of changing sex by means of operations, change of name and clothing habits. But from a psychological point of view it is by no means a painless transformation.

From a psychological viewpoint, however, it is also very interesting to see how most hermaphrodites prefer to retain the sex they have been brought up as belonging to even if anatomically and biologically they are proved to be of the opposite sex. This would seem to indicate that upbringing in one direction or the other can be even stronger than the anatomical facts and even stronger than the cellular sex.

There are probably between 3,000 and 5,000 persons in Denmark today who anatomically are hermaphrodites to a greater or lesser degree. (See also Homosexuality). But it must once more be stressed that the majority of these people probably lead entirely normal, or almost normal, sex lives.

In many religions the hermaphrodite who outwardly appears to be man and woman in one has been regarded as something perfect — an attitude we also find reflected in the romantic talk about an ideal marriage being a fusion of two who formerly belonged together, two halves that have finally found one another again.   *i.h.*

Hetaera: Greek term for a girl friend. The Greeks declared that one had a slave-girl for sexual pleasure, a hetaera as a friend and a wife to have children with. A hetaera was often intelligent and well-educated and had great political influence, just like the courtesans · of later periods. But one can hardly call them proper prostitutes · in the sense that they were supposed to go to bed with a lot of different men for money.

The position was more often that they were kept (in other words received money to live on) by one man or a few men. (See also Geisha).

Heterosexual, heterosexuality: Sexual urges directed towards the other sex, i.e. that of a man for a woman and vice versa, is called heterosexuality; the adjective is heterosexual. *Hetero* means *different from*, while *homo* means *the same*. Thus *homosexuality* means sexuality directed towards the same sex.

We of Europe and the USA, which we call our western civilization or western society, go out of our way to stress heterosexuality as being the natural · and only permissible form. Against our will we have had to accept the fact that persons exist whose sexual urges are directed towards others of the same sex, and that there are people who are interested in persons of the same sex as well as those of the opposite sex — bi-sexuals, as they are called. But we should always be on our guard whenever anything is called natural.

It would most definitely not appear to be nature's intention that we should exclusively direct our sexual urges towards persons of the opposite sex. That we can say that it is desirable, in the interests of continued human procreation, that sexual urges should only be of importance in heterosexual relationships, is something entirely different and fails to make heterosexuality out to be something sacred or right, nor homosexuality as something blasphemous, satanical and wrong. It is a matter of estimation as to what is practical. It would be desirable, practical and fortunate if heterosexuality were the only form of sexual urge in existence and that this form always enjoyed reasonable chances of obtaining satisfaction. But nature · is not designed with such singleness of purpose. Human beings are more complicated.   *i. & s.h.*

Homophile, homophilia: Expressions which Danish homosexuals prefer to homosexual and homosexuality. They mean *a person who likes the same thing*, in other words the same sex. The fact that homophiles prefer this expression is presumably because they want to stress — rightly — that their feelings towards the same sex do not merely involve sexual feelings, but the entire complexity of feelings which we call *love*, i.e. feelings

120

in which sexual urges play a large part, but which also include tenderness, respect and much else besides.   *i. & s.h.*

Homosexual, homosexuality: People whose sexual urges are directed principally towards persons of their own sex are called homosexuals and their interest is called homosexuality, both terms being derived from the Greek words *homo* (meaning *same*) and *sex*. (It has nothing to do with the Latin word *homo*, which means *man*).

When we speak about homosexuality and heterosexuality we should bear in mind that it would be more correct to speak of *homosexual behaviour* and *heterosexual behaviour*. If we add autosexuality — masturbation ⋅, for example — we may also operate with the concept *autosexual behaviour*.

Then we should furthermore accept the fact that, seeing that most people marry or begin to co-habit with another person comparatively late in relation to the time they reach sexual maturity, a great many are neither purely heterosexual or homosexual, but to an overwhelming degree (if we are to judge by their behaviour) autosexual.

If we elect to operate with the three forms of sexuality:

a) Sexual behaviour solo, i.e. autosexual behaviour

b) Sexual behaviour with a person of the same sex, i.e. homosexual behaviour

c) Sexual behaviour with a person of the other sex, i.e. heterosexual behaviour

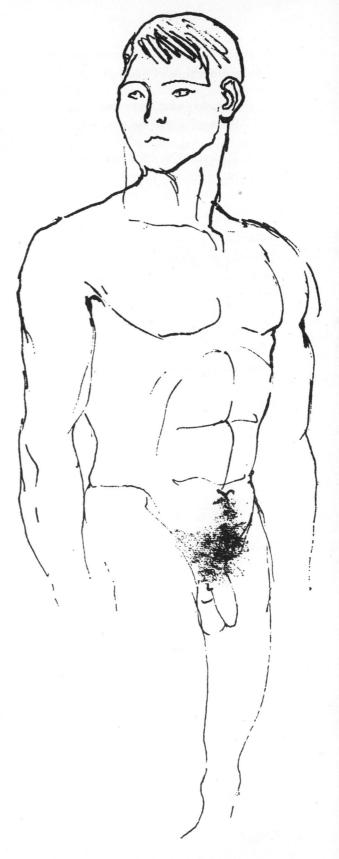

we find that we are obliged to draw up quite a number of main groups:

1) Persons who have never had any form of sexual behaviour.

2) Persons who have only had sexual experiences alone, i.e. through masturbation or some other form of autosexual behaviour.

3) Persons whose sexual experiences have been principally limited to autosexual behaviour, but who on occasion have had heterosexual experiences, i.e. practised some degree of heterosexual behaviour.

4) Persons with a considerable amount of autosexual behaviour but who have gradually taken to a certain amount of heterosexual behaviour and whose autosexual behaviour has thereby diminished.

5) Persons who fall into group 4) but who have had the odd (or slight) homosexual experience as well.

6) Persons whose sexual experiences have been more or less equally divided between the autosexual, heterosexual and homosexual, in other words quite a lot of bi-sexual behaviour.

7) Persons whose behaviour has been to a considerable extent autosexual, but gradually has included quite a lot of homosexual behaviour and resulted in a decrease in autosexual behaviour, apart from the odd (or slight) heterosexual experience.

8) Persons whose sexual behaviour has included a certain amount of auto-sexual behaviour, but gradually involved a good deal of homosexual behaviour and a decrease in auto-sexual behaviour.

9) Persons with principally autosexual behaviour but who have on occasion had homosexual experiences, i.e. some homosexual behaviour.

10) An extra group: Persons who have exclusively practised "other sexual behaviour", e.g. bestiality ˙, necro-philia ˙, etc..

In this way we obtain 10 groups. And these are only *principal* groups. And as always becomes necessary when we start pigeon-holing human beings, we have to overlook the intermediary groups and the transitional stages from group to group.

We know that group 1) is very small — if any human being should even belong to it at all. Group 10) is also problematical.

There are not many who have *only* had sexual experiences that cannot be classified under groups 2) to 9).

In other words it is in groups 2) to 9) that we find the greater part of humanity.

In groups 2) and 3) we presumably find the persons possessing what we call weak sexual urges. The same applies to group 9). The urges may be weak because they have been suppressed or because the needs are not so great.

Group 8) comprises people who have shown a certain amount of homosexual behaviour but have no knowledge of heterosexual behaviour. In other words, people whom one might genuinely call homosexual. We know that this group is very, very small. The persons we normally classify as homosexual belong in group 7). (This group incidentally also includes a number of people whom we would never dream of calling homosexual).

Group 7) is a comparatively large group. It comprises men in particular, but there are also a good number of women in it. Group 7) embraces many, many thousands of Danish men and women.

We can really call group 6) bi-sexual because its members have more or less the same degree of heterosexual as homosexual experiences. It is probably not such a large group as one might expect.

Our society · demands that we take a decision — either/or — in this sphere of our sexual lives too. (See also Practice).

In other words we are either pushed over into the one compartment or, more or less of our own accord, stick in the other compartment.

The majority of men and women are in group 4), where autosexual behaviour is gradually replaced more or less by heterosexual behaviour. Kinsey · has shown us that almost a third of all men and by no means so few women belong to group 5), which embraces people who have moreover had sexual experiences with somebody of their own sex. So many indeed, that we can say they do not differ from what is normal. Thus we can say that groups 4) and 5) together embrace the majority.

As outlined under heterosexuality · and bi-sexuality ·, one thing is that we are able to draw up rules for what is most desirable, most fortunate or most practical, but it is another matter to expect nature · always to conform to our wishes.

It would be more reasonable if we were to accept it as being a human fact — and likewise a natural · one — that human beings exist who are attracted by persons of their own sex to a marked degree, i.e. homosexuals. And that persons exist who are attracted more or less equally by both sexes, i.e. bi-sexuals. Things have always been this way. At certain times these fact have been far more accepted and far more widespread than is the case with us today.

For years it has been discussed whether homosexuality is something a person can be born with. Understandably enough, the homosexuals themselves have been interested in this aspect, because it removed all 'blame' from them, every thought of 'cure' and every problem connected with having to 'do something about it'. (See also Hormones). Added to this is the fact that homosexuals feel themselves to be just as naturally homosexual as heterosexuals feel themselves to be naturally heterosexual.

Let it be said once and for all: homosexuals cannot be blamed in any way for the fact that their sex life is different. They are very difficult to cure — and they cannot do anything about it themselves.

Exclusive homosexuality or fanatical heterosexuality can hardly be regarded as 'natural'. It is more likely that we all have certain tendencies, including homosexual ones, tendencies which may be developed if factors connected with our upbringing encourage them. When Greek culture was at its height relationships between married men and youths was a commonly accepted feature of life. We have no reason to believe that these Greeks should have been born with tendencies different to those we are born with today.

It looks as though nature in her multiplicity has given us a great number of possibilities for satisfying our sexual urges in one way or another, including heterosexuality — in other words with a person of the opposite sex — as the most attractive, likewise the one that ensures the future of the human race. We could say the same thing in a different way: the desire to be sexually satisfied by a member of the opposite sex must be the strongest — and it must be very strong — otherwise the human race would have become extinct.

But if we are deprived of this possibility for one reason or another, we are still able to take advantage of some of the other possibilities available — such as masturbation, or homosexuality.

Masturbation does not satisfy our need to be together with other people — the warming 'togetherness' that means so much to us. It is for this reason that masturbation as a rule is a temporary solution, or one made use of at intervals.

Homosexuality can arise in prisons, boarding schools, in wartime, on ships, during expeditions to the North Pole and other occasions when the lack of female (or male) company becomes so great that masturbation, in the long run, becomes merely a tame solution (see Sex life under abnormal circumstances). These are the instances when the possibility of sexual relationships with a member of the opposite sex does not exist. But we can also imagine a mental barrier. Thus if a person cannot, for mental reasons, tolerate the thought of being sexually satisfied by a member of the opposite sex, we still have a person who is longing for intimate human contact. Masturbation does not meet this demand; and so homosexuality becomes a possibility.

It is possible that boys who are brought up with a fear, terror or revulsion for girls can be 'seduced' · into permanent homosexuality, but then this means that it is not a question of a person to whom all possibilities are open that is seduced into adopting another course, but rather one to whom what is normally the most attractive possibility has become less attractive.

Kinsey · discovered that one man in three (37%) out of his examined material was able to relate having had one or more experiences of a homosexual character. In particular this referred to experiences during puberty, such as when two (or several) boys practise mutual masturbation together. But this sort of experience did not appear to have led to exclusive homosexual interest later in life — did not appear to have made them homosexuals, not even bi-sexuals.

The seduction theory must probably be discarded, at any rate in the form it has been upheld here in Denmark by those who fight against male prostitution. Here we must make brief mention of the identification theory (see also Identification), which is a more realistic explanation of how permanent, exclusive homosexuality arises. During upbringing, children as a rule have a father and a mother they can observe. Even when still very small they realize that a man does not use lipstick, that it is their mother who cooks and cleans, and many other things that tell them about the difference between the two sexes. (See also Sexual Differences).

As a rule a boy will decide he wants to be like his father, and a girl will identify herself with her mother. They will elect to play the roles which society allocates to men and women. (Margaret Mead, in her book "Sex and Temperament in Three Primitive Societies", gives a very interesting, detailed, but not exactly easily read account of the importance backgrounds of this kind can have).

As far as most people are concerned, this identification process takes place without any difficulty. We are perhaps not all quite as masculine or feminine as we would like to be, but we play the part reasonably well — it is not entirely strange to us. But in some cases this identification process presents difficulties. It may be difficult for them to play the part, difficult to live up to the part in question, or — and this is perhaps most often the case — it may have been difficult for them to identify themselves with the parent of the same sex. The father in question has perhaps been at sea for years, in prison, or the mother may have been divorced or unmarried.

In any case the boy may have been brought up by the mother alone. It may also be that the mother is such a domineering type that the father's role in the family has become indeterminate and weak. In all such cases the boy may have found it easier — for the possibilities have been greater — to identify himself with his mother. It is by no means rare for a single mother to bind her boy, in her loneliness, much too closely to her and actively oppose any kind of development towards becoming a man — without this necessarily taking place consciously. Many homosexual men have thus been extraordinarily firmly attached to their mothers, who are only proud of the attention and tenderness their sons demonstrate towards them.

The terms *daughters of Adam* and *sons of Eve* in connection with men and women who are homosexual originate from the same idea; the daughter who grows up to be like her father or the son who identifies himself with his mother.

Grown-up homosexual women can relate how they had a domineering father who tried to bring them up like a boy — with a correspondingly unfortunate effect on their sex life. (See also Oedipus).

Unfortunately our laws and jurisdiction concerning homosexuals here in Denmark are somewhat lacking in understanding. Let us say straight away that other countries are far worse, and that it has been far worse in Denmark too.

But it has also been better. The last raising of the minimum age for homosexual contact is a poor show. To be a 'fairy', a 'queen', a 'pansy' or whatever labels may get affixed to the male homosexual, or to be a Lesbian, or 'lesby' in the case of a woman, is not something the person concerned is suffered to be in peace. Homosexuals are looked down on. Just like all other human beings, homosexuals dream about finding someone — the one and only mate — with whom they can spend the rest of their lives in a sort of matrimony. A great number of these 'marriages' exist, happily established couples living in the same way as the rest of the more conformist world. In other words it is moreover completely wrong of us (looking, as we do, through the glasses of our prejudices) to lump all homosexuals together in the same pool. Just as big differences exist in their camp as in ours. (See also Male Prostitutes).

Our official moral code · completely forbids us to have even the slightest suggestion of a feeling that could be interpreted as homosexual, and the result is that we have built up a wall between ourselves and the others. We are a little afraid of these people. One can hear otherwise intelligent people saying: "Of course they must be allowed to live their lives in peace — provided I don't have to see or hear anything about them!"

But why in heaven's name not? When it is a question of different *animal* species we observe them with interest and like hearing about them, don't we? If homo-

A masculine woman is not necessarily homosexual — nor is a homosexual woman necessarily masculine.

sexuals really constituted a sharply delineated group that had no connection with us at all we would still have no need to react so violently — or so emotionally. (See Fantasies, sexual). This artificial wall also gets a few bricks piled on it by the homophiles themselves. "We were born this way," they say, because that is how they *feel* about it. But we cannot trust in our feelings.

Today homosexuals in Denmark have a chance of finding one another through clubs, magazines and advertisements. In spite of society's disapproval and the lack of understanding reflected in our laws hanging over their heads, it has become possible for them to live almost as happy lives with each other as the rest of us.

So far we have touched mainly on homosexuality between men, which is what our society knows most about and is most interested in — because it is regarded as a threat to young people during puberty ·.

Homosexuality between women exists too. But to start with women are permitted to fondle each other without immediately being accused of being abnormal, and girls have furthermore greater opportunities of identifying themselves with their mother. So it is believed that homosexuality between women is less widespread. Even so we must reckon with the fact that there are tens of thousands of homosexual women in a country the size of Denmark, and at least a hundred thousand men. They constitute a minority · with the same rights as — for instance — a racial minority would have among us.

Quite a number of women experience difficulty in achieving sexual satisfaction by means of normal sexual intercourse · with a man. It is natural that a number of these women are afraid without reason of being homosexual and some of them imagine that other women like themselves perhaps would be better able to help them. It is conceivable that the seduction theory — permanent seduction — is possibly more reasonable in the case of young women. It is not hard for us to imagine young women who have tried heterosexual relationships without result and who are unaware of the fact that as a woman it is necessary to make a personal contribution if satisfaction is to be obtained, and that it is common for

it to take quite a long time before a heterosexual relationship begins to give full satisfaction.

It is not hard for us to conceive of such women meeting a clever and experienced woman and being satisfied by her and thereafter perhaps immediately assuming — quite erroneously — that they must be abnormal and classifiable as homosexuals only.

Mistakes of this sort are due to the fact that we feign a state of exaggeratedly enviable sexual adjustment, and hold up relationships between a man and a woman as being, in the majority of normal ·, natural ·, cases, entirely uncomplicated affairs in which both parties rapidly obtain sexual satisfaction simultaneously.

This is a romantic lie that has caused many disappointments, many derangements and a great deal of loneliness.

Homosexuality can, in some cases, be altered by means of psychoanalysis ·, but not so that the person being psychoanalysed (in the same way as persons having had purely heterosexual experiences) comes to feel that this homosexuality is something for which he or she could never feel any inclination.

If a person has had considerable homosexual experience, he or she will of course still fully realize that in homosexuality there is a possibility of satisfaction. The 'cure' consists in helping, by means of psychoanalysis, a formerly exclusively homosexual person to experience, in some instances, heterosexual love.

This experience may prove more satisfying, equally satisfying, or less satisfying than the homosexual satisfaction previously experienced, depending on how successful the treatment is, or how fortunate the person being so treated is in the selection of a heterosexual partner.

Or the treatment may be entirely without effect. Here a certain amount of habit formation plays a part. A homosexual girl who has been used to cunnilinctio · with a girl friend will — quite erroneusly — feel it to be an admission of defeat if a man starts on the same thing, even though cunnilinctio is by no means uncommon in heterosexual relationships.

The same thing applies to fellatio · between men. If a woman suggests anything of this sort to a formerly homosexual man, he will experience it as an admission of defeat, even though fellatio is a feature of normal sex life too.

The widespread belief that homosexual men obtain satisfaction in particular by introducing the penis into the anus of their partner is just popular superstition. The practice occurs in heterosexual relationships and for anatomical reasons occurs more frequently in homosexual relationships, but it is not the most used method of obtaining satisfaction. Cunnilinctio ·, fellatio · and mutual masturbation are the common methods.

Homosexual men and women who try heterosexual relationships will often believe they are abnormal and hopelessly homosexual merely because they are unable to obtain satisfaction in the way they believe is the normal way, namely that in the course of an ordinary coition a man and a woman, by dint of inserting the penis into the vagina, achieve simultaneous sexual satisfaction within a comparatively short space of time. (See Simultaneous, Orgasm, Titillation, Impopotency). This is what is described in many books of sexual instruction as being the ideal — and the normal.

Ideal it may perhaps be, but normal in the sense of common it is most certainly not. — Many believe that all feminine men are homosexual. This is not the case. There are homosexual men who appear absolutely masculine. And there are masculine as well as feminine women who are homosexual. (See Transvestism).

Just as there are, amongst heterosexual persons, those who prefer prostitutes, there are male prostitutes · who provide some homosexuals with their pleasure.

Naturally there are people with masochistic · and sadistic tendencies amongst homosexuals — just as there are amongst heterosexuals.

Demonstratively feminine and affected homosexuals, likewise those who obtain their satisfaction from prostituted homosexuals, create a poor reputation for the entire peaceful remainder. The fate of a minority is so often that of being judged by appearances. Christianity has acquired a reputation for intolerance because a minority cries out — and in particular has cried out in the past — in a loud and condemnatory fashion. The milder souls are ill-suited to practice discipline and derive little pleasure from it anyway — as do their more demonstrative fellows.

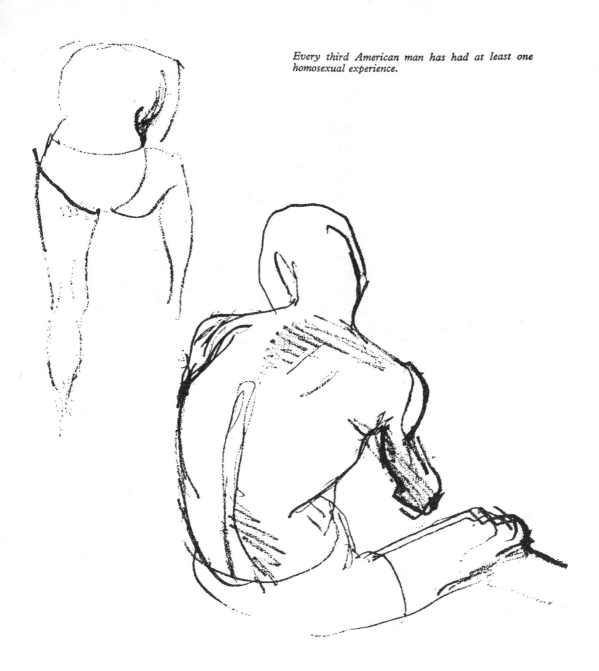

Every third American man has had at least one homosexual experience.

The extremists moreover possess a pronounced talent for setting themselves up as spokesmen. This is unfortunate, and we must take these factors into consideration when passing judgement on any social group. It is important for us to realize that the love life of homosexual persons can involve just the same tender, warm and human feelings as those experienced in heterosexual relationships, and that homosexual couples exist that might be just as happy as the happiest of married couples if society allowed them to live with one another in peace.

There are of course famous artists who are homosexual too. There are also extremely masculine men who are homosexual — and feminine men who are not the slightest bit homosexual.

We in Denmark have a long way to go before we can claim to be really tolerant towards those who feel differently. We look down upon the Americans for persecuting negroes; we smile at the clergy when they protest against women priests. We label such prejudices · racial discrimination and sex discrimination — but we practise several kinds of discrimination ourselves.

Just like Oscar Wilde in England, Herman Bang, a brilliant Danish writer, was subjected to the most cruel public persecution in his time, the attacks being led by another famous Danish author. Her-

man Bang was a homosexual, and the other writer, who was fully acquainted with the pleasures and problems of heterosexual relationships, should have been more open-minded — it is the duty of any practitioner of the arts to be so.

But sexual persecution is no mere question of past history. It still takes place in Denmark, albeit in a more discreet, camouflaged fashion.

It is claimed from many sides that homosexuality leads to criminality, but it should be borne in mind that if this is so it is not the fault of the homosexuals.

It is Danish legislation on the question that is to blame; for, even though more tolerant and humane than is the case in many other countries, it is nevertheless far stricter and more zealous in respect of homosexual love than it is in respect of heterosexual love. Homosexuality has been punishable by death, and no more than 30 years ago people were put in prison for having homosexual relationships with another adult.

Here in Denmark we have a minority of some 200,000 persons who feel differently through no fault of their own, people with sexual urges of the same intensity as those prevalent in heterosexual persons, in other words urges that cannot merely be "seized by the scruff of the neck and kept down" as some people believe. And these are urges that do not just demand sexual satisfaction, for that would be obtainable by masturbation ·.

They also involve a need for interhuman contact and tenderness of precisely the same kind as that which causes the heterosexual person to long for the warmth and company of the person he or she likes. (See also Satisfaction).

Heterosexual persons are permitted to have relationships with persons of 15 years and over, i.e. having just reached sexual maturity. But homosexuals can be punished for "abuse" of persons over 20, and a long list of instances could be cited in which the homosexual person can be punished but not the heterosexual. Such legislation has naturally been designed with the best of intentions, but is also the result of obdurate ignorance and a lack of interest in making unbiassed examination of the unfortunate consequences such strict legislation can produce.

It is hoped in this way to protect the young against seduction on the part of homosexuals ·. This hope is based upon a theory which we must still regard as dubious. On the other hand we find blackmail, robbery and violence following on in the wake of the strict line adopted.

All things considered, we can be thankful that homosexuals in Denmark nevertheless enjoy greater opportunities of getting together in peace than is the case in other countries. Special magazines exist carrying classified advertisements inserted by persons seeking others with similar interests, and there are clubs and similar meeting places where they can meet and find partners. "Vennen" (meaning "The Friend") P.O. Box 183, Copenhagen K., and "eos", P.O. Box 1268, Copenhagen S., are two such magazines sold in a number of newspaper kiosks in Copenhagen and in a few places in the provinces.

"Forbundet af 1948" (meaning "Association of 1948") is a social club that furthermore publishes a magazine called "Pan", P.O. Box 1023, Copenhagen K., from which address information concerning membership can also be obtained.

Those particularly interested in the subject will find an extremely sober review of the social problems connected with homosexuality in a series of articles published in a Copenhagen daily, the "Information", from 28th January 1961 until about the middle of February the same year. (Back numbers can be obtained on application to the editorial offices). Dr. Jarl Wagner Smitt has furthermore edited a book in which various specialists have contributed articles on homosexuality: "Why are they the way they are?" Also warmly recommended: Ford and Beach: *Patterns of Sexual Behavior*, published in 1951 by Harper & Brothers, N.Y. *i. & s.h.*

Honeymoon: A honeymoon is the period following after a wedding and the period to which many couples attach great and romantic expectations — so great that a honeymoon can often prove a serious disappointment and difficult to straighten out.

A happy sex life is not something that can be established in a matter of days, nor even of weeks or months. Each step forward may well take half a year or more. (See Wedding Depression and Cinema). *i.h.*

Hormones: Substances formed in closed glands in the body. They are carried round with the blood and affect the various organs in various ways. Thus insulin and adrenalin have different effects on the glucose content of the blood. Insulin promotes the deposition of sugar by the blood, while adrenalin impedes deposits.

Hormones furthermore exist that are of importance to growth, metabolism, development of the sexual organs, etc.

When hormones were first discovered — and sexual hormones in particular — it was thought that practically all the riddles of sex life had been solved.

It was believed that homosexual · men were merely men with too many female hormones, that impotency · was merely due to a lack of hormones, etc., etc., and that everything could be 'arranged' with the help of the appropriate injection. In fact it was even believed that the problems of old age were solved too, and that eternal youth would become a reality.

None of these expectations has been fulfilled. Hormones are not magical substances even though of extreme importance, and even though many diseases, e.g. diabetes, are now under control thanks to our knowledge and application of certain hormones.

But as far as sex hormones in particular are concerned, we have a long way to go before we can hope to know enough.

We know that hormones control menstruation ·, pregnancy, milk in the breasts and much else besides, but it seems very much as though psychic factors play a large and contributive part in our sex lives. The fact that hormone treatments gave such promising results when first started was largely due to the fact that faith can move mountains. Subsequent experiments proved that entirely neutral injections of salt water produced similar results as long as patients believed they were the new miracle drugs. But the effects of these 'miracle drugs' are unfortunately of brief duration, and as faith decreases, their effect becomes correspondingly less. Hormones would appear to play a part of greater importance in the lower mammalian orders.

Many kinds of hormone treatment can be of help, even though not so many as was at first hoped.

Faith does not always go on moving mountains. *s.h.*

Housing shortage: The unrestricted development of a person's sex life depends on so many external factors. It requires a place to be, a method of birth control · in which reasonable confidence can be placed, and various other arrangements.

A place to be. There are both women and men who groan, shout or even scream when they reach the point of orgasm, and they would probably be happiest if they could do their love-making in a completely detached house well-guarded against visitors. It is obvious that a two-roomed flat with non-existent sound-proofing between it and the flats above and below, plus children in the next

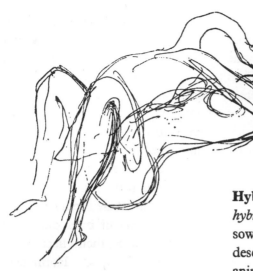

Leda and the swan.

room, would not be the ideal place for them. Neighbours once summoned the police to the home of some friends of ours because they thought he was murdering her. Little did they know.

The story may be comical, but it is also sad, because it stresses the fact that with the housing shortage as it is in our time, the opportunity of enjoying one's sex life undisturbed is a privilege.   *i. & s.h.*

Human being: It is not always easy to be a human being in this world with all its isms and the like. If we leave the lavatory door open we are suspected of exhibitionism ·, and if we lock it people think we are suffering from castration anxiety ·.

Let us cling on for all we are worth to the fact that what we call *normal sexual relationships* embraces a wide field. It is one-sidedness in our sexual relationships — not their multiplicity — that should make us uneasy.   *i. & s.h.*

Humaneness: See Intolerance.

Hybrid: Comes from the Latin word *hybrida,* meaning the offspring of a tame sow and a wild boar. Now used to describe the offspring of any two different animals (e.g. a horse and a donkey, the resultant foal being called a mule) or two different plants. Hybridization, or cross-breeding (or crossing) is common enough in botany, but in the animal kingdom that between a horse and a donkey is the most usual.

In the course of time the subject has fascinated many people. Countless cock-and-bull stories are told about girls who have managed to produce offspring with monkeys, dogs, donkeys, etc. Many scientists have experimented with the object of crossing various animals, for extremely practical results could well be obtained. One only has to consider the advantages to the farmer if a horse and a cow could be succesfully crossed and thereby result in a milk-producing beast of burden.

Throughout the entire course of humanity there have been no instances of a human producing any form of offspring with a non-human. Various religions, however, feature stories similar to that of Leda, who according to the legend had a child with a swan.   *s.h.*

Hymen: See Maidenhead.

Hypnosis: A somnambulent state in which a person has willingly made over part of his will-power to another person.

When in a state of hypnosis it is possible to hear the voice of the hypnotizer but nothing else. Used by responsible persons, hypnotism can be a pleasurable party game. When under hypnosis the person being hypnotized can have experiences similar to those in the most remarkable of dreams, depending on the imaginations of the hypnotizer and the person being hypnotized. Post-hypnotic suggestions are those placed in the mind of the person hypnotized during hypnotism by the hypnotizer, and can thus be made to take place after the actual state of hypnotism is over. It may be that the person hypnotized experiences a sudden, uncontrollable desire to drink a glass of water the moment the hypnotizer lights himself a cigar. It is also possible to hypnotize people into stopping smoking, not to be able to eat food from a plate, to remember better, etc., etc. But it should be borne in mind that things of this nature are really intrusions upon the personality · of the person concerned and may thus cause serious psychic damage.

If a person cannot stop smoking of his own accord, or start slimming, or whatever it may be, it means powerful forces must be involved, and such forces cannot be removed or brushed aside just by hypnosis. They can only be suppressed and kept down like a rubber ball under water — in other words hypnosis is a means of effecting a cure that should not be resorted to without precise knowledge of all the factors concerned, and even then only with the exercise of the greatest care. Many people are interested in knowing whether it is possible to seduce · a girl with the help of hypnotism. The point to bear in mind is that the actual fact of allowing oneself to be hypnotized is a declaration of confidence, and if confidence is held in a person, seduction is often possible. Or let us put it this way: it is possible to hypnotize a girl into going to bed with you provided she would have done so without being hypnotized. On the other hand it is likely that instances may occur in which hypnosis provides a girl with an excuse with which to appease her conscience. This is another reason why hypnotism should only be used by responsible persons, only as an interesting party game, or for serious, scientific purposes — in occasional instances as a part of a curative treatment.

There are many aspects of hypnotism that still remain unexplored. Experts find it hard to agree.   *s.h.*

Hypochondria: Imaginary illness. In a way the definition is wrong. Admittedly there are people who either believe they are suffering from a particular disease or who are constantly suffering from something new. They are very tiring to listen to and hard to take seriously, especially in a marriage or in a family. Nevertheless we should respect their hypochondria to a certain extent, for something really *is* wrong with them — hypochondria itself is a mental ailment.

attention wane, they talk about their illness — give it a little booster. The *malade imaginaire* is not merely simulating, nor is he an actor. The person who pretends knows he is really fit, and the actor knows he is playing a part. But the hypochondriac believes quite sincerely in his illness and clings to it.

One cannot remove the vital lie in a person's life without replacing it by something else. That something else should — for preference — be the ability to manage without his illness. Psychoanalysis · can help in some cases — but it is difficult, because psychoanalysis demands the active cooperation of the patient in question. *s.h.*

Hysteria: Violent reaction to comparatively petty provocation. If a girl tried to throw herself out of the window because she could not do her lessons in class we would classify her as hysterical.

It is a state of mental unbalancedness as a rule due to conflicts in completely different spheres to those we see. Sexual hysteria also occurs — and hysteria is often the result of conflicts connected with a person's sex life. (See also Psychopathy). The word hysteria comes from the Greek word *husterikos* meaning womb, because the Greeks had a feeling that a woman whose sex life was in order would not be subject to hysteria either.

Hypochondriacs are often people who feel themselves incapable of coping with the task of being a husband, wife, partner, or even just a human being. Maybe they find it hard to cope with their work. Some illness — or endlessly varying illnesses — therefore provides them with an excuse for not being able to cope with whatever it may be, and also draws attention to themselves. And should such

If mental problems manifest themselves through physical symptoms the condition is likewise known as hysteria. (See also Hypochondria). *i.h.*

I

Identification: Imitation — feeling like one's model. When a little boy saunters across the floor with a pipe in his mouth and great big strides saying, "Now I'm Daddy!" he is identifying himself fairly consciously with his father. But he will also imitate his father and assume his opinions and behaviour less consciously.

Of course we claim that young people during puberty revolt against authority on a number of points, but there are far more points where they entirely accept the norms with which they are confronted.

And when a mother said to her daughter: "Yes, sex is a curse inflicted upon us women because men are a lot of beasts" she was helping paint the picture the young girl formed of the business of being a woman.

In moments of difficulty later on it is possible that the girl will unconsciously act in accordance with the identification process which has taken place. She has formed herself in the image of the woman her mother has shown her in word and deed.

As a rule boys identify themselves with their father and girls with their mother. This is merely a theory, a hypothesis, but certain factors would indicate that permanent homosexuality · may be the result of a lack of identification with the parent of the same sex. If a father is very strict in his demands on his son it may well be that the son finds it difficult to respond to these demands and as a result turns more to his mother.

In this connection it may be mentioned that in our society we are far more concerned about our boys failing to grow up and be masculine men than we are about girls becoming feminine women. In other words we oblige boys to conform more strictly. Not all boys are by nature as masculine as we are so quick to demand of them. Most of us, however, live up to the expectations made of us and play the part society imposes upon us as men. In fact we identify ourselves entirely with the part we play — such is our nature. We are brave, vigorous, independent, creative, etc. — and women willingly give up their claim to these qualities. Being a woman in our society means not possessing certain qualities.

s.h.

Images, mental: See Fantasies, sexual.

Immodesty: Lack of modesty ·. Immodesty can be demonstrative or spiteful, but it can also be an expression of the fact that society has not succeeded in imposing a sense of shyness and shame upon us in the same way as on the others.

136

Modesty can be very sweet and charming, but it is rather impractical in a relationship between two persons. Immodesty, on the other hand, can have an utterly paralyzing effect on the other person.

The object here too must be to find a satisfactory balance.

Men are allowed to be a little bit more immodest than women, and women are expected to be more modest than men.

The best plan is probably to try and work away from too great a show of modesty so that, together, a little bit more immodesty is achieved. Then it hardly matters so much if the man still keeps the lead. (See also Taboo, Prejudice, Revulsion; and Breeding, good).

i.h.

Immorality: Everything that clashes with our moral code. Many things have been declared as immoral in the course of time. At various periods Christianity has classified every feeling of pleasure, every expression of joy and delight, as immoral.

Something of the same mentality still lingers in our Sunday restrictions, which attempt to force us to go to church by forbidding entertainments during church service hours. The peculiar thing about our Danish laws in this respect is that we are allowed to go and see 'cultural' documentary films on public holidays and early on Sundays, which as often as not means naked girls in the heart of the African jungle or on Easter Island. But not Laurel and Hardy.

s.h.

Impotency: Means that a person is incapable of performing the act of sexual intercourse ·. Even though women, in occasional, rare instances, can be impotent — unable to permit a penis · to glide into the vagina (see Genital Organs, female) on account of cramp in the muscles at the entrance to the vagina — the expression is mainly used about men.

Impotency in men can manifest itself in various ways. It may be the inability to have an erection ·, or it may be premature ejaculation. Both cases nearly always have mental reasons. Most men have experienced impotency at some time or other and most are a little afraid of it because we tend to demand of a man that "a real man is always potent". This is nonsense, but many believe it, and once the fear of becoming impotent arises, anxiety can very quickly provoke impotency. Thus there is often a question of a tedious vicious circle. Patience, love and a little praise on the part of the woman can do wonders (and have done wonders in the course of time).

The fear of being or becoming impotent hangs over some men like an obsession.

It is quite likely that it has made some turn to homosexuality ·. This is largely because we worship potency · and because we have come to attach too much importance to a man's erection and his powers of endurance. We now know that the chances of a woman's having an orgasm · is fairly independent, in the majority of cases, of any feelings up inside the vagina and there are therefore no reasonable grounds for maintaining this form of potency worship.

There is no reason why we should not endeavour to make a woman's sexual satisfaction · *independent* of a man's potency by choosing a form of intercourse or a technique · (see also Petting) that does not make these rigid demands on the man. (See especially Titillation). We men would so badly like to be indispensable, so some will perhaps interpret the suggestion as a sort of admission of defeat. This it is not.

Let us stop giving the word "potency" such a rigid interpretation. Whether one happens to be "able" in one direction or another is immaterial. If ordinary sexual intercourse were the only subject of interest, petting · would not be nearly as common as it is. In that case many would prefer masturbation ·, but this is far from being the case. We need each other. A man's sperm is admittedly important in the interests of procreation, but his potency · in the sense of his erection and ability to 'keep going' is nowhere near as important to a woman's sexual satisfaction · as has so often been claimed.

(See also Orgasm). In the case of impotency or cases of fear of impotency there is therefore no reason to regard it as a fiasco, but more as a particularly practical foundation for developing a happy sex life through choosing a form of intercourse that renders the woman's sexual satisfaction more independent. No matter what we do we will always be indispensable to one another. It is the sheer fact of being together that is the important thing in sexual relationships.

Disinclination · is worse than impotency.

In severer cases of serious impotency over a protracted period it is best to try doctors. Psychoanalysis · is likewise a possibility, but it is a lengthy and costly process. (See also Ambivalence and Form, being off).

Temporary impotency can be the result of confusion, shyness, inebriation, fear · of being disturbed, fear of catching a venereal disease, fear of causing pregnancy, violent infatuation, unconscious antipathy, etc. etc., or merely because of expecting it.

It does not make sex life any easier. But then nobody can claim that sex life is easy anyway. (See also Aggression, Refusal to eat, Sublimation). *s.h.*

Inbreeding: Means producing offspring by letting closely related couples mate with one another. If we want to pass judgement on the question of 'incest' objectively we should also bear in mind that 'incest' is widely practised by the breeders of agricultural animals in order to produce the finest and most desirable specimens possible.

Incest: Means sexual intercourse between persons who are so closely related to one another that such intercourse is forbidden by law. It is a rather delicate question sometimes difficult to reflect upon objectively seeing that we are all, or have been, emotionally implicated. A great deal of superstition and ignorance prevails concerning the reason why the law should forbid sexual intercourse between relatives. Let us therefore examine such facts as we can find.

If we go to the animal kingdom we find that in the majority of species fathers mate with their daughters, mothers with sons and brothers and sisters with each other (see likewise Inbreeding). It is not until we come to the higher orders, where there is a question of family groups, that we find restrictions bearing a resemblance to the incest taboos prevailing in the human race. In animal family groups there is as a rule a patriarch, or elderly male, who rules and dominates his wives and children and the family group as a whole. He will attack furiously any other male — whether of his own family or an outsider — who tries to get near his females. But once he has become sufficiently old and enfeebled, a younger, stronger male will topple him from his throne.

The good old Egyptians.

If from here we go to the human race, it is easy to see that it would be extremely unpractical if sons, as soon as they were able to overpower their fathers, could simply take over their mothers, marry them, and eject their fathers. Nor would it be such a good thing if fathers, once their daughters were grown up, merely abandoned their wives and married their daughters instead. The laws have therefore presumably been designed to protect the family group against internal strife and rivalry.

It must be regarded as probable that incest laws have been based on something of this nature.

Many believe that children of close relatives have hereditary taints, i.e. inherit their parents' poorest traits in multiple form. This is by no means the case. A marriage between close relatives may result in the strengthening of good as well as bad traits. For that matter we might just as well forbid people with poor genetical traits to have children with one another. In one circumstance, this is actually done, e.g. in cases where both parents are mentally deficient and a sterilization operation is performed to prevent their producing mentally deficient offspring.

If members of one family intermarry throughout several generations this may result in bad (but also good — see Inbreeding) genes becoming intensified and appearing in offspring.

Incest laws have existed in nearly all human societies ever since earliest times — with the possible exception of Adam and Eve's children. Laws against relationships between children and their parents are particularly common, but likewise those against relationships between brothers and sisters. We know, however, that both the Incas and the ancient Egyptians accepted marriage between brothers and sisters, and there are African tribes whose chief *must* have sexual intercourse with his daughters. In all these cases, however, the persons involved are the head figures of the societies concerned and thus placed outside the law. It is never permitted amongst the broad population.

Conversely, there are societies whose incest laws are so complicated and comprehensive that hardly any member is entitled to marry anybody else at all. In such cases the law has lost all common sense justification and has assumed a degree of omnipotence that can render life somewhat complicated.

Within our own cultural sphere too — that of the western world — what is understood by a 'close relative' varies from one country to the next. There are, for instance, modern societies in which cousins are not allowed to marry each other — which would seem to be stretching things a little far.

But all in all the majority of incest laws seem to be based on practical considerations. This, however, does not prevent erotic attraction arising between the parties concerned — an attraction which is suppressed very firmly during early years of upbringing and therefore not recognized by grown-ups. However, fathers now and again let themselves be tempted by their daughters, and in all probability it is even more likely between brothers and sisters. Most people can recall having experienced feelings of this sort towards their brothers or sisters, but of course direct sexual intercourse between them is a rarer matter and even rarer are children of such relationships, though they do occur. When they do they are generally kept secret.

If the family is otherwise fairly normal there is no reason why children from incestual relationships of this kind should not be entirely like other children in every respect. (See likewise Fantasies and Oedipus).

In our society, the normal parent/children and brother/sister incest restrictions are undoubtedly extremely practical in all general respects. But it is possible to conceive of situations in which they can result in tragedies — in cases of adoptions, for example, or when children of different marriages have been brought together. So it is quite a healthy thing to step outside our own society for a moment and try to regard the problem objectively.

— — —

As a curiosity may be mentioned the fact that in the Middle Ages, when the Black Death — the bubonic plague — was raging, it was widely believed that infection could be avoided by having incestuous sexual relationships on the altar of a church.   *s.h.*

Inclination: To have an inclination to do something means to want to do it.

We may want to drive a big red tram through a big city at rush hour, but we are not allowed to — being allowed to do what we want is not always so easy.

Obligations and responsibilities often follow in the wake of some of the things we feel like doing. We have to demand a minimum of proficiency, and certain rules must be obeyed. Those who want to drive a car are obliged to get themselves a driving licence beforehand and obey the rules of the road for ever afterwards.

In few spheres of activity does so much inclination — so much wanting — exist as in our sex lives. But we cannot always do just what we feel like doing here either (see Abnormal and Morals). We must have certain knowledge, a certain sense of responsibility ·, and we must obey certain rules. But what does inclination really mean, then? Do we know when we want something? Do we know what we want? Sometimes we spend a whole afternoon with a peculiar, restless sort of feeling in our stomachs.

Perhaps not until several hours later do we realize we clean forgot to have lunch — that we are hungry, that we want food.

Thus even a relatively simple thing like this can be quite complicated. Things become even more complicated when we have a look at sexual inclinations — the sexual urge ·. The desire for sexual satisfaction · is aroused at a very early age. Masturbation resulting in sexual satisfaction has been observed even in very small boys and girls.

In general, however, we reckon that the sexual need really makes itself felt with the commencement of puberty, i.e. close to the 13th year and during the ensueing years. Most girls have at any rate experienced some form of sexual desire — desire for sexual satisfaction — or other by the time they are 25, and men by the time they are 20.

Nowadays there is a good deal of talk about the fact that many Danish girls allow themselves to be talked into having sexual intercourse before they want to. This is probably both correct and incorrect.

A study of primitive peoples, of history and anthropology tells us that an early sex life is not uncommon. We have no reason to believe that our girls should be later developed — anatomically or physiologically — than others.

On the other hand it is not impossible that their mental — their psychic — maturity is often delayed. We try to keep back our young people's development in the hope that this will delay their sexual development. This is of course bound up with the fact that in our society we cannot marry and set up a home until we are 20 to 25 years old.

It is not our intention to encourage any girl to let herself be persuaded if she does not want to.

It would be better if we learnt to face up to facts · in all directions. Then at least it would be easier to decide whether one had the inclination or not — and to do what. _i. & s.h._

Incubation period: The period from the moment one catches a disease until the first symptoms appear. In the case of venereal · diseases, gonorrhea can be detected after a couple of days or so, but syphilis may take from a fortnight to several months to appear.

Incubus and succubus: The devil in the shape of a man or a woman. In the days of the witch trials · during the dark Middle Ages it was believed that the Devil had sexual relationships with human beings. These human beings were therefore his instruments, and as soon as the slightest suspicion arose that a person had any dealings with sorcery he or she was fanatically persecuted. When we learn anything about witchcraft in school nowadays we usually hear about evil eyes, black cats and broomsticks. These were certainly factors to be reckoned with, but the important part of all belief in witches was the interest in, and indignation concerning, witches' sexual excesses.

In this connection people let their imaginations go often to a frightening extent because the strict moral code of the day forbade nearly everything connected with sex life. The result was that the accusers projected their own lusts on to the accused (see Projection) and accused them of things they themselves secretly dreamed of doing and garnished such accusations with all the lurid details an incensed imagination is capable of formulating. _s.h._

Indifference: See Love Thermometer.

Indecency: Means an offence of a sexual nature. It may be a grown-up fondling a child rather intimately (see Crimes, sexual), or a man's taking advantage of a situation without a woman's agreement. (See also Seduction).

Indian art, literature and religion: Has dealt with in the past and continues to deal to a very great extent today with sexual questions and does so in a far more positive and accepting way than we are accustomed to. It is interesting to observe how a society that has been civilized much longer than we have can be far more sex-minded than we are.

Indignation: A very understandable feeling, even if it does not always manifest itself in the pleasantest of ways. If we push our bike the whole way home because we have forgotten our cycle-lamp, we feel indignant if somebody else, despite having no light either, jumps up and pedals off ahead of us, particularly if he gets away with it without being stopped by the police. If he is caught and fined we derive a certain smug satisfaction from the realization that the sinner has received his just dues. In other words: we become indignant if somebody else does something we would like to do but dare not — for example, if people pour scorn on the rules and traditions we do our best to uphold. *i.h.*

Infanticide: The practice of killing children immediately after birth has at all times and in many societies been a not uncommon, albeit drastic form of birth control ·. In some societies girl babies have suffered in particular, but there are also instances where only the boys have been killed.

Infantilism: Means childishness. It **may** be used in regard to physical characteristics such as chubby, childish curves, lack of hair even after puberty, etc. It may also be used in a mental sense, in other words about somebody with a markedly childish mind or mentality without the interest in sex life that comes with puberty. Infantilism may have hormonal · causes. We are also familiar with a purely physically determined form of infantilism in young, babyish girls who appear loath to comply with the demands which adult years and a mature attitude might be thought to inspire upon their surroundings.

Erotic infantilism may thus often be revealed as a marked anxiety about sex life and its 'brutal' demands.   *s.h.*

Infection: See Venereal Diseases and Prevention.

Inferiority, inferiority complex: A feeling of insecurity — uncertainty — that is very common especially in the years during and just after puberty.
(See also Disappointment and Conceit).

Young people have often discarded something of what the previous generation built upon, but have still not yet found their own way of life. (See also Gratitude and Responsibility, feeling of).

There is not so much to be done about this feeling of inferiority — it often disappears with the years. It may help to

143

find oneself a sphere one is master of — a sphere of activity in which one can have successs. Somehow it gives a point of departure — a wall to put one's back against. There is no need for it to be a large or important sphere. But like all advice of this sort it is easier to give than to follow. Important in this connection is the sexual inferiority complex, the feeling that in a number of matters one does not come up to scratch — sexually. It may be a matter of the actual appearance of the genital organs ·. A man may think his penis is too small. A woman may have a corresponding fear that her vagina is too big.

However, it cannot be said often enough, that in by far the majority of cases both these worries are entirely superfluous.

A woman with a very big vagina can lead a happy and satisfying sex life with a man whose penis is no bigger than his little finger. It is to a very greater extent a question of developing a satisfying technique in sexual intercourse. (See also Titillation).

As most women find it difficult to achieve orgasm · compared with a man's ability to do so, it is understandable, but no more true for all that, that many women imagine that a man with an ever bigger penis would work wonders. This is part of the superstitious load we drag round with us in the sphere of sexual relationships. (See also Sexual Similarities).

The presence of the penis inside the vagina, feelings up inside the vagina itself are — as mentioned in many other places in this book — relatively unim-portant to a woman's orgasm. To a man, on the other hand, the feeling of having his penis inside the woman's vagina is of much more importance to *his* orgasm. (And as his orgasm — unlike a woman's — is a prerequisite to fertilization, it is really quite practical if we think in terms of the procreation of our species).

The comparatively few women who attach decisive importance to feelings experienced in the walls of the vagina are furthermore often able to experiment their way to greater muscle consciousness by training the pelvic muscles. (See also Relaxation). Muscle consciousness is of far greater importance than the size of the vagina. (See furthermore Genital Organs, their appearance and size). Apart from the question of appearance and size, which are thus of comparative unimportance, there is the widespread sexual inferiority complex concerning a man's or a woman's potency · — their skill as lovers and mistresses. Men believe that other men are better lovers, that other men's erections· are better, that other men can keep going longer, can hold back their orgasm ·, etc. (see also Practice).

They fail to realize that the most skilful and experienced lovers are inventive and imaginative, and that they succeed in this way in making themselves fairly independent of both their erection and lasting powers. It admittedly demands a certain amount of authority and confidence towards women, who are more conservative and not quite so keen on experimentation. (See also Intolerance and Petting).

Women believe, just as erroneously, that other women only need to stretch out comfortably and kittenishly in order for a wonderful orgasm to come along within the space of a few seconds. (It may be mentioned in parenthesis here that the warmth, excitement and interest which men can report having met with in other women — and which they mistake for passion · — is in many cases hopeful expectation on the part of the other woman. Not the knowledge, but the belief that this time, with this man, she will experience the real, wonderful thing. A husband should not expect his wife to be able to trot out this sort of belief year after year). (See also Passion).

These are just a few of the misunderstandings that combine and cause us to feel that we each in our own lonely way belong to an inferior, impotent ·, frigid ·, abnormal ·, or perverse · minority ·. (See also Fantasies).

It can perhaps be added that what generally applies to an inferiority complex is that it prevents us from being fond of others and in trusting in the feelings of such others. If one regards oneself as a spineless squirt, a hopeless sort of person — or happens to feel crushed with shame from consciousness of one's own licentious train of thought — then one must either regard the woman who professes her love for one to be rather foolish — or refuse to believe her declarations.   *s.h.*

Infibulation: An operation that prevents sexual intercourse. It is not only in our time and in our society that cruel means have been invented to preserve the virginity of young men and women. In other societies young men's foreskins have been almost sewn up and similar embroidery performed at the entrance to young women's vaginas. A few threads were loosened when they got married and a few more when they were due to give birth. Strange things that people have put up with for centuries, and still do.   *i.h.*

Inhibition: A hindering, suppressive activity in the mind (see also Sublimation). An inhibited person is one who encounters difficulty in developing in harmony with himself — with his own personality ·.

Inhibitions may often be of a moral · nature, in other words acquired. In some instances it is a matter for regret that such acquired inhibitions have taken as firm root as they have. Many women (and a number of men) are able to ruin things for themselves by believing these inhibitions to be things they were born with and therefore of divine infallibility. It is not unusual for an inexperienced and uninformed woman to believe that a number of the approaches made by a man are immoral and wrong, because she has learned that this is so — it was always somehow in the air during her childhood and youth, *ergo* the man in question is a pig. (See Anilinctio, Fellatio and Cunnilinctio).

She is wrong. Nature · and what is natural are far more diverse when it comes to sexual activity than the official cultural attitude and code of morals ·

would have us believe (see also Kinsey). Many of the things we regard as abnormal or not very pleasant (see also Fashion and Taste) are entirely natural and ordinary things. On the other hand many things commonly regarded as right and normal are in reality no more than over-romanticized wishful dreams that are all too seldom fulfilled. (See Wedding Depression and Sexual Intercourse).

When we automatically look to our right and left before we cross a road it is because we have learnt to control something we have a spontaneous desire to do. The fact that before sinking our teeth into a slice of cream cake we wait until it is our turn, pay, and use a cake-fork, is because we have learnt to curb our impulses — we are inhibited. Most of our inhibitions are necessary if we intend living in a community, but individual inhibitions can none the less be downright harmful, especially if they prevent a person from developing reasonably. And a sexually satisfying life with another person is a human right.

"Inhibitions are soluble in alcohol," it is claimed. (But see also Alcohol).   *s.h.*

Most inhibitions are extremely practical, but a person with too many of them ends up by turning his back on life.

Initiative, sexual: In our society we have accepted the rule that it is up to a man to take the initiative. It is up to a man to telephone and invite, to take the lead. Many men would be paralyzed if their girl-friend were to take the initiative. It so happens that girls are often wily enough to do so in their own discreet fashion. (See also Conquer).

The same thing applies in most other societies, i.e. men officially take the initiative. And in these societies there are also women who plant discreet hints to the effect that now is the time to do something.

Thus there are girls who not only seek to establish contact and who are active during actual intercourse, both in societies where this has been accepted as being the task of the man and of course particularly in societies where the woman is directly encouraged to be active.

If we pass to the Animal Kingdom we find that mutual activity is far more pronounced, in fact is common. Both partners are sexually active and sexually aggressive ·. Both do what they can to excite the other. It would appear to be a rule that whichever partner happens to have the greatest inclination takes the initiative.   *i.h.*

Innate: We often speak of something as being innate, meaning that the person in question was born with it as opposed to having acquired it later in life either through environment or upbringing. We speak of innate modesty ·, innate dislike of homosexuality · and much else besides.

What applies to all these things and to many others which we regard as inherent is that it is nonsense and delusory to believe they should be as powerfully innate as we sometimes think.

We are not rational beings — and can only become such when we make it perfectly clear to ourselves that we continually allow ourselves to be fooled by our emotions. (See also Heredity and Upbringing).

Innocence: See Chastity and Virginity.

Inquisition: See Witch Trials.

Insemination, artificial: The notion that it might be possible to bring male and female cells into contact with one another by means of some other method than that employed by nature is a very old one. The easiest form of artificial fertilization is that which imitates the method used by bees to fertilize certain flowers and plants. The artificial insemination of cows by vets is already common in livestock breeding. But what we are interested in is the artificial insemination of human beings. Attempts have been made to make a woman pregnant by artificially introducing sperm cells for the past hundred years or so. The attempt is often made in cases where a marriage is childless for one reason or another. (See Childlessness). Occasionally there are cases of unmarried women who wish to become mothers in this way.

Thus the process involved is that of letting a doctor inject some male sperm cells up into the female womb. In approximately a quarter of the cases regarded as suitable this has resulted in pregnancy.

During the last war there were a number of women in the USA who became pregnant in this way despite the fact that their husbands were thousands of miles abroad.

If the cause of childlessness can be traced to some physical condition in the husband, there is the possibility of sperm being donated by an anonymous third person, who likewise remains ignorant as to the name of the person to whom his sperm is given. The use of a so-called sperm donor naturally presupposes the agreement of the husband. It can result in a great many moral, and in particular, legal problems. There have also been religious circles that have regarded artificial insemination as an impermissible interference with the course of nature. There is, however, little doubt that artificial insemination will assume increasing importance for the childless.

A very exciting side to artificial insemination, or rather, artificial fertilization in this case, is the attempt to achieve this without the use of a sperm cell. It has been found possible to make a female sea urchin's egg cell grow and turn into an embryo by tickling the cell membrane mechanically. So far advances have been made up through the ranks of the animal kingdom as far as rabbits. Experiments have also been made at removing the fertilized egg of a female that for some reason or other is unable to cope with a pregnancy. Thus there have been race horses that have 'foaled' and yet still won all their races. Perhaps there will be fragile little women in the future who will be able to hire big, robust girls to be pregnant for them — to hatch out their children for them. But it is all in the future. The same applies to the deep-freezing of the sperm of famous men. It would thus appear to be within the bounds of future possibility that women will one day be able to 'order' themselves artificially inseminated with the sperm of a man who has been dead for several years.

One of the more or less artificial methods that further the chances of fertilization is the use of suitable days. This method (which is especially used in reverse, i.e. to avoid fertilization, see Birth Control) — consists in having sexual intercourse principally on days believed to be conducive to fertilization, namely round about the 15th or 14th day before the next menstruation is due. This is because ovulation (see Fertilization) takes place just before this time. (See Menstruation Chart).

Of more surgical methods may be mentioned direct injection of sperm cells — either through the wall of the abdomen and in near the Fallopian tube — or up through the genital organs · and up into the womb itself.   *i.h.*

Instruction, sexual: See Enlightenment, sexual.

Intolerance, tolerance, humaneness: Intolerance is dislike of permitting other people to think, speak, believe, feel or act differently to the way one does oneself. Thus the intolerant person is far more tolerant as regards what he permits himself to do. Tolerance, on the other hand, is what is shown when a person respects other people's opinions and permits them to behave differently. It is a far more difficult attitude than that of the intolerant person. Intolerance would appear to be a psychological mechanism with which the majority of people are naturally equipped. Tolerance demands of a person that he make a conscious effort to understand himself, his feelings and prejudices.

Tolerance may be the result of inhibited aggressiveness ·; it may also represent an evasive mentality, a disinclination to take action.

Unfortunately, intolerant people always shout loudest and call upon God, the king, the fatherland and time-honoured traditions to be witnesses to their claim that their particular opinions are incontestable. It is, however, possible to be religious, royalistic, patriotic and conservative *without* being intolerant. And those who try to be tolerant have no need to tolerate intolerance like so many pious little lambs.

All of us have intolerant feelings in readiness to be unleashed. It is so easy, so obvious — one might almost say so natural · — to demand that the death sentence and punishment by flogging be reintroduced here in Denmark. Censorship is so logical, isn't it? And youth has never been so irresponsible, has it? (See Responsibility).

Tolerant people not only have to do battle with the intolerant ones. They must also be continously on the look-out for intolerance in themselves. (See also Christianity, Minority, Morals).

Tolerance in marriage is important.

Women with tolerant husbands often need to check whether their husbands are tolerant or just weak. Tolerance has its limits — weakness has none. It also applies to many other relationships in the course of life. We want tolerant parents, tolerant superiors and tolerant authorities — but there must be a limit. A clearly defined limit.

Humaneness means being humane, having human qualities. It demands a knowledge of how human beings are actually made up. It demands love for human beings as they are — and confidence in them.   *i.h.*

Inventiveness: It is van de Velde, who, with his books on marriage, has especially come to be known as an advocate of all sexual pranks and parlour games.

There is no need for us to belittle his contribution, which must be regarded against the background of a period when the presence of sexual urges in the woman were just being discovered. And there is most certainly no call either to minimize the value of the inventiveness and wish to experiment · which is also expressed in his books.

But just like courtship ·, it should not become an outward mask that in reality conceals a devaluation of the woman. Sexual relationships should not become

149

a matter of routine — of the kind in which both partners know each other backwards and are slightly bored by it all. (See also Practice).

Actually it is rather sad to think that we should have saddled sexual relationships — of all things — with such a violent taboo ˙.

There is no doubt that sex is the sphere of activity in life to have proved most inspiring and thereby caused human inventiveness to flourish most.

Yet we have forbidden each other to talk about it. (See also Masturbation Technique, Sexual Intercourse Technique, Titillation and Need).   *i. & s.h.*

J

Jealousy: Means that a person is unable to share the person he or she loves with anybody else. The jealousy of children when their mother is talking to other people can be particularly tiresome.

The incessant animosity of brothers and sisters and their disputes about who was given most are likewise pretty unbearable.

In general terms one can say that jealousy arises when one is uncertain about the other person's love. This uncertainty can be justified; and it can also be completely unjustified.

We have to face the fact that we do not own the other person and that we cannot impose our company upon him or her, nor our love; nor can we force anybody to love us. On the contrary, any sense of imposition may breed irritation, and the distance separating irritation and hate is not so very great. (See also Love Thermometer and Love Troubles). *i.h.*

There is a little psychological trick which has produced results in a number of cases. A young man had been associating with a young woman for several years when suddenly the lady began to show interest in somebody else. She turned down the young man's invitations and their whole world of mutual confidence seemed to be collapsing round them because she appeared to be severing the bonds. His first thought was to lay siege to her. Then he decided on a 7-page letter in which he wished her happiness and good fortune in the future and wrote sentimentally about all the things she had meant to him. Finally he came to his senses, tore up the seven pages and sent her 25 dark red roses accompanied by his card, on which he wrote:

Dear Else,
Thank you for the time we have had together. Thanks for — you!
Hans.

Whereupon she came back. They have now been married for 12 years.

This should not be interpreted as being a patent medicine or love potion that will always bring the loved one back.

It is only intended to illustrate that it may be more effective to loosen the bonds rather than tighten them. Clinging can chase people miles away.

It is dreadful to suffer from jealousy. Pathological, unmotivated, constant jealousy may have causes far back, possibly events during childhood and relationships with persons one loved at that time. *s.h.*

Jokes, naughty or dirty: Officially, all such jokes are classified as smutty, lewd or bawdy. Most of us know a lot of naughty (or dirty) jokes (see also Words, naughty). A blow should really be struck for the naughty joke and the naughty story. There are masses of them, both good and bad. Many of them are extremely funny. There are few spheres in which human genius and inventiveness, inspiration and imaginativeness is greater than in that of sex.

Let us take two examples from the vast number of anecdotes and jokes which it would be a pity to condemn:

— — —

A lecture on sex was being given to a group of university students in Copenhagen. The lecturer had got as far as to technique in sexual intercourse and introduced the subject as follows: "If we leave aside a number of gymnastic exercises of varying degrees of complication, we may say, broadly speaking, that there are four basic positions, that is to say four forms of sexual intercourse . . ."

At this point he was interrupted by a member of the audience in one of the front rows who looked up at him and said: "Five!"

The lecturer elected to ignore this interruption and merely repeated: "Broadly speaking, there are four positions . . ."

"Five!" said the student again, whereupon the lecture-hall started to buzz.

"Well," said the lecturer, "just listen a moment. First there's the one where the man lies on top of the woman . . ."

"Then there are six!" said the student.

And number two:

In England — at a large diplomatic dinner — a lady once had a Chinese gentleman as her dining partner.

In the course of their conversation, she asked:
"When do you have elections in China ?"

"When do I have elections in China ?" the gentleman repeated delightedly."
"Why, evely morning and evely night!"

— — —

A very important psychological mechanism in all jokes and funny stories is anxiety ·. The anxiety is not always equally obvious, but in the majority of cases it can be revealed by analysis.

A taboo · produces anxiety when we threaten to break it.

A joke — naughty or dirty — can almost be defined as a game played with a taboo ·. Few spheres are saddled with so many taboos as sex — which is why so many jokes on the subject turn up. *s.h.*

Joseph's Night, Tobias Nights: A custom that required a bride and bridegroom to refrain from having sexual intercourse for one or several nights after their marriage in order not to incur the wrath of the gods. The custom has been practised at many times and in many religions — and we are familiar with the mentality in many other spheres. (See also Epicurean). *s.h.*

K

Kinsey: Was an American professor of zoology. From his studies of zoology he was familiar with observations of the behaviour of animals. He was familar with the scientific thoroughness with which the sexual behaviour of many animals had been observed. His students then began asking him about the sexual behaviour of human beings, whereupon he tried to find books with equally objective, well-founded information concerning the behaviour of man. To his surprise he found the subject to have been sadly neglected. Although we have the most thorough reports on far more insignificant matters, he found nowhere a really comprehensive sociological · investigation on the behaviour of human beings in such a central sphere of human activity.

So in 1938 he began collecting interviews with the help of a number of highly qualified assistants with the object of preparing a gigantic report — to be known as the Kinsey report — which in statistical form provided information concerning the sex life of 5,300 white Americans. This report was published in book form in 1948: Kinsey, Pomeroy & Martin: *Sexual Behaviour in the Human Male*, Saunders.

In 1953 came report No. 2 about the sex lives of 5,940 white American women: Kinsey, Pomeroy, Martin and Gebhard: *Sexual Behaviour in the Human Female*, Saunders.

These reports received fantastically wide attention — and rightly so.

For the first time in the history of civilization we have been given the chance of finding out what is common in the sphere of sexual relationships and what is uncommon. Admittedly the report concerns white Americans, and admittedly Kinsey had difficulty in obtaining interviews with a wide and representative section of the population — nevertheless, it is a great achievement.

We have no better material if we want to study normal · sexual relations in western culture. Naturally we would like to see a Danish report on the sex lives of Danes too. (See also Report).

Until such a report is forthcoming we must therefore be satisfied with Kinsey's trail-blazing work, which is also quoted in every book on the subject that has ever been published since. Here are just a few figures — and it must be repeated that they apply to white Americans:

95% of the men had had an ejaculation · by the time they were 15 years old.

(Women do not have ejaculations so here we must use sexual satisfaction — orgasm · — as a yardstick.) Not until the age of 35 did 90% of the women report having experienced an orgasm. (If instead of an orgasm we speak of having sensed sexual urges — having had sexual feelings and sexual desires — the figures are naturally different). Puberty · begins in women at the age of 12 or 13 (with the appearance of hair round the sexual organs), and 30%, that is to say every third woman was able to state that at this stage she had noticed her sexual urges, and had had sexual feelings. Only 2% of all the women declared they had never — whether when young, grown-up or old — experienced sexual feelings. (See Frigidity).

One of Kinsey's most interesting results was that he discovered that men's sexual powers, sexual urges, interest or potency, measured in terms of sexual ejaculations per week, was greatest between the ages of 16 and 20 and thereafter decreased steadily until about the age of 60 (though there was also sexual activity after the age of 60). Women, who might well appear to be a little slow in getting off the mark, retained on the other hand their potency — their weekly number of orgasms — at a fairly constant level — in fact they possibly increased a little.

Kinsey also mentions — very significant-ly — that nearly all men and two-thirds of the women reported being able to remember that they had tried to mastur-bate with the object of obtaining sexual satisfaction. Erection is seen on many boys even in their cradles, and orgasm has been observed in boys and girls no more than 6 months old! One girl in ten and one boy in five could report having masturbated as early as at the age of 12.

Girls discover the possibility as a rule by themselves, while boys often learn about it from each other.

One man in three (37%) could report having tried sexual satisfaction with the help of a person of the same sex (in other words what we term homosexual · behaviour). And one woman in eight (13%) reports being able to remember similar experiences with other women.

If we imagine these figures transferred to Denmark it would mean that a million Danish boys, girls, women and men alive at the present day either have had or will have sexual satisfaction with the help of a member of the same sex; and of these, 100,000 to 200,000 have or will have permanent or exclusively homosexual relationships.

Bestiality · — sexual satisfaction with the help of an animal — was also investigated by Kinsey. Almost one man in ten (8% — especially in country districts) could report having obtained orgasm with the help of an animal, while only 3 to 4% of the women could report having had sexual experiences with animals.

In short, Kinsey revised the American public's ideas — in a statistical sense — as to what could be called normal. He showed us the colossal difference there can be between what we *say* is right and common and what we really do.

It is understandable that Kinsey's two reports have become a kind of Bible in the sphere of sexual research. It is not because they are either complete or exhaustive, but because we have nothing better and they are what we have needed

154

But we have the most detailed reports on the sex lives of mandrills and Danish sticklebacks.

ever since the very first peoples on earth began to lay down rules for behaviour (see Morals). *i. & s.h.*

Kiss: We all know what kisses are. There is the indifferent, cool kiss; the affectionate, but non-sexy kiss; the passionate, burning, sizzling kiss; and then all the intermediary forms.

A hot, passionate kiss of love likewise has its different degrees of intensity from the lightest touching of the ear, the neck, the breast or the backside (see Anilinctio) to the demanding, violent tongue-kiss in which the two tongues struggle with one another deep inside one another's mouths.

There are peoples who never kiss at all — and peoples where every instance of sexual intercourse is introduced by the man's first caressing the woman's clitoris with his lips and tongue. (See Cunnilingus).

Kinsey's report tells us that all these forms of kiss occur within what we call normal sexual relationships. He adds: (Report 2, p. 588). "It is not so strange that the two parts of the body that are the most sensitive erotically, namely the mouth and the genital organs, should be brought into contact with one another so often."   *i. & s.h.*

Kiss, passionate: A kiss that encourages or invites the recipient to show equal passion — as opposed to the paternal kiss ·, the courteous little kiss of welcome between husband and wife, women friends and so forth. It does not necessarily have to be a kiss on the mouth — it may be anywhere on the body, especially on any of the erogenous· places.

Amongst many peoples the kiss has been unknown, or at any rate so indecent that it was reserved only for the most intimate moments.

Knaus, Herman; Knaus' method: A method of birth control· that requires no mechanical appliances, merely a calendar and accurate knowledge as to the next date of menstruation. (See Menstruation Chart). It is the only method of contraception towards which the Catholic Church makes no objections — the so-called Rhythm method.

It is not entirely reliable but can be used independently of other methods if it is not absolutely imperative to avoid pregnancy. If used in conjunction with other methods it naturally offers additional security.

It can also be used for the very opposite purpose, in that it indicates the days when the chances of fertilization· are greatest, i.e. in instances where children are wanted.   *i. & s.h.*

If the woman is afraid of sexual relations the man should be patient, but not weak or indulgent. To achieve the right balance requires skill.

L

Lambitus: The same as cunnilingus ∙.

Lapis: See Prevention.

Latrine Drawings: See Erotographomania.

Lesbian: Homosexual∙ woman.

Lie: To tell somebody something that is not true is called to lie. When bringing up our children we always tell them it is wrong to lie — sinful. Nevertheless, children and grown-ups all lie. Polite lies, white lies and necessary lies.

It may well be the person who asks who forces the lie. (See also Simulate). Those who cannot bear hearing the truth are better advised not to ask in the first place. Many lovers torment each other with questions like: Do you love me? Are you faithful to me?

Of what use are the answers?

The truth can also be used as a form of aggression ∙, as a biting weapon with which to annoy the other party. There are husbands who simply have to entertain their wives with tales of their unfaithfulness ∙, or who 'forget' compromising letters in the hope that their wives will discover them. Such action may be revenge and may reflect a bad conscience.

Or a woman may suddenly reveal, in a fit of temper, that she has always simulated her orgasms. These are not always cases of praiseworthy honesty.

It is only in the novels of Sir Walter Scott and in cowboy films that the hero is honest to the core and rides on a white horse.

In real life the liar may well be a finer person than the stickler for truth. (See also Unfaithfulness).

But lying can also become a bad habit.

i. & s.h.

Life together: Married life, marital relations, cohabitation, living in sin — all are forms of life as led together by two persons. In our society the term *married life* mainly implies being respectably and cosily wed, whereas *marital relations* is a more direct implication of the sexual side of the relationship. *Cohabitation* is the strictly legal way of stating that two people live together, married or not; and *living in sin*, while originally a shocked and censorious way of inferring that two people were enjoying marital relations without being married, is nowadays generally used in cheerful acceptance.

An old Roman senator named Metellus once said: "Nature has arranged matters so that we can neither live with women nor without them."

He was evidently a genial fellow and according to reports happily married, but not unaware of the difficulties involved in living together: namely that the relationship demands understanding, tolerance (see Intolerance), patience ·, practice · and likewise a little knowledge about what is normal ·.   *s.h.*

Lodgings, landladies: Many young people live in rented rooms. Many landladies (and landlords) make a point of prying into the private lives of their tenants. They butt their noses in the most revolting fashion into the question of when, how long and who is visiting whom.

The same thing moreover applies to parents with grown-up children.

It is understandable that one likes to have a tenant who is easy and almost unnoticeable. But to interfere in the question of whether women have men in their rooms (or vice versa) after 10 o'clock at night is an intrusion on human rights. (See also Housing Shortage).

Sexual relationships are difficult enough as it is.   *i. & s.h.*

Loneliness: Being alone, feeling lonely, is something that hangs over civilized man like an ominous, dark cloud, particularly during youth, during and after puberty and before one has found somebody one likes — and who reciprocates the feeling. But loneliness exists amongst couples too. It is possible to feel lonely in a marriage. (See Inferiority Complex).

We place the individual higher than society, and it is possibly this we have to pay for in the form of loneliness. Where the individual occupies a second place and the community is number one, people have to pay a different kind of price, but are rewarded in the form of increased group feeling.

We can seek out groups and become members. Boy scouts, clubs and associations — whether political, religious or social — unite their members into a community. The reverse side of the welfare state medal is that many become self-sufficient and close their doors.

But we are now enjoying good times and have no wish to revert to the old days. What can lonely people do? The advice may sound banal, but is none the less effective: cultivate some interests in life, seek out some groups and enter into the spirit of their activities. For those who are lonely with their partner, the answer is the same thing: try to pursue common interests!

An important point to remember here is that you often work up an appetite as you eat. Nobody starts by being an expert in a field, nobody knows everything about something before even beginning. Whether it be Persian rugs, bridge or football, whether it be dancing, chess, books or anything else, in each case it demands a positive effort, a serious attempt to grasp what it is all about — and as likely as not it will end up by becoming an absorbing interest or hobby. But it also demands an effort to find somebody — or each other — to share it with.

It is possible to be lonely in a group, too.

There are many lonely people waiting to meet each other. (See also Advertisements, matrimonial). Being alone can, however, also be a delightful thing — provided it is voluntary.   *s.h.*

Looking-glass: As a rule it is regarded as ridiculous and reprehensible to look at oneself in a looking-glass. We blush, feel ashamed and thoroughly put out if we are caught doing so. It is called vanity · and conceit. (See also Self-satisfaction). Here again we have an example of some-thing entirely human and natural which we have encumbered with a pointless taboo ·. Why on earth should we not take an interest in ourselves? We are the most obvious people to do so.

Both men and women inspect themselves interestedly in a mirror when they are alone. Why should we not be pleased with ourselves? How will we ever be able to accept all the human, natural · and normal · things in others if we do not even allow ourselves to accept our-selves?   *i.h.*

Love: We are familiar with many kinds of love — motherly love, love for one's neighbour — also called charity — self-love, love for one's country, and so forth. In a way it is a little sad to think how often we use love for others as a *weapon*. In the play *Lysistrate* by Aristophanes · the girls refuse to go to bed with their husbands until they have abolished all war. Their intentions were certainly noble.

But it happens often in daily life that we deprive each other of our love when we are dissatisfied. We close up like clams when we are angry with our wives. They go as cool as water-melons when they are fed up with us for some reason. And when it comes to upbringing of children we do the same thing: we show children quite clearly that we don't like them if they don't behave themselves. We close off the channel of contact, and this can often hurt much harder than blows, for neither children nor grown-ups can manage without love.

A very considerable part of this love is our sexual feelings, our sex lives, eroticism — but there is much more in the concept of love: the feeling of affinity, of solidarity, tenderness towards another person, mutual respect and confidence and a great deal else besides.

Sexual feelings have been underestimated for a long time. Many women have never permitted themselves to acknowledge them. Love has been over-romanticized because it was felt that sexual feelings dragged the more delicate feelings down to a lower level. (See also Troubadour).

It has therefore been necessary, and is still necessary, to stress the fact that sexual relationships constitute a very considerable part of love in all people no matter whether they choose to suppress them, deny their existence, exaggerate their importance or let them assume their rightful place.

Some will exclaim unctuously: "We must not forget love for the sake of sex!" It is the old discussion about body and soul. Why undervalue either? They are two sides of the same question. What is most important, human happiness or a microscopic piece of coal? If one happens to have the bit of coal in one's eye it is difficult to be happy.

People so often talk about sex *or* love as if it were a case of *either/or*. Is it?

i. & s.h.

Love, free: Means the right to love, in particular sexual love, without the responsibilities of marriage. Free love has been a motto, a slogan for a cause. (See also Christianity, Trial Marriage, Emancipation).

Love, homosexual: See Homosexuality.

Love, lesbian: Love between women. (See Homosexuality).

Love life: The term is applied to the entire vast sphere of feelings concerned with love · but with slightly more stress on sexual love. Two weighty volumes edited by Dr. Tage Philipson are thus entitled *Kærlighedslivet* (Love life), Lund & Andersen's Forlag, 1952.

Love-making, the art of: Means getting the most out of that important side of our lives which we call our sex life. Like other arts of living, it cannot be learnt merely by dry theories, but by a happy combination of knowledge, inspiration and genuine wish.

Love-play: The prelude to actual coition ·. What we are thinking of here is all the many deliciously stimulating things a couple can do with each other. In few spheres of activity is man as imaginative as in this particular one. (See also Petting and Titillation, sexual).

Unfortunately we have our taboos concerning all sides of our sex lives, and so there are many things about which we never hear. It has been stressed that love-play may be of special importance to the woman, who as a rule experiences more difficulty in becoming interested (see Erogenous Zones) and therefore requires a very protracted session in order to obtain sexual satisfaction. But there are also women who are not interested in preludes of any sort, but prefer more direct forms of excitation ·. (See also Sexual Intercourse, techniques).   *i.h.*

Love thermometer: It is a little odd to   write about something that is not something, but it is because of the widely held theory that love and hate are two opposite poles on a scale. We have made a diagram of this idea (see also Ambivalence) and would like to explain that this is not the way things are. People often imagine that burning love is more or less boiling point, or 100° on a Celcius thermometer, that indifference

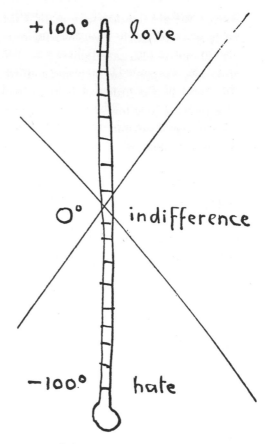

It is not as simple as this.

is at 0° and that savage hate must be far down below freezing-point. But this is not the case. Love and hate are relative. If love happens to be slightly less burning it can be felt — experienced · — as hate. If one's hate is slightly less savage it can be experienced as sympathy.

Thus the correct scale simply cannot be drawn, because the two emotions may moreover be reversed: the person one loved, but now loves a little less, one may end up by hating; and the person one hated so bitterly before may be found to be quite pleasant after all. (See also Wedding Depression and Cinema).   *s.h.*

Love troubles: In most cases these involve the crossing or jilting of one partner by the other. The ailment is also known as unrequited love, and is a miserable state of affairs and usually a hard time to get through. Those of us who are older now and can remember having been through it can of course smile in a superior fashion and say it passes, that it is what happens when you are very young, and that it is wonderful to have such intense feelings. Just like seasickness, it is something other people seldom bother to take seriously.

— — —

All that can be said is that the outlook that only one single person in the whole world is the right one for us — is not right. There are many people with whom we can live happily provided we happen to have what it takes to live happily.

— — —

All this talk about 'the one and only' is romantic nonsense with which we have succeeded in thoroughly fooling ourselves. Unfortunately we believe in it, so on the other hand we must also respect the love troubles of very young people, for they are often experienced deeply and sincerely. It is no help treating them superficially and breezily.

— — —

When the beautiful Helen was carried off by Prince Paris because of being the world's most beautiful woman she was 12 years old. Daphne and Chloe were 15 and 13 respectively when they fell in love with one another, and when Romeo became enamoured of his Juliet so passionately the young lady was 14.   *s.h.*

Love, to: The ability to be fond of another person — in all senses of the word — must be regarded as being of great importance. Considerable stress is laid on this subject in psychoanalysis ·.

It may well be combined with healthy egoism · and is much less demanding than consideration · may often be. It is therefore much more important to say:

"I love you!" than to ask: "Do you love me?", which may become a nuisance — the question is as a rule superfluous anyway.   *i. & s.h.*

Lubricant: Rubber goods shops sell a vegetable jelly which is practical as a lubricant. (See Intercourse, sexual). A little jelly can be used on the tip of the penis before drawing on a condom. It will make the condom less noticeable and the risk of its breaking is also reduced — but the risk of its sliding off becomes greater! The woman can also use the vaginal jelly and place a little of it at the entrance to the vagina. It is by no means unusual for a woman's vagina to be rather dry to start with. Many women wash and dry themselves before going to bed with a man.

— — —

The jelly costs a couple of *kroner* a tube and only a little is used at a time. Special condoms also exist that are prelubricated.

For want of anything better, ordinary spitle can also be used.   *s.h.*

Lust: See Sexual desire.

M

Maidenhead, maidenhead worship: The fold of mucous membrane present round the edge of the entrance to the vagina (see Genital Organs, female) on young girls until removed by a doctor, through masturbation, washing, intercourse or in some other way, is called the maidenhead, hymen and probably many other things. Its removal is known as deflowering. It would appear to be only in human beings that the maidenhead is found. (Some scientists maintain, however, that a similar obstacle exists in nearly all female animals, but that it bursts shortly before sexual maturity is reached).

There are — and have been in the course of time — many peculiar ideas attached to maidenheads and their deflowering. When deflowering takes place (which is rarely difficult) there is usually a little bleeding because a slight break occurs in the mucous membrane. It is an entirely undangerous and physically unimportant affair. In some cases defloration is not even noticed at all.

In many peoples there has been a complete lack of interest in whether a girl should have had sexual intercourse before or whether her maidenhead happened to be still there or not, but in certain peoples the custom has existed of displaying the bridal sheet duly stained with blood after the bridal night as proof that the bride has not had sexual intercourse before. This has given rise to many ingenious inventions such as a little pig's bladder filled with pigeon's blood and placed up inside the girl's vagina with the object of satisfying worshippers of the virginal state.

We see the same importance attached to 'purity' in present-day societies. In the USA as well as in Europe there are women who are well-versed in all forms of sexual activity with the sole exception of having actually permitted a penis to enter their vagina. (See Virgin, technical).

The thought of reserving particularly loving feelings for the man who removes a girl's maidenhead is naturally an outcome of maidenhead worship. If a maidenhead is to be kept carefully for the one and only man in a girl's life, well then, the man who finally does the removing simply is that one and only man.

The idea has probably been somewhat over-romanticized. In our times, in which sexual intercourse and the deflowering of maidenheads often take place without subsequent marriage with the person concerned, it would be impractical to try and keep the tradition going.

It has been claimed that it is an inherent feeling in the woman, but there is nothing to support the theory even though many continue to do so. On the contrary, there have been several cases observed in

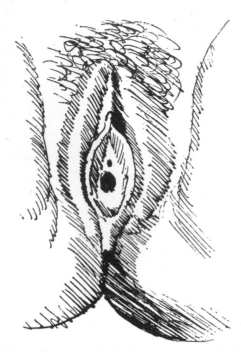

This is what a maidenhead, or hymen, can look like in a woman who has never had sexual intercourse · with a man.

which it appeared that for her first sexual intercourse the woman in question deliberately sought herself out a man with whom she did not later intend to continue relationships. Many have stated that it was something it was best to have got "over and done with".

The fact that a number of men still attach importance to pure untouched virginity is thus partly due to these traditions (though of course they would never dream of making the same demands on themselves) but there may also be a question of a fear of sexual inferiority ·. Men have little experience of what other men are capable of. They have no idea whether they are 'good enough' sexually. And women are not always the ones to praise them and tell them it was lovely.

Saddled with a fear of this nature, i.e. of being compared with others — and perhaps rejected — it is understandable (but no more the reasonable for all that) that they want to find themselves a girl who has nobody with whom to compare them.

And if a girl has previous experience with which to compare, a man makes entirely unreasonable demands · on himself as well as her and insists on her having an orgasm.

The first experience of sexual intercourse · is likewise burdened with great expectations, with fear and trembling and many other feelings.

Let us make it quite clear: it is not the wonderful experience so many like to make of it. Most people are so confused, shy, tensed, etc., that as a rule there is a disappointment, a feeling of "Was *that* all it is?" afterwards. (See also Wedding Depression).

To any girl who may be afraid can be said this, that it is not nearly as bad as she thinks. Fear can cause one to tense one's muscles unnecessarily, and this can cause a little pain that would never have come otherwise. Even the removal of the hymen is very rarely so difficult that intervention on the part of a doctor proves necessary. It may be so in some instances, but even then is a simple affair that can be managed in the course of a normal consultation. (See also Gynaecological examination). *i. & s.h.*

Majority: See Minority.

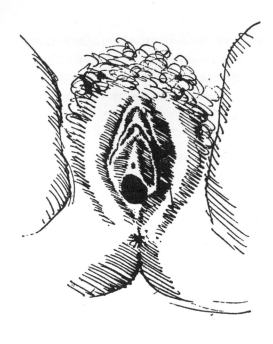

The first time a woman has sexual intercourse with a man the mucous membrane which hitherto has partly covered the entrance to the vagina is ruptured; some of the remains of the hymen can still be seen here.

Male brothels: Brothels · where women can buy themselves a man are much rarer than ordinary brothels; but instances of them do occur. (See also Gigolo).

Male wedding, male marriage: Many peoples have existed whose laws fully permitted marriage between two men — or two women. The Greeks, the Romans and the Indians had all provided for this sort of thing. Many homosexuals · live private married lives in our own society. They would very much appreciate it if such marriages were accepted and recognized in the same way as ordinary marriages.   *i.h.*

Mamma: The female breast.

Man auction: The counterpart to a woman auction . Said to have taken place in England right up to the days of our grandparents.

Mandrake: A plant root in the shape of a man. (Latin name: *Mandragora officinarum.*) According to the legend it was supposed to have grown forth from the seed of a hanged bachelor and in olden days was regarded as a love charm, furthermore capable of easing birth and promoting fertility.

Masochism, masochist: A speciality in the sphere of sex life ·. A person who becomes particularly sexually stimulated by being tortured or humiliated is called a masochist. But let us not forget that we are all slightly familiar with the sensation — with masochism as well as sadism · and all the other isms we call perversities. All these things exist in normal · sexual relationships. It is when any one of them is pursued to the exclusion of all others that it becomes dangerous, for it then indicates a twisted mind.

Masochism — the name — is derived from a German author, Leopold von Sacher-Masoch, who lived during the 19th century and described in his books the pleasures he obtained from being mishandled by his wife. Religious history furthermore provides us with countless examples of people who have tortured themselves because in so doing they satisfied the sexual urges they were otherwise forbidden to permit a more natural · release. We have instances of it amongst nuns obliged to live in celibacy but who derived intense pleasure from the cruellest tortures and forms of humiliation of their own selection, from hunger and whipping to drinking the blood of persons infected with the pox and licking the wounds of the leprous. Some of them were made into saints. Nation-wide movements of religious flagellants have also existed — but their supporters never realized that sexual urges were behind it all.

As will be seen from a small-scale investigation referred to elsewhere in this book (see Governess) many fairly pronounced practitioners of masochism exist in Denmark today. In the case of a great many of them it is obvious that the seed which has resulted in these special wishes was sown long ago during childhood. In respect of the remainder it is less apparent, but probable none the less, that childhood experiences bound up with humiliating, sadistic forms of punishment have been the cause.

We have many other proofs of the way upbringing · can form personality ·, but few give such food for thought as this.

Both men and women can become masochists; the fact that the 'governess' material in question principally involved men who longed to be "brought up" by a dominating type of woman is probably bound up with the fact that it is easier for women to find a dominating type of man in our patriarchal society.

It may be added that for a woman who possibly finds it a little difficult to have sexual feelings (see Frigidity), even her husband's 'misuse' of her, i.e. using her

to obtain his own sexual satisfaction, can sometimes give her a passive form of pleasure reminiscent of masochistic feelings. (See also Deformity Fetishism and Transvestism).   *i. & s.h.*

Massage, massage clinics: Understandably enough, quite a lot of prostitution has gone under the name of *massage* in the course of time.

Masturbation: Also known as onanism, auto-erotics and many other things — "self-abuse" is one of the worst of them and dates from the days when it was believed that masturbation was dangerous and abnormal. It is not so very long ago that people used to tell their children as well as themselves this lie.
Masturbation means trying to satisfy one's sexual urges alone and unaided.

(But we also speak of mutual masturbation, by which we understand that two people, instead of trying to satisfy themselves, try to satisfy each other with the help of a technique used in masturbation. But mutual masturbation is thus not really masturbation). (See also Kinsey and Homosexuality).

Of the many thousands of Americans Kinsey interviewed, 62% of the women and 93% of the men reported that they had tried masturbating once, several times or many times. Prior to Kinsey's reports on sex life in America it was widely believed that masturbating was rare, abnormal or even perverse ·. Of course there were sexuologists · who had a well-founded hunch that masturbation was perfectly common, but it was not until the Kinsey reports that we obtained proper documentation that was to prove convincing in wider circles.

Thus it is highly possible that Kinsey's figures are too low, i.e. that masturbation is still more common and widespread amongst both men and women.

But it is unlikely that the figures can be too high. People are usually loath to admit anything of which they are ashamed — and until the Kinsey report was published many have believed themselves to be alone with their 'sin'. As we have no reason to assume that conditions in Denmark should be different from those in the USA — on the contrary, we have many reasons for assuming that they must be more or less the same — we can safely state that nearly all men and at any rate far more than half of all the women have masturbated, do so now and will in the future for varying lengths of time.

We find masturbation in very small children, small children, slightly bigger children, in teenagers and in adults — married as well as unmarried. Unfortunately a bad conscience is often bound up with these experiences.

Many still believe that masturbation is something to be ashamed of — in fact there are even those who believe it can be harmful. Even in open-minded, sensible Danish books of sexual guidance one can come across the turn of phrase: "Masturbation is entirely harmless provided it is not practised to excess." (See Excess).

Nobody need be ashamed of masturbating. It is not harmful — and it cannot be practised to excess. It is really quite incredible that it should still be necessary to say: "It is quite harmless. It is quite normal." (It is incredible that books should still be published that say that "an effort should be made to make a person who masturbates start thinking of other things — if necessary via treatment by a psychiatrist" — to quote a German book published in 1955).

We have sexual needs — sexual urges — just as we need to pass our water. If we don't see to it that we pass our water at intervals we may pee in our pants. It is

the same thing with 'wet dreams' — nocturnal emissions. It is just as reasonable to satisfy one's sexual needs as to satisfy one's urinary needs. But we don't speak about "making the urinator think of other things — if necessary through treatment by a psychiatrist" — on the contrary. It is involuntary urinating — uncontrolled satisfaction in this sphere we think we should treat.

We cannot always draw a conclusion from the one sphere to the next. But it might help us a little to regard the problems connected with masturbation in a clearer light. For masturbation is still a problem for young and older people alike.

Therefore it must be said again: masturbation is one of the quite definitely commonests methods of satisfying one's sexual urges — in fact if we want to count orgasms · it is probably *the* most common — and always has been. Just as common and natural as eating when we are hungry.

By far the majority of people — perhaps almost all — have tried masturbating for longer or shorter periods.

It is not something that is always admitted during a short interview or that is mentioned during the first hours of a psychoanalysis ·. A very, very strong degree of mutual confidence has to be built up first.

Women would appear to be particularly reserved on this point. This possibly explains Kinsey's, likewise Kirsten Auken's (in "Unge kvinders sexuelle adfærd", Rosenkilde & Bagger, 1953) lower figures for women.

After several hours' talking about masturbation and a final confession accompanied by a violent emotional outburst, and after subsequently hearing about all the pangs of conscience that have tortured the person concerned like a nightmare, and about the colossal relief it has been to have a proper talk about it all — not until moments like these does one understand how foolish and ignorant people have been and still are concerning such a natural side of sex life. Masturbation is one of the many possibilities we have of satisfying our sexual urges ·.

And as very few of us can marry at the age of 10 to 15 it is a very common and normal form of satisfaction. Not abnormal · — not wrong — in no way a substitute of inferior value as it is so often made out to be — not anything childish or immature either.

Sexual urges in many ways resemble hunger for food.

And in the same way that we may resort to a snack if we happen to get hungry, and enjoy it because it satisfies our craving for food perfectly well, we can also (whether as children, in our teens or as adults — married or unmarried) — let masturbation settle our sexual hunger and leave us free to think about other things again.

We can draw the parallel even further: of course it is more pleasant and more festive to dine with our beloved and enjoy the choicest of dishes. And it is reasonable that married people should have their daily meals together whenever possible.

You can control your appetite a little bit to suit the other person — we are not always hungry at the same time. And of course it is loveliest to be able to satisfy one's sexual needs in the company of the person one likes. And just as little as it is a matter of filling one's stomach when it is food we want, equally little is it a question merely of being sexually satisfied in the company of one's loved one.

There is much more to it — otherwise masturbation would be the easiest and simplest form of sexual satisfaction. But many men and women are still inclined to regard masturbation as a fiasco — a defeat — particularly if they are married and have the opportunity of being together. There is no need to take this whole question so earnestly. Just because one happens to go out to the kitchen and help oneself to an evening snack of some sort alone there is no reason why anybody should think that from now on this is the only form of meal one wants.

Just like the in-between-meal snack, masturbation is an excellent safety valve that enables us to satisfy a need when it turns up at moments when we have neither the opportunity nor the time for satisfying it in a more festive fashion.

Far too many men's vanities are deeply wounded if they discover that their wives masturbate. They take it as a personal defeat because we are living in a period of transition during which we have just permitted a woman to have sexual urges. Nice ladies were not allowed to have such urges at all a few generations ago — and the way it has developed nowadays is that a man should "permit" a woman to have sexual satisfaction — provide it for her.

Society · has also put up a number of ideal demands — that both partners should be satisfied at the same time and by means of ordinary sexual intercourse ·.

But this is not the usual case.

It is only in very few cases in very few marriages that the joint sex-life fulfils these ideal demands — in other words they are not normal at all, but represent a romanticized dream — a hope — an objective we have declared to be the only right thing.

Idealistic demands of this kind do untold damage because we have for far too long been ignorant in regard to ordinary sexual relationships as they manifest themselves for most of us.

Just think of masturbation, which right up until our own lifetime has been decried as rare, abnormal, an 'infectious' disease.

Curiously enough, the common word for masturbation used in Scandinavia is *onani*, onanism, derived from Onan in the Bible, who did not actually masturbate at all, but had *coitus interruptus* · (see Birth Control) with his deceased brother's wife. He was *supposed* to be having intercourse with her according to the levirate law, because he was supposed to see to it that his brother had some children. But he withdrew his penis from the woman and "let his seed fall upon the ground" in order to avoid making her pregnant. In doing so — practising *coitus interruptus* — he broke the levirate law and was sentenced to death. People have since chosen to misunderstand this.

As they wanted to condemn the satisfaction of sexual urges as practised separately from the interests of procreation, they quite erroneously called masturbation onanism and pointed to the fact that the Bible condemned Onan. A complete misunderstanding from start to finish — and a misunderstanding that has caused untold suffering and still causes a good deal of entirely unnecessary pangs of conscience. Now and again young men still try to castrate themselves because of their bad consciences about something that is and always has been natural and common.

It is only in very rare cases, when masturbation continues to be the only way in which a person can obtain sexual satisfaction, that we can speak of unfortunate one-sidedness — that is to say if a person is unable to obtain sexual satisfaction with another person.

i. & s.h.

Masturbation Technique: (See also Masturbation; Titillation, sexual; Orgasm, Satisfaction and Fantasies). Men, women, children and young people use all sorts of different methods when they want to satisfy their sexual urges alone.

The commonest are those in which the hands, fingers and thighs are used in one combination or another.

The central stimulative point in a man is the head of the penis · and in a woman the clitoris ·. (See Genital Organs, female).

Many have believed that most women used some form of substitute for a penis which they pushed up inside their vagina when masturbating. And many have been afraid that things of this sort might perhaps disappear up inside them or bring on cancer. An extraordinary amount of fear and superstition exists on this particular point.

A few women use penis substitutes of this sort, but in the majority of cases titillation of the vagina itself in this way is not necessary. (Incidentally, these things cannot disappear up into the womb. The vagina (see Genital Organs, female) is a comparatively short tube that is completely closed at the far end by the neck of the womb. There is only a very narrow canal leading on into the cavity of the womb. In other words the neck of the womb is joined to the end of the vaginal tube in a continuous, unbroken piece of flesh).

It must be mentioned that by far the majority of things people have thought up in the course of time are entirely harmless. Both men and women have used telephone showers, the heel, pillows, brushes and many other things. Some have derived pleasure from tickling the urinary canal, the anus · , the breast, testicles and other parts of the body.

Masturbation usually results in orgasm and seldom lasts more than 5-10 minutes. Masturbation is probably the commonest form of sexual satisfaction · if we count total orgasms in a person's life. So we might as well show man our confidence and believe that in the majority of cases it works fine.

It is all the very prohibitions and fear-inspiring policies themselves that have led to the over-refined forms of masturbation which, in a few isolated instances, have proved harmful. There *are* women who have used hairpins which have disappeared up their urine pipe and have had to be removed by surgical intervention. There *are* men who have suspended themselves beneath chandeliers in special masturbation apparatuses put together with boards and nails — but they constitute the rarest of isolated instances. A very considerable part of masturbation is the fantasies · which accompany the act.

These flights of fancy are among the most private things we human beings have.

But in the majority of instances these fanciful images accompany masturbation — i.e. parallel acts that supplement each other until the desired sexual satisfaction has been achieved.

Nor is it unusual for these erotic fantasies, these sexual 'accompanying' dreams, to be somewhat bolder than the reality which surrounds us. It is not unusual for our dreams to be somewhat wilder than our daily lives.

It is not unthinkable, for instance, that a woman may select images of a homosexual nature — without this meaning that she would enter into homosexual relationships in real life. There are others who possibly toy with the thought of prostitution — without our therefore being entitled to assume they intend to start walking the streets.

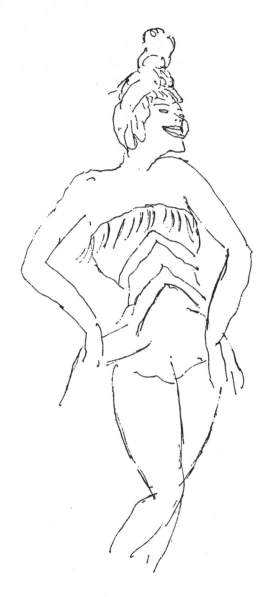

Even though a man may let his imagination run wild on the subject of daring and uninhibited girls, he may well be quite satisfied with the more peaceful type he chose for a wife.

In the same way there are men whose images may be tinged with sadistic · or masochistic · ideas, but who in the course of their sex life keep strictly to the conventional, accepted pattern.

This applies to the majority of what we call perversities ·, namely that they are things of which we can find traces in normal, natural sexual relationships.

What applies to an even greater extent to these sexual flights of the imagination is that we clearly see how the framework surrounding what is normal is much larger. Much more is permissible in the world of our imaginations.

So it must be stressed that nobody need feel himself or herself abnormal, perverse or diseased because their flights of erotic fancy happen to be much bolder than their real lives.

It is not uncommon for particular themes to be repeated again and again in the course of these erotic flights over which we in many cases exercise control — which we ourselves direct. Such fantasies happen to constitute one of the various forms of safety valve that make it possible for us to adjust ourselves to life in a society.

How often may one masturbate? This question can be answered quite clearly: as often as one wants to.

It has become a custom to say that masturbation is not harmful provided it is not practised to excess ·. In doing so, mankind has been done rather a bad turn, for nobody knows what constitutes excess in this connection. We know, on the other hand, that there are people who masturbate several times a day and that there are others who do so once a week — and that both types of person are equally healthy.

We are perfectly capable of forcing a little food down our throats even when we are not hungry — or drinking a little when we are not thirsty. In the same way it is naturally possible to masturbate without particularly wanting to — without being sexually satisfied.

The nicest kind of meal is probably the one when we are feeling just pleasantly hungry — in the same way the most satisfying masturbation will take place when sexual needs — the sexual urge — have reached a suitable intensity. But just when one's sexual urges have reached a suitable intensity is something we can only decide for ourselves — and it should not be allowed to become a problem. There is no need to take the matter too earnestly.

The only harmful thing we find in connection with masturbation is the enormous feeling of guilt ·, the bad conscience · which society in a foolish and entirely unjustified manner has imposed upon us. Society has a peculiar knack of making us feel as though we were the only child in the world that picked its nose. The same thing applies to masturbation ·.

i. & s.h.

Mating time: See Heat, to be on.

Matriarchy: Our society is a society controlled by males — a patriarchy — in other words men enjoy the greatest privileges and decide more things. But a few instances of matriarchal states exist, i.e. states in which women play the more important part.

Member: The penis · (see Genital Organs, male).

Menarchy: A young girl's first menstruation ·. As a rule it occurs at the age of 13 or 14, but may come earlier, may come later. (See also Puberty).

Menses, menstruation: Once a month blood starts coming from a woman's vagina (see Genital Organs, female) and the occurence is known as menstruation, menses (the plural form of the Latin word *mensis*, meaning a month), the monthly period, or just 'period'. Many women speak of their menstruation in tones of contempt, referring to it as "the curse", etc. — the colourful ways of describing it are legion. (See also Abstinence, period of).

Even though the anatomic factors of menstruation are dealt with in the article on Genital Organs, female, it may be mentioned here that the blood in a woman's body is normally closed off from the menstrual blood. The bleeding which takes place is thus not like the bleeding from a wound, but a precise quantity of blood that is found in the mucous membrane discarded every month.

Menstruation plays quite a large part in a woman's life. A girl is often quite unprepared for her first menstruation and very frightened by it. Menstruation can also be painful and accompanied by mental instability. Unfortunately many mothers encourage this instability although it does not necessarily accompany the monthly bleeding period at all.

Menstruation is also sometimes used as an excuse for not having sexual intercourse. Many wives regard sex life as a necessary sacrifice, and all the revulsion with which women are often brought up to regard menstruation makes it easy to use menstruation as an excuse for not having to make the 'sacrifice'.

A violent taboo · exists about talking about menstruation, particularly when men are present. It is something about which one is ashamed. When menstruation fails to happen though, it is something that arouses a good deal of talk, because it may be an indication of pregnancy, of the fact that a fertilized ovum has lodged itself in the mucous membrane of the womb (see Genital Organs, female) and has begun to develop into a child. In many instances however, it will prove not to be a case of pregnancy after all. The wisest thing is always to consult a doctor, but not before one week after menstruation should have come at the earliest (see also Pregnancy Reactions, Tampon).   *i. & s.h.*

Menstruation chart, rhythm chart: If a woman is very anxious to have children, or very anxious not to have children, a practical idea is to keep a chart of her menstruation ·. We know that as a rule the egg, or ovum, can be fertilized 12 to 17 days before the first day of the following menstruation. This period, i.e. about 15 days before the next menstruation, is particularly fertile, in other words the chances of fertilization taking place are greatest. As menstruation can vary a couple of days one way or the other — in other words come a

173

day before or a day later — it is best to add a little at both ends and for safety's sake reckon on the period between the tenth and the twentieth day as being the fertile period, and the rest of the time as the unfertile period.

Note that the counting must be done backwards, i.e. from the first day of the *next* menstruation. In keeping count it is thus the first day of menstruation that is of interest — and not how long the actual bleeding lasts. (See also Knaus and Birth Control).

Let us take a practical example: a woman has menstruation on the 1st January (i.e. this is the first day her bleeding starts) and expects to have it again on the 28th, 29th or 30th January. She has kept count for so long she knows this as a rule is the interval.

So we count 19 days backwards from the 28th January: 27, 26, 25 .... 11, 10 ... the 9th January is thus the 19th day.

From this day onwards the chances of fertilization increase. On the 9th and 10th they are not so great, but on the 11th, 12th, 13th, 14th, 15th and 16th January they are quite large; on the 17th and 18th a little less, and for the rest of the month less still.

If this woman wants to have children she will try to have sexual intercourse · on the 12th, 13th, 14th and 15th January.

If she is anxious not to have children she will stick to the days prior to the 9th January and after the 18th. (See also Abstinence, periods of).

This method is not safe if used as a form of birth control ·, but used in conjunction with a condom · or a pessary it provides an increased measure of safety — something one can hardly have too much of.   *i. & s.h.*

Menstruation, double: Menstruation · every 14 days instead of — as normally — every 28 or 30 days. Comparatively rare.

Mental disorders: We realize today that complete abstinence · must be regarded as unfortunate. In the course of time we have seen many examples of unpleasantly twisted minds resulting from fanatic attempts at abstinence.

Kinsey ·, in his report on the sex life of men in the USA, showed that there was a statistical relationship between abstinence and the possibility of suffering from mental disorders. Our violent prejudices · and taboos · concerning masturbation have indirectly been the cause of countless mental suffering on account of guilt complexes · and bad consciences produced by these misunderstood prohibitions.

There is no sharp division between mental sufferings and mental diseases. They are sufferings and diseases in the mind, and they can have many causes besides the sexual ones. But as the sphere of sexual relationships is one in which society particularly sets up prohibitions and taboos, a connection to or from the sex life of the person concerned is not rare.   *s.h.*

Minority: A small group within a large group.

Here in Denmark we have a number of minorities, e.g. Jews, Catholics, Salvation Army, Jehovah's Witnesses and other small groups. Nationally speaking we have a number of Germans in North Slesvig and other small groups. Common to all these groups is that they are not wholly accepted by the majority — the larger group surrounding them.

Even though it will be denied by many, we still have a good deal of antisemitism (see Prejudice) in Denmark. The other religious groups cannot be said to be entirely left in peace either. Germans in Denmark and Danes in Germany are all able to say a word or two on how unpleasant it can be to belong to a minority.

Within the sphere of sexual relationships we have a number of minorities: fetishists ·, sadists ·, masochists ·, and many others.

Until the Kinsey Report · came, 90% of the white population of the USA believed it belonged to a minority that had transgressed the strict American laws concerning indecency ·.

Absurd conditions of this kind are what may result when a strict public moral code imposes restrictions that are transgressed by the majority — when sexuological · science is suppressed and enlightenment opposed — likewise in the name of morality.

It is the hope of morality and discipline that the majority of healthy, warm-hearted, vigorous people will go round each believing himself or herself to belong to an imperfect, slightly perverse · or indecent minority. Once the real majority has been split up in this way, an over-moral minority stands up and says:

"We represent the majority. We decide what is right. All you people who might like to think a little differently — suppress and deny these feelings!"

And the majority of us are fairly obedient provided the moral code in question is not too strict. Things are not too bad in their way, but a few people cannot submit to the commandments of the moral code. These are the persons whose behaviour is furthest from that prescribed by the said official moral code, and society thereupon expels them even further out into the darkness. They are called antisocial, and society builds up a wall between them and us by chivvying us into the same fold and pushing the others away.

It is the same as declaring that all men between 5′6″ and 5′10″ tall were 5′8″. Then we would bawl out all those who were 5′10½″ or taller for being giants and all those of 5′5½″ and under for being dwarfs. We would be denying that transitional heights existed at all.

If we regard each person's sex life as a jigsaw puzzle, a mosaic, a pattern, we find there are just as many patterns as people. Each person has his or her own little pattern. There may be a number of patterns that in their broad outline resemble one another, but this does not justify our saying they are exactly the

This is what a strict moral code tries to make us believe we are : a normal, central group, all of whose members are alike; and, at a suitable distance from us, the abnormal, perverse · , animalian rest.

same, that they are the majority and have nothing in common with the minorities. The classification 'majority' which we, in the name of morality, claim for ourselves, in reality consists of a lot of minorities which we pool together into one large group. Here in Denmark we have a numerically strong minority consisting of several hundred thousand persons whose lives we make miserable by denying their existence. We annoy them, talk behind their backs, look down our noses at them, pass special laws to control them — all in the name of morality. Very few people show any interest in scientific research of the kind that could really provide us with the facts and a background against which to deal with this group in a humane fashion. Here we are thinking of the permanently homosexual · and those who are periodically bisexual — people to whom otherwise quite open-minded citizens choose to close their eyes.

But we too, i.e. the compact majority, all belong to a minority in one sphere or another as far as sexual relationships go — and in many other ways for that matter too. The pattern of our individual sex lives is in fact so distinct that it is **not** precisely like anybody else's.

No more than a generation ago it was believed that an indecent, perverse, sinful, morbid minority existed called masturbaters · . Headmasters at boarding schools in Denmark asked their pupils whether they 'suffered' from masturbation. Nowadays we know that masturbation is just as natural · as drinking water.   *i. & s.h.*

Miscarriage: See Abortion.

Mixed marriages: A term used as a rule to describe marriages in which man and wife have different religious beliefs or skin colour. Such marriages may result in violent and unforeseen complications connected with the bringing up of children, also at religious festivals, family gatherings etc. Their sex habits and sexual upbringing may prove so incompatible that the marriage has to be abandoned.   *s.h.*

176

But this is what we look like in reality : there is a gentle transition from the majority in the middle to the very few really different cases at each end.

Modesty: There are societies in which the women are so modest, so shy, so reserved and chaste, that a doctor is not allowed to examine them if they are ill. If they have a pain in their back the place is pointed out on a doll. This is probably carrying modesty a little too far. On the other hand our ancestors in the Middle Ages allowed their friends and acquaintances to come and watch their first coitus on their wedding night — and this appears to us a little on the immodest side.

These are the extremes — but who on earth can say that we in Denmark, today, have selected just the right amount of modesty to practise? Because we feel it to be so right, so sensible, so ingrained and so natural ·? But that is just what the others felt too! Nakedness is also a kind of measure of modesty. Nakedness varies from society to society, from period to period, from place to place. In the USA tiny girls wear bathing suits with tops to them on the beach. A girl wearing a bikini would be a sensation in

a main street in Copenhagen, but a girl wearing a big brassiere and a pair of cami-knickers can be more exciting on a beach than even the most diminuitive of bikinis plus contents. Our great-grand-fathers' hearts began beating fast at the sight of an ankle, but our ancestors further back were more frank about things. However, it seems women in all societies cover up their genitals from curious eyes. There is possibly a biological explanation, as in many animal species the baring of her genital organs by the female is a direct invitation to the male to copulate.

In our society, modesty is held in high esteem by women — possibly because we men feel a little more confident?

There is, however, nothing to indicate that women should be so very much more shy, reserved or sensitive from birth on this point than men. There is the possibility that women in certain societies — like ours — learn, during the course of their childhood, to play

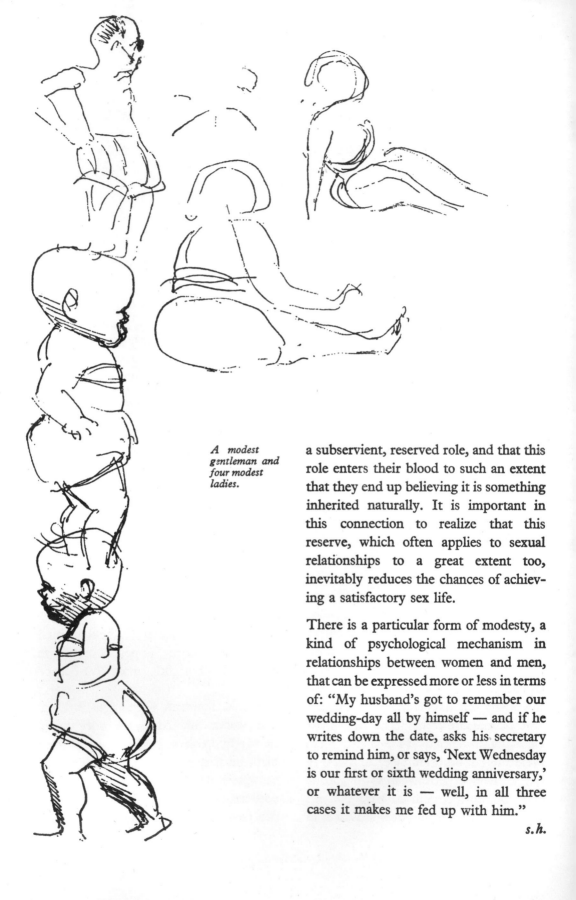

A modest gentleman and four modest ladies.

a subservient, reserved role, and that this role enters their blood to such an extent that they end up believing it is something inherited naturally. It is important in this connection to realize that this reserve, which often applies to sexual relationships to a great extent too, inevitably reduces the chances of achieving a satisfactory sex life.

There is a particular form of modesty, a kind of psychological mechanism in relationships between women and men, that can be expressed more or less in terms of: "My husband's got to remember our wedding-day all by himself — and if he writes down the date, asks his secretary to remind him, or says, 'Next Wednesday is our first or sixth wedding anniversary,' or whatever it is — well, in all three cases it makes me fed up with him."

s.h.

It would appear to be seldom that women forget their wedding anniversaries, but extraordinarily common for men to do so. We women presumably attach far more importance to it than men, and regard it as a kind of negligence of ourselves and our importance in the family (perhaps justifiably?). But at all events I think there is little to be gained by letting our husbands forget it and then sulking about it. Admittedly *we* are not the ones who are supposed to do anything on the day in question. He is supposed to buy the flowers or chocolates. So why don't we give each other flowers? Or, what might be easier for us — just remind him of it the day before.   *i.h.*

This, of course, is merely one example; there are others more serious. The same law seems to apply during sexual intercourse ·, when it manifests itself in a slightly different way. Misplaced modesty often results in a woman's completely omitting to inform a man that what he happens to be doing at any given moment is not making her the least bit excited, and her muttering under her breath:

"He'll have to find out for himself."

This, of course, is the worst thing that can happen, and naturally hinders and delays matters a great deal. It is much better if, without displaying too much irritation, she can guide her lover. But at this stage, unfortunately, psychological laws once more impose themselves. Far too many sensible girls forget to say when everything is lovely and just the way they like it. They expect a man to be able to guess by himself, or from hints that are so discreet the normal block-headed man

has not the slightest chance of understanding them. In other words, it is not quite enough to complain when things go wrong — a plain word or two when things are going right would help enormously.

We men, on the other hand, must be prepared to accept the fact that it is not easy for a girl; that she would prefer us to discover things for ourselves; and that generally speaking girls are not so very keen on helping us — not for any reasons we can scold them for, but because it is almost insuperably difficult for them to get themselves to do it.

There may be a touch of superstition · attached to the question too. Many girls say they have a feeling that if they say:

"Oh, just like that! That was simply wonderful!" — then the wonderful part will simply disappear — dissolve into thin air. This is superstition, all right — but it is possibly connected with Kinsey's· hypothesis to the effect that women are more liable to let themselves be distracted at the loveliest moments of all and that it is very much more important to a woman that coition and a man's movements be performed in an entirely regular, unbroken rhythm — while a man is perfectly well able to make pauses, try variations, etc., without his excitement being affected.   *s.h.*

I am quite sure that many girls would be happy to give guidance — if they dared. But to start with there seems to be a sort of instinctive feeling that if you are a girl it is just something you don't do. Secondly, it so happens that there are men who take it as a deadly insult: "Well, since I don't seem to be able to please you . . ."

Thirdly, the fact is that when you are a girl there is a great possibility of your not knowing exactly what it is you want anyway. (See Inclination).

Probably the most important thing is for both parties to realize that it is not something one just 'does', but something it should be possible to talk about and gradually work out between you.   *i.h.*

Monogamy: Means being married to one person only. Most other combinations exist too: one man married to two or more wives; one woman married to two or more husbands. But in our society · a person is only permitted to be married to one person at a time. As is always the case with such things — because they are connected with morality · — we have hastened to elevate this to the status of being natural ·, the 'right thing'.

Of course people will go so far as to say that men are polygamous ·, that you can never give a man enough women — but "women are monogamous by nature".

There is *nothing* to indicate that women should be more monogamous by nature than men — i.e. that it should be an inherent quality in women.   *s.h.*

Morals: A set of rules for human relations. Now and then people will talk of sexual morals, by which they mean a special set of rules for sexual relations.

— — —

This is an extremely difficult question and one on which learned persons find it hard to agree. It demands not only knowledge but also the ability to put aside one's own prejudices and standards.

— — —

Let us start by agreeing that there must be rules in any society ·.

There is furthermore not much point if we have to weigh up in our minds whether something is right or wrong before each act. It is more practical if we automatically look to our left (or to our right, depending on what part of the world we happen to be in) before crossing the road. But this is not to say that our national highway code should be regarded as something divinely infallible and irrevocable. Laws have a habit of lingering on in force even when they have become antiquated and pointless.

Moral codes are even worse because they are nearly always classified as a divine institution, or something inherent in man, so that no form of revision can be tolerated. Thus it can be quite useful to examine morality from the historical viewpoint. Christian morality in particular, Catholic as well as Protestant, has undergone great changes in the course of time. (See also Church Murals). Going for a walk on Sunday mornings has been regarded as highly sinful at one time.

Polygamy has been permitted by the Protestant Church on several occasions.

Luther, for instance, approved of Philip of Hessen's second, bigamous marriage. During the 14th century all experiments in physics were forbidden by law because the Church regarded them as sinful. The Catholic Church forbids nearly all forms of birth control · — and for that matter the Protestant Church did so until recently too.

There have been Catholic cardinals who had children with their sisters without this being regarded as any hindrance to a career (see Alexander VI). State-authorized brothels exist in many countries, particularly Catholic ones. Protestantism has regarded the woman as being very "unclean" and therefore far removed from everything godly. And in our own times, not so long ago, a large number of Danish clergymen protested against permitting women to become priests.

Other clergymen, however, regarded it as reasonable.

From these examples taken at random it will be apparent that the right code of morals is not something unequivocal and applicable at any time in any society. The ideal code of morals would presumably be a set of rules which most people found it possible to obey without such obedience costing too much in terms of human happiness and harmony; rules that are strictly necessary in order to prevent encroachment on others or abuse; rules that can ensure the right of development of the individual. (See also Shoes). In other words, rules that as many people as possible can observe — and still be able to accept themselves.

This sounds all very well and good, but it is of course extremely difficult to draw up a set of rules of this nature.

The way one draws up any code of morals likewise depends on the kind of belief one has in man. If one believes that man is evil and bad and foolish one naturally draws up a different set of rules to that one draws up if one likes people the way they are and can accept their less fortunate qualities as well as the more fortunate.

A religion is nearly always obliged to draw up a strict moral code that can make people conscious of sin and give them bad consciences. This strengthens their faith and maintains discipline. On the other hand a code of morals that is too tolerant would make those seeking religiousness — others, too — uncertain and unsatisfied. Happy people are not created merely by suddenly relieving the moral pressure, by suddenly declaring that what was previously forbidden is now permissible — even if the restriction in question was unreasonable. The pressure must be relieved gradually — keeping pace with the development of the individual. But it should not be used as an excuse for maintaining a too strict code of morals. The unsettled conditions in the Congo after its liberation can also be used to prove that the negroes there are not yet mature enough to govern themselves. But if constantly suppressed, a people will never become mature.

In the name of religion and morality very nearly 10 million Europeans have been put to death during the past 500 years. (See Witch Trials).

Unfortunately a few strict moralists as a rule are strong enough — and energetic enough — to get their ideas introduced into a society normally marked by its joy of living. (See also Minority). They are able to use up all their repressed, unused sexual energy (see Sexual need) on acquiring influence on national legislation and the official code of morals.

We are made to feel the pinch of this sort of thing very clearly by present-day Sunday and public-holiday legislation, which from a democratic viewpoint is entirely unreasonable as it compels sundry entertainment establishments to remain closed with the object of forcing a minority to go to church — and a majority passively puts up with this.

We also see it in a ridiculous little thing like the fear of the magic power of words (see also Words, naughty) in that a minority protests fanatically against swear-words on the wireless.

This minority tries to impress its morbid attitude on as many sides of our lives as possible — is mistrustful of science, research, enlightenment and social institutions. It may seem unfair to lump all these things together, but there is often a psychological bearing · on the subject resulting in the fact that we find all these things turning up in the same people.

There is reason to believe that the current code of morals at any given time is always behind development, seldom dares to accept man as he is, often is opposed to pleasure, is always used by the older generation to keep the younger generation down, and is nearly always regarded as infallible and unalterable.

We shall never achieve the ideal code of morals — like so many other ideals. But that should not deter us from trying. We should incessantly be taking our code of morals up for critical revision in accordance with the continual discoveries about man being made in the spheres of anthropology ·, psychology ·, and other sciences. In particular we should endeavour to learn from the history of morality.

What we should endeavour to eradicate are the superfluous, traditional restrictions that have outlived themselves and seized themselves a kind of unjustified absolute monarchy, a functional autonomy.

i. & s.h.

Morals, double codes of: It is not rare for a person to believe that one code of morals applies to himself and another, stricter code, to others. A woman should be a virgin, but a man should, for preference, have had some experience. (Just who is supposed to marry the non-virginal girls with whom he gets his experience is something he never bothers to think about). Ever since Adam and Eve (or whatever their names were) most men and women have masturbated but forforbidden their children to do so. Kinsey mentions repeatedly in his reports the chasm that exists in American society between the official code of morals and the actual state of affairs. The healthiest society is the one in which the difference between the official code of morals and the actual state of affairs has been reduced to a minimum.

s.h.

Mother Fixation: Sometimes a mother may, during the upbringing of her children, try to bind them very closely to her. It happens particularly with sons, whom a mother often finds it hard to see grow up and go their own ways.

It often takes place in the case of single mothers or mothers who find their husbands are unable to give them everything they expect from him and whose lives therefore begin to revolve around their son instead.

Most sons will experience a certain amount of this sort of thing during their puberty ·, and it can give rise to a certain amount of conflict in a home, but in the majority of cases the mother capitulates. In some cases, however, it is the son who capitulates instead and stays living at home with his mother up to the age of 30 and even 40 or so.

Corresponding relationships naturally occur between fathers and daughters too, also between mothers and daughters — but more rarely. (See also Identification and Oedipus complex).

i. & s.h.

Mouth: See Nose.

Muscle consciousness: There are muscles in the walls of the female vagina (see Genital Organs, female) that are grouped in rings and can be contracted.

At the base of the pelvis, at the entrance to the vagina and in the last part of the anal canal there are muscles which a woman can contract and release at a rhythm of her own choosing. By means of relaxation · as a preparatory exercise to birth she can become very conscious of these muscles. They can be of great importance to a woman during intercourse · in general and her orgasm · in particular.

i.h.

Music: Just like many other things which influence our senses, music can have an enchanting, charming ·, sexually stimulating effect — its powers are often described in various artistic mediums.

Mødrehjælpen (Mothers' Aid Centres): A Danish institution corresponding to the English National Council for the Unmarried Mother and Her Child. It was started by the state and is run partly by means of borough council funds and partly private subscriptions in order to help mothers (whether married or not) or women about to become mothers.

Married and unmarried pregnant women as well as married or unmarried mothers with children can get various forms of help at the offices of the Institution all over the country.

As mentioned above, the purpose of the Institution is to help in particular those about to be, or who are already, mothers.

Such help is provided in the form of recreation arrangements, advice in family matters, help with clothing, finding adoptive homes for children whose mothers cannot keep them and many other kinds of help.

A dot · after a word refers to an article under this heading.

The premises of "Mødrehjælpen" in Copenhagen.

Nevertheless, *Mødrehjælpen* stands in the minds of many people as an institution that helps pregnant women not to become mothers. For this is the place you go to if you want to have an abortion ·.

Many have applied to *Mødrehjælpen* with this end in view. And we have heard bitter comments. "Don't talk to *me* about *Mødrehjælpen*" is what many have said, because they have been disappointed.

They feel they have not met the understanding for their problems they had expected, nor that anybody tried to help them in their desperate situation.

Many have applied for an abortion · and have been infuriated at the length of time that has passed before a decision has been communicated. Time is valuable in view of the fact that an abortion is easiest and least dangerous during the first three months of pregnancy. Naturally episodes will occur at a *Mødrehjælp* office just as anywhere else — not least on account of the fact that its clients are often unbalanced because of the nervous pressure an unwanted pregnancy can bring on.

But there is no point in just criticizing the *Mødrehjælp* institution itself. It is not there the mistakes have been made. *Mødrehjælpen* is merely the institution entrusted with the administration of a law concerning abortion that is not worthy of human beings.

Mødrehjælpen actually does help a few thousand people every year to have an abortion. The fact that many thousands more are obliged to go to quacks — and do so despite their fear and the risk they know is involved — is neither the fault of *Mødrehjælpen* nor that of the women concerned. It is the law that fails to conform with the needs of the people.

And whether we are confronted with a ridiculously low speed limit on some by-pass or some far more serious matter like the right to abortion by medical intervention, both merely contribute in the long run to decrease our respect for the law when it is so much out of step with actual conditions.

An unreasonable law fosters crime. The thousands of abortions that take place in Denmark every month are illegal. But it would be more reasonable to say that the law is inhuman.   *i. & s.h.*

N

Nasty man: See Crime, sexual.

Naturalism: See Nudism.

Nature, natural, naturalness, unnatural, unnaturalness: We so often use the expression "naturalness" or "of course it's only natural" — by which we mean that of course it is completely normal and ordinary and acceptable. It is in the sphere of sex life and sexual questions in particular that it has become modern and emancipated to say things like "... as long as we deal naturally with matters which, after all, *are* natural".

Conversely, nature is dragged in when the object is to condemn: "Ugh — it's not natural! It's against nature!"

Let us for a moment examine this nature we call upon to be our witness in moral · questions. What is nature actually like?

Zoologists (Kinsey · among them) and botanists will be able to tell us that amongst both animals and plants a wealth of things take place which we are in the habit of calling perversities ·; that nature, in her bountifulness, offers us many more possibilities of sexual satisfaction · than those that lead to fertilization; that propagation takes place in so many remarkable ways and with such an extraordinary display of imagination we ought to go home and quietly bury ourselves.

Anthropologists will likewise be able to shatter our belief that we, in our society, should happen to have hit upon the real and genuine form of naturalness. Nature gives us no reason whatsoever to assume that we should all place ourselves at the service of procreation in the same way, employing the same manner of procedure and the same serious singleness of purpose; nor that sexual relationships should only take place in the interests of procreation. This is not the case in the animal kingdom either. On the contrary, in fact, nature seems to offer us a tremendous number of imaginative ways in which to obtain sexual satisfaction — and encourages us to make use of them. (See also Inferiority Complex). In view of the upbringing we have received and the customs we unwittingly declare to be inherent in us, it is doubtful whether any single one of us is capable of behaving entirely naturally. On the other hand we can also contend that human beings can never be unnatural.

At all events all those who wish to express themselves on the subject of what is "natural" should display the greatest tolerance. *i. & s.h.*

Naughty jokes: See Jokes.

Naughty words: See words.

Necrophilia, necromania, necro-sadism: Are all the sexual things people can think of doing with dead persons' bodies. It is not exactly an unknown phenomenon for people whose sexual urges have not found outlet in the more normal fashion to allow themselves to be tempted by corpses.

These things naturally take place in particular amongst people whose profession causes them to deal with corpses in their daily work. For such people death is not so frightening, and respect for dead persons therefore decreases in the course of daily routine.

The Danish Arctic explorer Knud Rasmussen once told of a Greenlandic couple who lost their only child on their way across the ice. The husband consoled his wife in her grief by saying that their own love would have to take the place of that they felt for their son and replace the loss.

Just before reaching the next settlement his wife was killed by their sledge and as the other Greenlanders came out to receive them he threw himself, beside himself with despair, over his dead wife's body "and for the last time took his marital rights". This is another shade of meaning of the term necrophily.

Of all the many things we relegate to the world of perversities · this can probably be classified as the rarest. Many of the other so-called perversities are to be met with in the course of normal sexual relationships. Necrophilia is as a rule encountered in one place only: in somewhat macabre naughty jokes ·.

s. h.

Needs, urges: Also called sexual needs. Something we are born with. The need for food, for drink, for sexual intercourse — all are particularly strong forces at play. The sexual urge is perhaps most clearly comparable to the desire for food.

The way in which the need makes itself felt is much the same in both cases too.

When our stomachs have been satisfied we give little thought to food, but as our hunger grows, our thoughts gradually turn more frequently to the subject. Finally, we can hardly speak or think about anything except food — whereupon we eat and satisfy our hunger. The thought of food fades away for some time, and then starts all over again.

All human beings have sexual urges that make themselves felt at intervals and demand satisfaction in one way or another — including people who deny having them, and even those in whom we find it hardly credible. Even women who fanatically oppose themselves to any form of sex life whatsoever have sexual urges that demand satisfaction. Various restraining factors during upbringing — amongst them our strict taboos · and resultant anxieties — have, however, rendered it difficult for them to obtain satisfaction by means of what we call normal sexual relationships. They may get their satisfaction through masturbation, in their sleep, or via other, more camouflaged means. (See also Sexual need).

s. h.

Neuroses, sexual: The term is variously defined, but we choose to define sexual neuroses (see also Psychopathy and Personality) as neuroses resulting from conflicts between the conscience and the manifestations of the sexual urges.

Against this background, neuroses have been observed that have been the result of the prohibitions of former times against masturbation · — in the same way that one can still find neuroses in many people whom a harsh public code of morals (see Morals) has threatened with ejection from the group.

If the mental conflicts are so great that one finds it impossible to do one's job satisfactorily, or that one cannot cope with one's relationships with other people, various forms of treatment — of psychotherapy — can help. (See, for instance, Psychoanalysis).

Sexual neuroses can manifest themselves in the form of impotence ·, premature ejaculation ·, false frigidity · and many other ways.

It must be stressed, however, that all human beings become familiar with these symptoms at one time or another. Thus one can also say that we all suffer from sexual neuroses for shorter or longer periods, for here, just as in so many other spheres, there is no abrupt transition from the normal, or common, to the pathological. Young couples will experience this sort of thing particularly during the beginning of their relationship. A harmonious sex life takes time to build up. Mutual confidence is needed, likewise patience and respect, but not misplaced consideration ·. Some experimentation is also necessary — with self-confidence, and in externally secure conditions. (See also Practice, Housing Shortage, Lodgings and Birth Control).   *s. h.*

Neurosis: See Psychopathy — but they are not the same.

Nightdress: A contemporary Englishman has said: "The transparent and seductive nightdresses of to-day suggest that women have learnt to accept the inevitable where men are concerned — and, if possible, to enjoy it." Let us hope he is right.   *s. h.*

Noises: Many women — and some men — have, in the course of time, been ready to sink through the floor with shame on account of all the various noises that can come from their various organs during the extremely intimate business of sexual intercourse. It is therefore important to realize quite clearly that such noises are very normal, ordinary happenings and perfectly human. They are things Marlon Brando, Rex Harrison, Brigitte Bardot, Bette Davis and you and I all have in common.   *s. h.*

Norm, normal: A norm is a rule. Social norms are rules of behaviour in a society ·. They are the things "one" ′ does and thinks. So what is normal is what is ordinary, common. We often use the words normal and natural · promiscuously. This comes from the fact that we believe all people do as they say they do.

Kinsey · showed us clearly that the normal, i.e. what everybody really did, was not officially regarded as normal at all but as abnormal ·. In other words one should be very careful about using the word normal seeing that we have no idea what really is common. For many years masturbation ·, for instance, has been howled down and called abnormal, perverse and diseased. Today we know that it has always been normal — that it has been common for as long as human beings and animals have inhabited the earth.

Kinsey documented convincingly that we should widen our concepts of the terms normal ·, natural and the like.

From many other sources (see also Society) we have learnt that we are actually born with a multiplicity of possibilities of obtaining sexual satisfaction. (See also Masturbation, Bestiality, Bi-sexuality, Homosexuality and Perversity).

Despite a great deal of difficulty the majority of people in all societies end up by adopting heterosexual · love, i.e. that between a man and a woman, as their preferred form.

But not without deviations en route. If therefore on the one hand we close our eyes to all difficulties in entirely normal cohabitation and on the other hand deny that normal boys can be attracted by other boys and that normal girls can have 'crushes' on each other — well, it means that we push a great many people away from us. We chase a large number of them out into an unpleasantly lonely life in which we force them to believe that they are impotent ·, frigid ·, homosexual ·, perverse ·, warped ·, etc.

i. & s.h.

Nose and mouth: It is a fairly widespread idea that the nose of a man and the mouth of a woman should be able to give an indication as to the appearance and size of the sexual organs of the persons concerned. In other words that a man with a big nose should have a correspondingly large penis · and that a woman with a little nose should have a correspondingly small vagina ·.

The first comment to be made to this is that there is no reason for attaching so much importance to the size or appearance of the genital organs ·. This is something young and inexperienced people do. It is a superstitious belief that presumably originates from the fact that many people feel they might have got more out of their sex lives. So they think: "If only I'd got a bigger penis!" Or: "If only I had a smaller vagina!" But as already said, the idea that size should have anything to do with it is a much too widespread and obdurate superstition.

To this must be added the fact that we have no proof that there should be any connection between the nose and the mouth on the one hand and the genital organs on the other. Nobody has as yet ever gone round with a tape-measure in order to measure ladies and gentlemen at both ends.

So we can either believe in the theory about large nose = large penis or not believe in it. The important thing to remember is that it has nothing to do with size anyway. (See also Inferiority Complex).

i. & s.h.

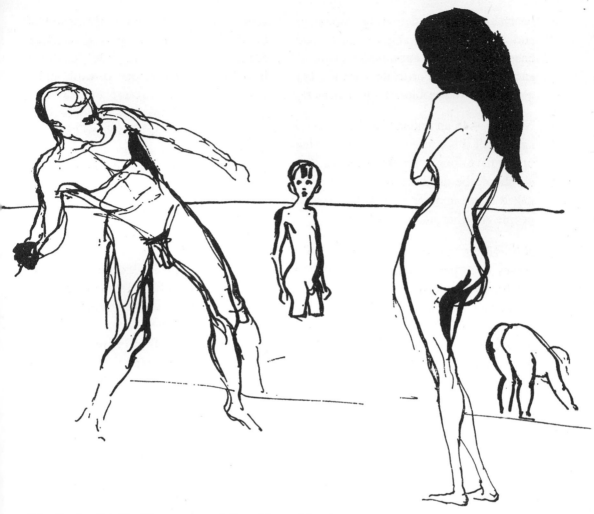

A family of nudists like this can scare a whole parish out of its wits.

Nudism, naturalism: A movement that is an understandable reaction to the form of suppression from which we still suffer.

We have at times been very much ashamed of what we have been supplied with physically. Men as well as women have used wigs, perfume and make-up, and have tried in all sorts of ways to make themselves look different.

Married folks of the past generation never saw each other naked — some of them at any rate — and their children were on no account permitted to see their parents naked.

— — —

In many countries even a 1-year-old little girl is obliged to wear a brassiere before she starts running about on the

189

beach and the very notion that little boys and girls should be able to run around naked on the sands appears to them to be entirely absurd. Fortunately we are not quite this old-fashioned in Denmark.

Nudists — in an understandable reaction against all this concealment and covering up — have fought for the principle that we should be unafraid to show ourselves naked to one another — including several people together and of both sexes.

Naturally a touch of fanaticism easily comes over people who go against the "ordinary run of the mill" — but a little fanaticism can definitely have a great mission — particularly on this point, for it reminds us that we are in the process of an artificial development.

A few nudists are very much afraid of being suspected of having unclean thoughts behind all their nudism. But it is hardly likely that one discards one's sexual urges just because one discards one's shirt and trousers. We can only hope that a nude girl is able to have just as sexually stimulating an effect on nudists as a fully dressed one can have on the rest of us.

"Back to Nature" is not a new slogan, but when we consider how much fun and how inspiring nature · can be in all its fantastic multiplicity we have to admit that there is probably something to it. We are all nudists in the eyes of God. *s. h.*

Nymphomania: Is an expression meaning female erotomania ·.

When we consider how thoughtlessly unclothed dogs manage to go round and behave towards each other, it is really astonishing that it should have been tolerated so long. And to think most of it takes place at toddler height too! But this will probably only be until somebody realizes what is going on.

O

Obscenities: The name we give to all the things we have accepted as being indecent, unsuitable, naughty. What we understand by obscene is somewhat relative. The Indians have temples containing statues which by our standards would be obscene. Mural · paintings in old Danish village churches uncovered in modern times now and again have to be whitewashed over once more because by present-day standards they are obscene.

We can say things to the person we love — things that are merely sweet and loving and fun — but which in the presence of others would seem obscene.

In the company of good friends we can say things which would seem obscene to our superiors or inferiors.

When we are at a reception at an embassy we ask in a low voice "Excuse me, could you tell me where the toilet is?"

If, instead, we said what we usually say in less delicate circles we would be regarded as obscene. Incidentally, where do members of the diplomatic corps learn such dreadful expressions? (See Words, naughty). *s.h.*

Oedipus, Oedipus complex: It was Freud · who, amongst many other things, pointed out the deeper emotional ties that can exist between a mother and her son. Particular bonds also exist between a father and his daughter.

Mother's boy and Daddy's little girl can have quite big and serious conflicts with the other parent, i.e. of the same sex.

And the strong bond can make it difficult for the children to break away during puberty ·. Mothers in particular can be bad about clinging to their sons. As a rule it is fairly easy to be a son-in-law.

Mother-in-law is glad to have one more admirer and to be rid of the daughter, who competes with her for father's favours.

It is seldom that any girl is good enough to become mother's daughter-in-law. And the young man can drive his beloved out of her mind by talking about his mother's meat balls, the way his mother washed up, and so forth. Mother, on the other hand, is helpful and naturally does so badly want to give an irritating hand in her son's home. *s.h.*

Onanism: See Masturbation.

"One": "One" is a factor to be recognized. In the sense of what "one" does or does not do — what is done and what is not — it is probably one of the most powerful factors in all societies ·. "One" is the voice of conscience, the voice of society and of its moral code.

"One" is often enough a perfectly sensible sort of fellow. "One" looks both ways before "one" crosses the road.

But "one" can also be the most dreadful tyrant. "One" wears high-heeled shoes ·, shoes that are too small. "One" declares that 'big boys' never cry and similarly monstrous things. "One" is the world's mightiest dictator, because every revolution is doomed to failure. For it so happens that we all — even the most revolutionary of us — have, to a varying extent, a touch of "one" in us.

Thus the revolutions always fail. But during a slow process of development it is possible to change "one" either for the better or for the worse. Youth rants against "one", whereas older people submit a little to "one". The funny thing is that the power of "one" becomes less the more we accept it, particularly when we acknowledge "one's" power over us.

i.h.

Oral Erotics: The mouth is very sensitive and takes part in our sex lives in many ways. (See also Kiss, Fellatio and Cunnilingus).

Orgasm: The feeling — or all the feelings — that comes just before the moment of complete sexual satisfaction — the peak of sexual enjoyment, the culminating point of erotic pleasure.

In a man, orgasm is usually accompanied by ejaculation — the squirting of sperm from the penis.

No corresponding ejaculation takes place in a woman. Even though certain glands possibly produce a little more secretion at the moment of orgasm, there is no actual ejaculation.

There is nothing to which orgasm can be compared — with the possible exception of a proper sneeze ·. Orgasm is also a form of release, or liberation, because the neuro-muscular tensions gradually built up in the course of mounting sexual excitement are suddenly liberated, or relaxed, after a culminating point of erotic pleasure has been reached.

"It is as though every drop of blood in my body were tickling me in a wonderful fashion" is one way it has been described. "Sodawater in my veins" is another. And a Danish author, Poul Henningsen has described it as: "Joy and aching — the flight of clouds in blue and green..."

Orgasm can be analyzed and described in many ways. Much advice and instruction can be given. But there are no patent answers, no miracle cures. Neither we nor anybody else know enough about coital satisfaction, the greatest possible mutual pleasure, the deepest and most complete mental and physical release. We human beings should really be a little ashamed that we know so much about technique and so little about being human beings.

We can safely state that the majority of men have orgasms. They obtain them through masturbation or ordinary sexual intercourse without any great difficulty.

There can be some difference — one orgasm can be better than another, but on the whole the problems connected with a man's orgasm are not particularly big or complicated. We know that this does not apply to all men, but only to the majority. A man's orgasm up inside a woman's vagina is necessary to fertilization — and the majority of men attach great importance to having their penis up inside a woman's vagina. A woman's orgasm is entirely immaterial to the fertilization process. Of course it is by no means immaterial to her. But the sensation of a penis up inside the vagina is not nearly as important to a woman's share of the pleasure of sexual intercourse.

Most women have orgasms too, but not nearly as easily as men in the course of ordinary intercourse — not nearly as often from having a penis inside the vagina.

The majority of women can obtain orgasm from masturbation ·. And if we were not so secretive concerning masturbation as practised by grown-ups and married people we would be able to learn a great deal from masturbational orgasms concerning the nature of a woman's orgasm. But we know a little. We know that it is relatively seldom that women use penis substitutes when they masturbate ·. The few that do, do so because they feel they should do what they can. to make it resemble actual intercourse.

This is why the myth about *vaginal orgasm* has arisen. But we know that the majority of mature and experienced women obtain clitoral orgasms, whether directly or indirectly. We know that the skilled and experienced lover concentrates on the woman's clitoris to a far greater extent than the vagina.

In this way both parties become independent of what otherwise is known as potency ·, namely a man's erection and ability to 'keep going'. The result is a greater degree of ability — real potency.

During a woman's orgasm many muscles are in function — including muscles in the walls of the vagina. Many women are unaware of these muscular contractions.

This muscle-consciousness can become greater. Most women can report discovering more and more things about their own orgasm with the years. Many women thus discover that their vagina contracts rhythmically during orgasm — something they had not realized before.

And even though the erotic pleasure thus always originates from influence brought to bear, directly or indirectly, on the clitoris, orgasm can be experienced either to a greater or lesser extent as a diffused sensation spreading round the abdomen, or as a more direct sensation round the clitoris. But in both cases it is the influence brought to bear on the clitoris that is the important thing.

During intercourse most women — of those who experience orgasm at all, that is — obtain orgasm by means of some direct form of titillation of the clitoris.

Here it is important to mention that a woman as a rule prefers a calm, constant, regular form of titillation without interruptions. The intensity of the titillation may vary during the period concerned and the woman may wish to have the rhythm changed a little, but as rule she is less able to tolerate direct interruptions than a man. She is more easily distracted and then has to start all over again from beginning in order to build up the tension that is to culminate in orgasm. Her orgasm would also appear to build up more slowly, remain at its peak longer, and ease off more slowly.

A man as rule becomes stimulated by the thought of the intercourse about to come, by talking about it, by the sight of the naked woman, by caressing her.

Men believe that what is normal for them applies to women too. But this cannot always be counted on.

There are a few women who react in the same way as men on a few or all of these points. But probably the principle rule for women in our society — for it is also a question of upbringing — is that they do not become nearly as excited by the thought of intercourse. They have also learned that it is not something to be talked about; the sight of a naked man seldom excites them, and when they caress him it is often more for his sake rather than because they have a direct wish to do so.

There can of course be exceptions to this in that the individual woman may on a particular occasion become excited at the sight of a man or by caressing him. But a woman's reactions are not as regular and marked as in the majority of men.

Nor is it all women who become excited from having their breasts caressed. Men often assume that since they themselves find it so wonderful to caress a woman's breasts, surely she must find it so too.

Conversely, women cannot always understand a man's enthusiasm for talking about what they are going to do.

Various fantasies · would appear to be of importance to both men and women.

It is difficult to say whether there are differences in regard to sex here because it is something one does not talk about.

The sexual urges of the woman possibly increase a little with the years, whilst those of the man dwindle slowly after his twentieth year. Thus there is a chance of partners meeting each other more or less half way — and after all one can adjust oneself to one's partner to a certain extent. Both partners can select a technique that does not make such great demands on either their vivacity or powers of endurance.

We know that mutual, simultaneous orgasm is something that takes place very, very seldom and that it is by no means the normal, natural thing so many have tried to make of it. As a rule both first concentrate on the woman's orgasm, after which the man has his. Or one of the partners may peacefully go without once in a while if the sexual urge does not happen to be so great.

During orgasm breathing becomes deeper and faster. Blood pressure rises, the heart beats faster; most of the mucous membranes increase their secretion; most of the senses become slightly blurred and the muscles tensed.

Kinsey is of the opinion, incidentally, that fewer and fewer women believe they are frigid. Since 1900, more and more have derived pleasure from sexual relationships with men.

Women can experience great differences in their orgasms — they can have small ones and big ones. Many women can 'divide up' their orgasms, or rather, they can have several small ones instead of one big one. Some women can have up to 20 or 30 orgasms in the course of a 24-hour period. In due course these orgasms can become concentrated — fewer, but more intense; finally a woman may have one or two powerful orgasms. The Kinsey report on women would appear to show that the more orgasms a woman had in her younger years — and the earlier on she had them — through masturbation, petting · and the like — the more frequently she has orgasm in her subsequent marriage. Which may be interpreted as one likes: whether it is the particularly passionate ones who merely go on being passionate, or whether there may be a question of the value of early practice, cannot be determined.

It is likewise interesting to note that a number of the positions adopted in sexual intercourse that are officially regarded as very bold would appear to be somewhat more widespread in the higher social spheres — among those who have received higher education.

Greater muscle consciousness can be a contributative factor to greater pleasure.

The muscles on the floor of the pelvis, for instance, the muscles round the entrance to the vagina and the anus can often be rendered far more conscious by deliberate training.

One can be cheated out of an orgasm just as one can be cheated out of a sneeze ·.

One feels the tension rise and rise, but the culmination — the relaxation and satisfaction — fails to come. It is not nice to be cheated out of a sneeze. It is a hundred times worse to be cheated out of an orgasm.

It must be stressed that a harmonious, profitable, warm sex life does not come wandering along by itself. It has to be sought out and cultivated. The notion that a man should be a master of the art of love on behalf of both partners is out-dated superstition. A negative, rejecting woman can in the long run quench the glow of inspiration in even the keenest man. The man has admittedly been made a present of his orgasm by nature.

Unfairly enough, the woman has been rather let down on this score. She is therefore obliged to make a greater effort herself. She should not be afraid to make sensible use of pillows, stools, bed-ends etc. What two people happen to like doing together is nobody else's business.

Now and again it may be necessary for a man to use his authority — a mild form of pressure — in cases where a woman is too violent in her rejections by allying herself with the keepers of public virtue and the pillars of society, i.e. with the most tiresome of all the light-snuffers that labour in the name of morality. And these rejecting powers unfortunately have a slight hold on his own soul too.

A large number of orgasms is not necessarily proof of a great degree of happiness ˙. Twenty meals a day is no way to paradise either. But we should be enabled to satisfy our calorific as well as our sexual needs. *i. & s.h.*

Orgasm, simultaneous: In many books of sexual enlightenment, simultaneous, or almost simultaneous orgasm is put forth as being the normal, common and desirable thing. It is, however, a lie that has caused much damage in the course of time because it has resulted in many couples feeling abnormal or 'no good' without reason.

The misunderstanding originates in wishful thinking. Simultaneous orgasm is of course lovely and delightful on the rare occasions when it does actually occur. But simultaneous orgasm is by no means a common thing. (See also Intercourse, sexual; Orgasm; Satisfaction, sexual; Titillation, sexual; and Masturbation). *i. & s.h.*

Orgasm, vaginal: Is a bit of a superstition. It is supposed to be an orgasm that takes place in the actual vagina as opposed to a clitoral orgasm ˙. Also sometimes called a 'deep orgasm'. This misunderstanding has unfortunately caused many men and women to believe that their sex lives were not normal.

It must therefore be repeated: the clitoris ˙ corresponds to the tip of the penis ˙ in the man. The clitoris is the focal point of erotic pleasure in the woman. The clitoris is the switch that turns on all the sensations all over the body, i.e. in the

musculature, in the vagina, in the floor of the pelvis — in other words all the sensations that go to make up what we call orgasm.

It is the monotonous, undistracted, direct or indirect titillation ˙ of the clitoris that produces an orgasm. Such direct titillation can take place in many different ways (see also Petting). Indirect influence can be brought to bear via the muscle fibres that extend from the clitoris to the entrance to the vagina, from the muscles around the anus ˙ and from the small and large vaginal lips (see Genital Organs, female).

The commonest thing, the normal thing, is a fairly direct tickling of the clitoris.

Indirect influence is rarer. It may, for instance, be the root of the penis that influences the muscle fibres round the entrance to the vagina. But it is still an indirect clitoral orgasm. (See also Satisfaction, sexual; Simulate, Consideration). *i. & s.h.*

Ovary: Derived from the latin for egg, *ovum.* A woman has two ovaries and it is in these sexual glands that the eggs are formed every month. (See Genital Organs, female).

An ovary is about the size of a plum: $1\frac{1}{2}'' \times \frac{3}{4}'' \times \frac{1}{2}''$, perhaps slightly almond-shaped; it weighs 7 to 8 grammes and contains the potential for producing some 100,000 eggs of which only a few hundred are developed — one for each menstruation. Correspond to the testicles in a man ˙.

196

P

Parts, private: We in our society choose to keep our genital organs and anus concealed. We have somehow come to be ashamed of these parts.

In Africa the Tuaregs are instead ashamed of the lower part of their faces just like the veiled women of the harem.

There are other societies where both men and women walk round with their genital organs and their breasts entirely uncovered.

There are other societies even stricter on this score than ours.

We are not suggesting that from tomorrow onwards everybody should proceed to his office or place of work in his birthday suit (even though it would undoubtedly be a festive sight), but we do feel the present-day fanatical taboo · to be misplaced.   *i.h.*

Passion: Many men complain that their wives are not passionate enough. By George, they once knew a girl, and she was always as passionate as anything . . . The passionate little girl they once knew has also in the meantime married, and her husband also tells her about a passionate little girl he once knew . . .

Does it mean that women get less passionate as soon as they get married?

In a way, yes! During the first passionate period of acquaintanceship they often only managed to sleep together at protracted intervals. Everything was new and exciting, and they expected everything of each other. Then there possibly came disappointments ·, and the more peaceful, more frequent form of sex life did not lead to the pleasures they had expected.

The man increases his demands and believes his wife cannot be normal. Misunderstandings on the subject of clitoral orgasms · have contributed to estranging couples from one another. (See also Inferiority Complex).

It is also easier for a woman to simulate · tremendous enthusiasm in a relationship of briefer duration. And far too many women have got off to this false start.

All these factors — and more besides — result in a number of men being dissatisfied with their wives' passion.

There are also women who are dissatisfied with their husbands' lack of passion.

They think he has slackened off. It may be due to fear of being impotent ·, and thus for this reason alone it can also be of importance to experiment · early on with the object of developing forms of intercourse · (see Petting) that make them independent of the man's potency ·.

197

Now and again we hear that our times are over-sexed. If by this is meant that we talk more about sex than previously in history — or more in our society · than in others — it is simply not correct. But on one point our times are over-sexed: our entire culture is directed by men, who have cultivated the myth about sensual, passionate girls. Through books, advertising, plays, films, and so forth, men have constructed an over-sexed 'ideal woman'.

All lively, warm-hearted, sweet, lovely and normal women can easily begin to regard themselves as sexually inferior if they try to live up to these ideals. Each feels herself to be a frigid · exception because men have persuaded them that all other women are always so wonderfully on form. Men believe in this myth them-selves and are all dissatisfied with the fact that they are the only one to be un-lucky.

Men admittedly know what it means to feel sexually inferior ·, but the sensation has particularly good chances of thriving amongst women.

The result is that women often promise more than they are able to fulfil. In tight sweaters, short dresses and with flashing eyes, they compete for the attention of men in quite an acceptable manner.

Across their tempting chests is the word — in big block capitals — LIFESAVER.

But when a man falls into the water and the promise is due to be fulfilled, the girls stammer: "Oh, but I didn't actually mean it like that — to tell you the truth

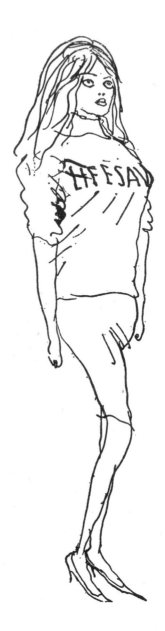

I can't swim at all . . . at any rate only a little bit."

And they have suffered from bad con-sciences, for they believe all other women can. Perhaps the couple agrees to pretend outwardly that they have taken their big swimming test together. And the man consoles himself perhaps on the sly with looser acquaintanceships who, by flapping energetically with arms and legs, just manage to keep themselves afloat.

But much improves with the years. A woman's best years often start during her thirties. Patience · and practice · can often help a good development · on its way. A man's fieriness falls off slowly after the age of twenty, while a woman's possibly increases a little. Together, they manage to work out a form of life together that suits them both. It begins to dawn on most of them with the passing of the years that they are possibly not so abnormal after all. Naturally the majority of women are warm-hearted and passionate; but not so burningly as some of their feverish sisters now and then would like others to believe.   *i. & s.h.*

Patience: In few spheres is there so great a need of patience as in living together with another person — sexual relations in particular require great patience. One should not expect great progress in the course of days, weeks, or months, but more in the course of half-yearly periods, for it takes time to win confidence in each other and loosen the bonds, just a little, of the straitjacket to which society has tailored each one of us.   *s.h.*

Patriarchy: See Matriarchy.

Pavlov: A Russian Nobel Prizewinner who, at about the turn of the century, worked with *conditioned reflexes* in dogs.

He proved experimentally that reflexes could be built up. If a dog, for instance, always heard a bell ring just before it was given food, Pavlov managed to prove that the sound of the bell thereafter was enough to set the salival and gastric juice glands in function.

An American, *Watson*, had a similar experiment with a little boy who was repeatedly frightened while at the same time being shown a toy rabbit (an iron bar was banged behind little Albert's back and he cried). Finally it was enough to show him the toy rabbit — he cried.

We probably also acquire a number of conditioned reflexes — reflexes, attitudes and ideas that can be a hindrance to us in our sex lives. We are equipped with distaste, revulsion ·, anxiety ·, violent modesty and other unfortunate feelings that turn up in an impractical fashion in situations that are really supposed to be pleasant. Conditioned reflexes of this sort may disappear again — become 'de-conditioned'. Little Albert (the boy who was made afraid of the rabbit) was happy to see the toy later on after he had been shown the rabbit again and again together with nice, pleasant things — carefully and patiently, without going about matters too hastily.

Something of the sort happens in our sex lives. Gradually many people discover that this nasty business of sex is actually quite a pleasant affair that can involve the loveliest of pleasures. And gradually the terrified attitude cultivated during upbringing is given up.

     s.h.

Pederast, pederasty: If a grown-up has sexual relationships with children he or she is called a pederast and the relationship pederasty. As the terms have come to be used in particular about relationships between a man and a boy and about the particular practice of introducing the penis into the boy's rectum, they are often used to mean the same as analcoitus ·.

Peeping Tom: Also called a *voyeur*. The name is given to persons who like to espy upon others unseen, especially naked people or people engaged in sexual intercourse. Now and again shocked reports appear in the press describing chases after perverse · persons who have been caught in the act of peeping. Not long ago a big Copenhagen daily printed a story of this sort with the headline:

"Heroic deed by male nurse at hospital".

It appeared that a 17-year-old youth had been peeping at a young nurse who was in the process of undressing. She had forgotten to pull the blind down. The male nurse spotted the youth, dashed after him in a hectic chase and knocked him down so efficiently he had to be admitted to the casualty ward. Here and now I would like to request male readers, who had they been in the 17-year-old's place claim they would not have seized the chance too, to raise their hands. I am pleased to see there are no more.

— — —

When I think of the gratitude with which I recall the forgetful ladies who, in my youth, undressed in front of uncurtained windows, I am thankful too that I was never discovered by any male nurses.

And I promise you that if the actress who lives opposite us appears by her window-sill either partially or wholly undressed, I shall, with my wife's permission, fetch a pair of binoculars.

Unfortunately the above is not the only example of the irresponsible way in which the press often handles sex stories. Such stories are always 'good copy' and a spot of flaming indignation always boosts circulation much better than boring and tiresome tolerance ·. If Danish women were really as modest as certain journalists think they would never ride bicycles in windy weather.

If peeping is perverse, then the majority of men are perverse. Oh no, sexual aberrance only starts when peeping becomes the *only* thing that excites us and we start chasing round with the sole object of peeping. The fact that young people at the stage of puberty, likewise others whose sex life or curiosity is unsatisfied (curiosity, incidentally, is probably difficult to satisfy in this connection) make a practice of peeping whenever they get the chance can on no account be labelled perverse. Give us a chance!

Of course it is not necessary to tolerate meekly persons who peep through your letter-box or who grab ladders and peer in through your bedroom window. But such people deserve neither lynching nor castrating ·. We all share the responsibility for the fact that it is difficult to obtain a satisfactory sex life. (See also Understanding). *s.h.*

200

Penis: Also called the male sexual organ, John Thomas and various other more or less unprintable names (see Words, Naughty). It is — together with the anus — what a grown man is not allowed to reveal on a bathing beach. All this has resulted in a curious mixture of worship, pride, boastfulness, shame and fear.

We know of other peoples who are unfamiliar with this prohibition against revealing oneself in the nude — and nudists · try in their own way to weaken the power of this taboo ·.

The penis is a sensitive organ (see Genital Organs, male) and it is understandable that it was once found wiser to protect it against insects, thorny grass etc. But it is also an organ that can be filled with blood and swell up, become firm and erect when a man feels sexual desires.

201

We know that the ancient Greeks (amongst others) worshipped the penis (see Phallos) and made amulettes for their children and baked cakes in the shape of a penis. In other words, an entirely different way of accepting the organ from what we are familiar with.

Ancient Greek cakes of this type (outsize ones) can be seen round the Stork Fountain · in the main shopping street of Copenhagen.

Amongst men in our society there exists a certain form of penis pride, and in a number of women a more or less conscious form of penis envy (penisneid, penis jealousy) (see Superiority, struggle for; and Castration Anxiety).

In other words a negative form of worship. And thanks to the fact that the penis is concealed, especially in its erected state, many women to start with are somewhat unfamiliar with the phenomenon and slightly frightened because an erect penis bears no resemblance to the kind they have seen on statues in parks or on small boys paddling by the seashore. (Though even newborn babes can have erections·.)

A number of primitive peoples use penis sheaths, or holsters, originally they were intended to protect the penis, but have been made larger and more striking with the years. (See also Breeches).

As a rule the penis is slightly more 'suntanned' than the rest of the skin on the body — more brownish. In its erected state it points horizontally out into the air or slightly upwards at an angle and the thin soft skin on it becomes taut and slightly retracted from the faintly bluish-red, earthenware-like tip, which is also called the *glans* (the Latin for acorn) even though it looks more like a plum.

The veins that conduct blood to the penis pass through the middle of the penis. But the veins that lead it away again are just below the surface of the skin. Thus if the foreskin is narrow and tightly stretched over the penis when it is pulled back over the glans, the blood may have difficulty in running away again. This can be painful.   *s.h.*

Penis envy, penisneid: See Superiority, struggle for; and Penis.

Penis in the female: See Sexual Similarities.

Perineum: See Genital Organs, male and female. During birth a woman's perineum may split a little — this happens in about every fourth case.

Period: Another word for menstruation ·.

Personality; the psychoanalytical personality theory: A person's personality is the sum of all the things in a person that go to determine the said person's relationship to other people.

Many theories have been expounded concerning human personality. Many models have been made in an attempt to show what actually happens. Some of these theories are more practical than others, but none of them is correct. We still know too little — perhaps we shall never find the right one. The one which

A model of what we call a person's personality. At the top the Superego, in the middle the Ego, and at the bottom the Id.

will be described here is of course not the right one either. It is the one used in psychoanalysis ˙.

This model — like so many other theories — is a picture, an attempt to explain something unknown with the help of something known. If we think of personality as an Indian totem pole with three faces corresponding to three persons it will give us an idea of the model.

The three persons have names and are very different in character:

1). The top face is rather strict and censorious. A bit of a light-snuffer. We call this person the *super ego*, and it represents everything we have learnt concerning what is right and wrong. The *super ego* reminds us how to drive through traffic, how to hold a knife and fork and generally speaking how "one" behaves. It is also the voice of conscience ˙.

2). The bottom face on the totem pole is a person we call the *id*. This person takes care of our wishes urges and needs —, the very honest, primitive, but likewise somewhat ruthless powers within us. The face of the *id* is therefore a somewhat primitive, uninhibited, wild and brutal mug.

3). The middle face is our own. It is called the *ego* and is a little squashed between the other two faces. While the upper face possibly resembles our parents, and the bottom face appears a little strange to us, we find it easiest to accept the middle face — a compromise between what we want to do and what we are allowed to.

Our own face, the one sticking out a little perplexedly between the other two, is known, as already mentioned, as the *ego*, and it is this person who thinks and acts. (See also Psychopathy).

We are a little perplexed because if we are very good and reserved — then the bottom person thrashes his tail and rebels while the top person nods approvingly. And if we are too abandoned and let the bottom person have his own way — well, we find ourselves landed with a bad conscience, because the upper person grumbles.

So we have to strike a balance. We have to stick to a certain moral · code — stick to certain rules of the road in order to mingle with the traffic. But we must also pay attention to our 'nature' — our *id* — who likewise demands his rights.

The above is — as already stated — only a model; but quite a practical one.

The things we have a genuine desire to do come from our *id* — from our primitive, greedy depths. But we cannot merely satisfy our desires, do just whatever we please in an entirely unrestrained fashion. (See also Abnormal).

If we suddenly want to dash across the road to say hullo to a friend we have, fortunately, a 'built-in' inhibition · that says to us: "Look out!" This inhibition becomes part of our *super ego* during upbringing. And we — the *ego* — then act according to a compromise between these two forces: we look out — and then cross over to our friend.

Thus it is very practical for us that in by far the majority of situations we embrace all three persons in ourselves:

1. A monitor who sees to it that we cause no offence and stick to the rules. (The upper face).

2. Somebody who makes sure we do not die of hunger, that we procreate our kind and a few other important things. (The bottom face).

3. A person who can think and act in accordance with directions issued by the other two. (The middle face).

The difficulty lies in the fact that the *super ego* and the *id* never come out into the open. They are not conscious.

We can only deduce their directions by observing how our *ego* thinks and acts.

If the *super ego* is very strict and censorious — because our upbringing has been strict — the result is that certain wishes and needs are completely denied and subjugated. Then we get what are called *repressions*.

And there is one repression which makes it appear that there are women who are frigid · — i.e. without sexual needs. However, the sexual need is there all right — in the *id* — but the *super ego* prevents it from making itself felt through the *ego*'s thoughts and actions — or at any rate only in such heavy disguise that psychiatrists, psychologists, psychoanalysts and others with knowledge of the workings of the mind are necessary in order to see through the camouflage.

The wishes and needs of the *id* can thus fool the *super ego* by putting on a mask.

This is what happens (for instance) in dreams (see Psychoanalysis and Freud).

In dreams, wishes make their appearance in disguise — wishes that have been repressed because the *superego* has forced them down by censoring their behaviour.

The ideal personality would thus be one that embraced a more or less mild *super ego* which, although it guided and controlled our actions to a reasonable extent, at the same time permitted us to recognize and accept all the wishes and urges of the *id* the way they are — yet without allowing them to get the upper hand.

The ideal personality is in harmony with both itself *and* society · provided this society does not make inhuman demands on its members.

In the course of history we have seen societies whose demands were so strict that many people were mentally destroyed.

Definite rules provide on the one hand a feeling of security — but security should not cost too much human happiness in the form of personalities in conflict.

i. & s.h.

There is no need for us to tap away at the same note the whole time. Every person has been supplied with rich possibilities. Naturally there is no need to use all the notes of the keyboard, but let us admit that they are there. The melody of life is played upon a judicious and festive selection.

Perversity, perversion, perverse: In everyday speech we call things like erotomania ·, exhibitionism ·, pederasty ·, homosexuality ·, deformity fetishism · (and other types of fetishism), masochism ·, pornography ·, sadism ·, bestiality · and many other things perversities or perversion, and persons accused of these things are called perverse.

We should be extraordinarily careful about pinning labels of this sort on people who do the things we dare not do — or have no inclination to do.

Thanks to the growing understanding of the workings of the normal · mind given to us by psychology (and psychoanalysis · and psychiatry ·) we now know that most of these things hover quite mildly in the minds of most people.

In some cases they are suppressed and kept under strict control (see also Minority and Personality); in others they manifest themselves in an acceptable and lawful manner (see Erotographomania) — or else they are not talked about.

Take a matter like masturbation: we have mentioned it often in this book, but as an example it becomes none the worse for that: — until our own generation, masturbation was regarded as a perversity — a youthful sin, a frightful vice. Let us be human beings — even though it can be abominably difficult to be allowed to!

Real perversity is a deformity of the mind, a fanatical, one-sided choice amongst the many possibilities existing within the range of natural, comprehensive sexual relationships.

But no sharp dividing line is drawn between normal sex life and perverse sex life. If a man for instance, gets particularly excited at the sight of his wife in a black brassiere and girdle there is no reason to be shocked · by it — so why not let him have the pleasure? (See also Orgasm). (Incidentally there are probably many girls who would gladly do so.

But there are men who openly proclaim their admiration for some film star or other in a marvellous transparent get-up, but would not care to see their wife or girl-friend in the same thing; men who talk about how exciting it is to see a black brassiere and girdle but who, when it comes to the point, think it is the sort of thing that spells prostitute or at any rate a not-quite-nice girl.)

If a girl for her part feels that a couple of pillows here and there would give a completely new feeling there is no need for her to feel herself perverse on that account. In the sphere of sexual relationships there are so many pleasant possibilities of using one's imagination.

Kinsey, in his report on the sex lives of white men and women in America, proved that more than half could not only be called perverse — but that they could be punished according to American law.

This is a good example of how wide of the mark a society can hit in its efforts to be 'justly' censorious.

It is those who are inhibited (see Personality) who become one-sided and therefore only able to manage in one particular fashion. A harmonious person acquires more and more strings to his bow. If a person's perversity tortures him, if he feels that it is harmful (either to himself or to others) then there is reason to do something about it. Something can be done about it, even though it takes a long time and is therefore expensive. Psychoanalysis can (for example) often bring relief to troubled minds and help clarify a number of matters. *i.h.*

Pervert: See Crime, sexual.

Pessary: A rubber bowl or cap that can be inserted into the vagina (see Genital Organs, female) in order to prevent sperm cells from making their way up into the womb and on out into the egg duct, where they may fertilize · the female ovum.

Pessaries have only been used for about a hundred years. Prior to that time other things were used — for instance a little sponge of the yellow kind we use for washing.

Pessaries can be bought at chemists · and at rubber · goods shops. But a pessary has to fit exactly and one needs to learn how to insert it. For this reason it is necessary to go to a doctor first so that he can take measurements (see also Gynaecological Examination) and give instruction in how to put it in properly.

It should be possible to feel the front edge of the pessary pressing against the lower edge of the pubic bone (see Birth control.) And it should be possible to feel the tip of the womb bulging out through the thin rubber of the pessary.

A pessary is possibly a little too difficult and complicated a thing for a very young girl to use. It is probably easier for the man to use a condom ·. But for slightly more stable and settled relationships a pessary is in many cases probably the best contraceptive aid we have today.

Pessaries are obtainable in many different sizes from an inch or two right up to about four inches in diameter. As the pessary is placed inside the vagina at an angle, it is not the actual size of the vagina itself but the distance from the womb to the pubic bone that determines how large a pessary it is necessary to use.

Many women are dissatisfied with the pessary because they have to see a doctor about it and learn to insert it. And generally speaking because they have to take over the bother and be prepared for sexual intercourse beforehand. It appears to them both unromantic and unreasonable.

A new method of contraception made its appearance in Denmark in the autumn of 1961:

A woman can take a pill every evening during the period between her menstruations. Every evening, for a total of 20 times in a month, she has to take her tablet. Thereafter she is not supposed to become pregnant for the following month.

The cost of these pills (at the moment of going to press) is approx. 30 kr. a month; but if the pills really do what they claim they will constitute a revolution in sexual relationships.

The new pills contain a hormone preparation that prevents the production and loosening of the egg (ovulation) and thus fertilization from taking place. The pills have been tested abroad since 1956 and sound promising. Here in Denmark a series of tests are being conducted but no results have as yet been published. If they really prove to be both effective and harmless there could hardly be a simpler method.

We already know that they are excellent 'birth-controllers'; but whether or not possible side-effects will prove harmless will remain an open question for some years.

But to return to the pessary, which for the time being is the most recommendable, even if not the ideal contraceptive aid.

A pessary will not tolerate ordinary fats, which make the rubber go brittle. For this reason a special cream is used, partly with the object of making the pessary fit more tightly against the walls of the vagina, and partly in the hope of killing the sperm cells.   *i.h.*

Petting: Is the American expression for sexual relationships in which everything is permitted with the sole exception of actually introducing the penis into the vagina (see Genital Organs, female) the object being to preserve virginity at all costs. Both partners can obtain orgasm through petting.

As the presence of the penis inside the vagina is of nowhere near as much importance to the woman as it is to the man, it is often easier for a woman to make do with petting. For the more experienced, petting can furthermore develop into many things such as cunnilinctio · and fellatio · and mutual masturbation in various ways. We often speak about petting in somewhat derogatory tones, and about 'technical virgins' (see Virginity), but in societies like ours that have a fairly strict moral code, petting can undoubtedly be quite a useful prelude to subsequent love life. It can remove some of the fear, inhibitions and scruples.

Out of sheer fear that not enough children should be born we have seized upon ordinary sexual intercourse as the only approved method of enjoying oneself.

This is an entirely unjustified fear and shows a one-sidedness of mind that is not far off being perverse ·.

Petting that does not lead to orgasm can give a man sore testicles ·.

Petting as a result of virginity worship may be classed as somewhat off-the-rails, but as an introductory form of love-play that involves no risk of untimely fertilization it definitely has its mission.

i. & s.h.

Phallos: The Greek word corresponding to the Latin word penis, both meaning the male sexual organ. Phallos is used especially to describe the penis in its erected state. An extraordinary large number of peoples have used phallic amulettes and worshipped the phallos as a symbol of fertility. There have been festive celebrations involving large pictures and statues of a phallos. Children were given amulettes in the shape of a phallos. The idea of making columns in the same shape is one we have adopted from Greece, and examples of this can still be seen round the Stork Fountain · in Copenhagen.

Phimosis: Means contraction of the foreskin ·.

Picnics: The desire to sit out-of-doors under a nice blue sky and eat the food one has brought with one probably orig nates in a genuine relationship with nature. But now and then this desire manifests itself in a rather bizarre fashion.

We see families, for example, who have gone out into the country for their holidays, allowing mother to drag all the dinner or unch or tea things out into the garden. And there they sit under the burning sun, while the butter promptly melts, on uncomfortable, rickety chairs, with flies, ants and wasps in the food and up their trouser-legs instead of fixing things simply and quickly at a table in the kitchen, which would give mother a chance of a holiday too. Or they could each butter themselves a few sandwiches and take them outside.

Others drive out into the country and pull up right at the edge of a main road, fix up a camp table and four pokey little camp chairs and sit and enjoy their sandwiches amongst the stench of petrol and the roaring exhausts of all the other cars racing past their noses.

That is of course their business, but it only goes to show how a perfectly normal and sensible desire can take on a somewhat twisted form of expression. It tells us that even in the sphere of eating, where we have far fewer taboos than in that of sex, we are still capable of going off at a tangent. *s. h.*

Pillow-book: See Bridal roll.

Pimp, pimping: When a man lives entirely or partly on money which his girl — or girls — earn by prostitution ·, he is known as a pimp and his occupation as pimping. It is punishable by law, and in recent years between 25 and 100 men have been punished for the practice annually in Denmark. The real figures are naturally much larger, and of course it is also very hard to define a pimp or the practice of pimping accurately. Is a young, impecunious student a pimp because he falls in love with a prostitute and starts living with her? *i. h.*

Plastic Surgery: By plastic surgery we understand operations performed with the object of improving a person's appearance. It may be a matter of making the ears lie closer to the head, breasts that hang or are too big, crooked noses and many other things. Although it is mainly used in connection with crashes

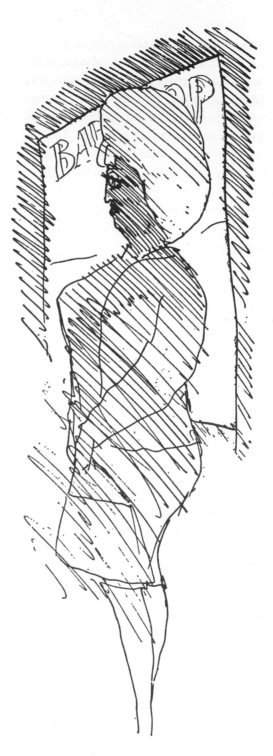

This is not a nymphomaniac trying to combine the pleasurable with the profitable.

and accidents in which a person is badly hurt, it is becoming more and more common. Considering how much some difference in appearance can cause a person mental pain — far more than the physical pain of appendicitis or a broken limb — it is really disgraceful that plastic surgery is not treated with greater respect. It is not considered nice to be vain about one's appearance, but none the less we all are more or less (particularly the latter) openly.

So it is "just not done" to have some minor defect put right and thereby make life a little more tolerable. We speak so sentimentally about freckles, about how sweet the little girl looks with them, and we tell a little boy not to be so silly if he gets unhappy about the way his ears stick out — but it only shows a lack of respect for the feelings of a fellow human.

If a person is really desperately unhappy about his or her appearance it should be an entirely reasonable thing to have something done about it — and by one of the finest surgeons in the country at that. Today the very idea is relegated more or less to a place in the corner. It is not entirely a natural thing to go to one's doctor and have him pass one on to a surgeon. But the position is improving here and there. And one *can* get help if one shows a spot of insistence.

It has to be something pretty bad before people will accept one's wish to have something done about it. This is really rather unfair when one considers how much people do for cosmetic reasons.

Women wear brassieres, corsets, pointed shoes etc., etc. — so why should people not be allowed to do something really effective about their physical appearance? The fact that one's nose is a little too long and one would prefer it shorter is not enough — it practically has to be like a corkscrew with a big lump on the end before we think it reasonable that anything should be done about it. And even so, shyness on account of a long nose can be enough to make a person screw up his or her face so much that it becomes stiff and ugly.

Of course it must also be stressed that freckles can be charming. It is possible to be a happy person with flapping ears or an unhappy one with a nose like a Roman god. On the other hand there is no reason to be desperately unhappy about some unfortunate physical feature if it is something that can be corrected.

It is during our young years in particular that we can suffer mental torture about this sort of thing. Because we who are older have partly forgotten how hard it was and partly discovered that we have managed all right none the less does not entitle us to make little of things that can ruin a person's young years.

There is nothing to be gained by our all becoming film stars — on the contrary.

And many of the things we can get desperately unhappy about when we are young seem far less serious when we are older. On the other hand there are people who need a little encouragement to have something altered if it is unbearable mentally.

The sweetest freckles.

Here are a few prices — approximate, of course — charged for some of the commoner operations:

Too large breasts: 1,000—2,000 *kroner*

Fat on the hips and stomach: 1,000—2,000 *kroner*

Nose corrected: 800—900 *kroner*

Ears corrected: 500—600 *kroner*

Face lift: 1,000 *kroner*

There are various places one can go. Some hospitals undertake some of these operations on occasions. There are furthermore a few specialists and clinics specializing in plastic surgery. Talk to your doctor about it if you have a problem that worries you particularly.   *i.h.*

Pleasure, sensual: Like everything that is really lovely, intense erotic pleasure (see also Epicurean) is likewise regarded as sinful. Anybody who wallows in sensual pleasure is a shocking person and we fail to see what right they have to wallow. But we may just dare to admit that what we feel when we have an orgasm is intense sensual pleasure.

Polterabend: A German term denoting a man's last evening as a bachelor, i.e. the last evening before his wedding. It used to be celebrated — especially in olden days — by going out and having a party with all his men friends.

Polyandry: A special form of polygamy· (see Bigamy and Monogamy) in which a woman is married to several men. This practice has existed amongst certain peoples.

Polygamy: The name given to the practice of permitting a person to be married to several others. The harem custom is probably the best known form of polygamy. (See also Bigamy).

Ponce: See Pimp.

Pornographomania: See Erotographomania.

Pornography: Is a term of abuse for all the things which offend us, i.e. offend our standards of sexual morality on account of their sexual content. Thus we can speak of pornographic films, books, photographs, postcards, figures and much else.

It is a subject in which many people are extremely interested, either because they think all sexual things are exciting, or because they are shocked ˙. Sex concerns all of us so personally we are unable to remain entirely passive and disinterested.

Some people have liked to call everything in any way sexually stimulating pornographic. Using this definition, woman herself would be pornographic — and in fact she has been regarded as such. And if the sexual needs of an individual have grown sufficiently we can observe how literally everything can have a sexually stimulating effect; while conversely nothing will be able to stimulate the person who is entirely satisfied. It is the unsatisfied who become most excited.

Funnily enough there has hardly ever been anybody who has claimed to have been 'made brutal' by pornography, comic strips or pornographic books. On the other hand there are many who read such literature in order to be able to warn others against reading it.

If anything offends the public moral code it is stamped as pornography. But we have seen how such moral codes can vary from country to country and from age to age. If we were to use this definition of pornography the world would never make any progress in any direction.

There would appear to be a human — not legal — law which says that the more good pornography a country gives its citizens, the less need there is for the bad kind. The more a fruit is forbidden, the better it tastes. (See also Censorship).

i. & s.h.

212

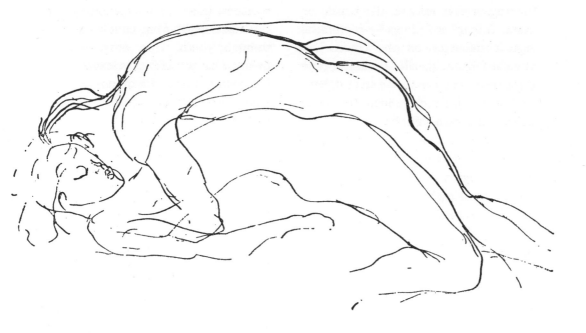

Potency: Really means ability, power. The word is used in particular about sexual capacity, and in an even narrower sense as the ability to have sexual inter-course ·. Impotency is thus used to mean inability to have sexual intercourse; perhaps more particularly lack of ability to 'keep going' during actual intercourse.

It may be lack of desire ·, lack of erec-tion · or premature ejaculation ·. As a woman is as a rule always capable of having intercourse we do not speak of potency or impotency in women.

It was formerly believed that the usual thing — and therefore the normal thing — was for both the man and the woman to have their orgasm · simultaneously as a result of ordinary sexual intercourse ·.

Thus many men thought they were impotent · — or they made the woman believe (unless she already believed so herself) that she was frigid ·.

Dangerous misunderstandings developed from the fact that a false ideal, or stand-ard, was created: "Look, this is the way normal people function! If your sexual relationships are not like this it means that either you are impotent or your wife is frigid!"

Today we know — thanks to Kinsey, amongst others — that this kind of potency worship and frigidity anxiety of former times is unfounded and super-fluous. The erected penis has admittedly a certain importance to the man's orgasm.

But it is not the sensation of the penis in the vagina that releases the female orgasm. It is other feelings — rhythmical, regular influence on the clitoris (see Genital Organs, female) — and to cause these there is no need of an erected penis. (See also Titillation). Such an intense penis-and-vagina cult has been created it is high time it was firmly established that a man with a tiny penis and a woman with no vagina at all can have a lovely sex life with each other or with others. (See also Petting).

The most important advice (and the best one can give) is that both parties make themselves as independent as possible of the man's potency. (See also Form, to be off). As a rule this will prove beneficial to both.

The fact that both partners are able to obtain an entirely satisfying · orgasm · without being dependent on the man's powers of endurance will make for greater peace and harmony in their lives.

What is normal · and natural · consists in the very fact that many possibilities of sexual satisfaction exist. To be capable of taking advantage of them — *that* is real potency.   *i. & s.h.*

Pouch: The scrotum · (see Genital Organs, male).

Practice: A happy, harmonious sex life is not something we are born with. Experimentation and practice is required — and this applies to both animals and human beings. We can draw this conclusion by peacefully observing animals and human beings in other societies.

Amongst animals and in many human societies, this experimentation and practice starts right from childhood and up through youth ·, in other words far before what we refer to as sexual maturity has been reached. We do not permit our young people and children to experiment and practise. During the first twenty years of our lives we are kept away from the water and we are forbidden to swim.

Apart from a few swimming strokes practiced on the sly on dry land we are entirely unprepared when we take our first plunge off the top of the high-diving board. Sex life in our society is a matter of either/or — with no transitional period.

Forgetful old people console themselves with a knowing grin and mumble that "human beings have always managed to find out what they're supposed to do."

It is too facile an observation. When we grown-ups finally start our experimenting, start practising, it is with all the things we have been told not to do fresh in our minds. We are like a subjugated negro tribe that is suddenly given its liberty.

"Can't you see you aren't mature yet?" yell the old people, delightedly. "There you are, it's a good thing we made you wait. It wouldn't have harmed you to have waited a couple years more!"

The fact that we are kept back, year after year, the fact that we are not allowed to experiment and practice, means that we have to do a lot of catching up within a short space of time. Being impatient and full of expectations, many stumble as soon as they start. Not only do we have to learn to love and be loved — we also have to minimize the power of some of the prejudices, prohibitions and delusions with which we have been so thoroughly imbued. This is why it is not a mere matter of days, weeks or months before we notice any progress — it may take six-month periods at a time. (See also Disappointments).

— — —

Why is it only in the field of sex that we believe that lack of knowledge, inexperience and lack of practice constitute the best driver's licence?

i. & s.h.

Praise: We all know how encouraging it is to be praised. This knowledge should make us readier to give praise to others.

Pregnancy calendar: If one wants to work out when one can expect a birth to take place one can take the date of the last menstruation and *subtract* three months. Birth may then be expected 1 week after this date. Thus if the first day of the last menstruation was 18th August we subtract three months from this = 18th May + 7 days = 25th May.

i.h.

Pregnancy test, pregnancy examination: One can visit one's doctor and be examined (see Gynaecological Examination) in order to find out whether one is pregnant. It can only be felt 3 to 4 weeks after menstruation should have come — at the earliest.

One can find out faster by having one's urine tested. A Friedman reaction can be used as little as one week after menstruation should have come. In Denmark it costs 45 *kroner* and the answer can be picked up a couple of days later. A Bufo-reaction is a little cheaper (20 *kroner*) but cannot be used until 2 weeks after menstruation should have come. In the case of both these tests one should apply to one's doctor — or to any doctor — who will supply a bottle for a urine sample.

A couple of fluid ounces of *fresh* urine should be delivered at the Serum Institute, Amager Boulevard, Copenhagen.

For those who live in Copenhagen it is easiest to go out and deliver the bottle personally. Otherwise it can be sent in by post. But remember, a doctor first! If you discover you are pregnant, i.e. going to have a baby, and it is a catastrophe for you, and if you are thinking of going to see *Mødrehjælpen* in order to try and arrange to have an abortion, it is wisest to find out quite definitely first whether you really *are* pregnant.

The examinations and decisions made by *Mødrehjælpen* take time. Help should preferably come during the first three months of pregnancy, and those three months pass quickly.

i.h.

Prejudice: A prejudice is a condemnatory attitude resulting from ignorance, but especially an emotionally dictated attitude. It comes from the Latin *prae judicium*, i.e. 'preceding judgement', and is thus a judgement passed prior to acquaintanceship with the facts of the case.

We all have our prejudices, and it is by no means always that they disappear with the acquisition of greater knowledge. We are never keen on giving up the things we feel. Many scientists have prejudices, too. The story is told of an extremely intelligent and clear-thinking professor, now deceased, to the effect that one of his pupils told him that he (the pupil) had just become a lieutenant in the reserve. The professor growled bad-temperedly: "All officers are fools!" The lieutenant was somewhat taken aback, but then said: "It surprises me to hear a scientist generalize like that!" — whereupon the professor leapt to his feet, dashed out of the room and away down the corridor. Presently he returned and croaked grudgingly: "You are right!"

Prejudices against negroes, Jews, homosexuals · and women are by no means uncommon in Denmark. (See also Minority).

Prejudices are things we wear rather like glasses. They distort the reality around us. It is a tough job trying to look at things over or round these glasses. They have grown almost permanently to our noses. Many never realize they are wearing them at all. If prejudices are the same in all the members of a community · it would perhaps be better to call such prejudices a common window through which they all look.   *i. & s.h.*

Pretending: See Simulation.

Prevention: Pregnancy can be prevented. (See Birth Control). Women cannot protect themselves against catching ven-

A box of 'Samarit', or prophylactic kit.

ereal diseases. As far as men are concerned, a condom affords fairly good protection provided it does not break. One can furthermore rub calomel ointment into the unprotected parts of the genital organs · and the surrounding skin both before and after intercourse. Calomel ointment can be bought at any chemist's in a little box marked 'Samarit'. A man who uses this to protect himself can be reasonably sure of not infecting the girl he sleeps with. All you have to say at the chemist's is: "I would like to have a box of Samarit," and you will be given one. It costs 3 or 4 *kroner.*

Calomel ointment should be left on for about four hours (to be on the safe side.) It can be washed off with soap and water — above all not with spirits or anything similar, as it stings abominably. 'Samarit' is actually a box of prophylactic kit containing other things for additional protection, including a lunar caustic solution. Instructions for use are included with the kit.

s.h.

216

Private parts: See Parts, private.

Problems, sexual: Means all the difficulties we have met, meet, and will meet in connection with our sex lives.

If we regard the approximately 5 million Danes who live their lives between 1930 and 1970, we can draw up various tables concerning the number of sexual problems which must exist in one way or another. We know that during this 40-year period, approximately 600,000 abortions·, legal and illegal, will take place. Several thousand hermaphrodites · will be living amongst us. 200,000 children will be born out of wedlock. There will be approximately 200,000 homosexual · and bi-sexual · men and women, several thousand prostitutes of both sexes, several thousand persons with various perversities of which a number must be classed as sexual criminals, etc., etc.

Making a vary cautious estimate we could place the total number of sexual problems at about 1 million. If we count on the fact that some of these problems will occur in the same person we can say that approximately 500,000 persons will be concerned with, indirect or direct sexual problems of this kind.

This is not even to say that the most obvious ones are the most serious. We all know that a whole lot of people furthermore exist who go round with serious sexual problems that do not happen to come to light via such an artificial kind of calculation as that made above. (And all these people have wives, girl-friends, boy-friends, husbands).

No matter how cautious we may be in our experimental estimation of the total number of sexual problems in Denmark, we still end up with quite a considerable figure.

We have not found the ideal solution to the abortion · problem as long as there are still chemists and customers who stand blushing when a purchase of contraceptives is being made (see Birth Control), nor to the homosexual problem as long as a very large minority of homosexuals are not allowed to insert straightforward advertisements for their membership magazines in the big daily newspapers, nor to the simple business of peaceful co-existence even within our own society as long as it is regarded as 'perverse' if a young man peeps (see Peeping Tom) up at a window in which a girl is undressing and has 'forgotten' to draw the curtains or pull down the blind.

The sole object of the above is to stress the fact that we have not — as some of us now and then would appear to think — established a little human paradise on earth, and that we, in little Denmark, do not live under such harmonious and open-minded conditions as to entitle us to rest at our ease on all our laurels.

The majority of these problems can be reduced and should be reduced.

i. & s.h.

Projection: A mental mechanism we all know. It really means 'casting across on to'. We know how a film projection apparatus in a cinema projects light and pictures on to the screen.

As a mental mechanism it means that we cast our own, possibly forbidden or unconscious or secret wishes and motives, across and on to others.

A very innocent kind of projection often takes place at the dinner table: "Wouldn't you like a little more gravy, Mr. Winkleby?" usually means: "I'd rather like some more gravy myself." Thus we cast, or project, our own desire for gravy over on to somebody else.

During quarrels we often experience being accused of something we regard as unjust. Often we answer: "Where did you get that idea from? I suppose it's something you wouldn't mind doing yourself?" Or else we say about somebody: "Just because he's such a pig himself he needn't think everybody else is too."

But we know of far more serious examples. The witch trials · were a very marked example of inflamed imaginations, namely those of the upholders of a strict moral code, being projected on to others who were thereafter burnt as witches. (See also Incubus).   *s.h.*

Promiscuity: Means going to bed with anybody, indiscriminately. Amongst certain primitive peoples young persons have been permitted to choose themselves a sexual partner for a limited period and thereafter change to another.

In our society this is not entirely permissible.

We are afraid of venereal diseases · and illegitimate children, but many also believe that such licence would result in the leading of a wild and uninhibited life, which in turn would result in nobody's wanting to marry and thus an absence of stable marriages in our society.

This fear is probably unfounded. After all, we have been able to observe how the above-mentioned peoples have managed to have peaceful and stable marriages all the same. The longing to find somebody with whom one can live happily for the rest of one's life is something deeply ingrained within us. Those who continue jumping from one bed to the next even when they have reached quite a mature age have not developed such habits merely because promiscuity is permitted, but more likely because it is something of which society 'disapproves' — and it is neither a happy nor a richly satisfying life. (See Erotomania).

— — —

Those who condemn and use expressions like 'promiscuous living', 'goes to bed with any Tom, Dick or Harry', 'indiscrimate fornication', and so forth are usually extremely moral · and indignant · persons who — in Denmark, for instance — talk scathingly about 'sucked sweets', by which they mean women (not men, who are allowed much more liberty) who go to bed with men without marrying them. This strictly moral and condemnatory attitude is particularly common in countries where prostitution · is actually encouraged, where state-authorized naughty girls take care of the bad men so that the nice girls can carry on being chaste and virginal until the one and only man in their life turns up.

Probably nobody goes to bed with 'anybody', no matter how many they go to bed with; but there are many who try to find the 'one and only', namely the person with whom they can live the rest of their lives. There is nothing to indicate that the less one searches the better equipped one is to have a happy marriage.

Nor is there anything to indicate that the more one searches, the worse one must be fitted for a stable marriage.

But it does look as though a certain measure of experience before marriage results in greater sexual success in marriage. In Kinsey's report on women there are figures which point in this direction.

This is not to suggest that we should all just let ourselves go.

As indicated elsewhere (e.g. in the articles on Personality and Morals) we are obliged to observe certain rules and regulations, and nobody becomes a happier person from having disregarded the moral code of his society, no matter how unreasonable it may appear.   *s. h.*

Propagation: The business of having children, producing offspring, reproducing our own kind. Those parts of our bodies which are necessary to the propagation of our species are called genital organs or sexual organs.

Fertilization · is essential to the self-reproduction of human beings. Fertilization demands a mature ovum, or egg, in a woman and sperm from a man. Most women between the ages of 20 and 40 are able to supply a mature ovum. Men have excessive supplies of sperm. A man does not need to have an erection ·, but it is not very easy for him to supply sperm cells without pronounced sexual desires, without an orgasm ·. His ejaculation · is combined with the crucial moment of his intercourse. Whether a woman has an orgasm or not is entirely immaterial to the business of fertilization.

This is a regrettable fact. This is naturally no explanation of why men have orgasms much more easily and much more frequently. Of course we could use Darwinian argumentation and say that men who do not have orgasms do not reproduce their kind and become extinct as a race. Women, who have difficulty in experiencing orgasm, can perfectly well continue the race.

This is merely armchair philosophy. Of greater consequence is the fact that from time to time it has been held that sexual urges should be restricted to the interests of propagation. The result was that it was not necessary to pay attention to a woman's share in the pleasures of sexual intercourse.

There have even been periods when what was regarded as suitable attire for a woman engaged in the business of sexual intercourse was a sad-looking shift with a hole in it. That jolly well served us men right. We have no need to go back further than one generation to find many married couples who never saw each other naked. Such couples still exist to this day. (See also Nightdress).

Nowadays sex life is accepted as something that can be lovely for both parties.

We have even been allowed to keep the business of the propagation of our species out of it.

We may do so with composure. It is not underpopulation that threatens us. *s.h.*

Prophylaction: See Prevention.

Prostitutes: People who live partly or wholly on prostitution ·. We call prostitution jokingly 'woman's oldest profession', and scores of films have been made on the subject, for it is one that interests. The life of the prostitute is romanticized and there is no doubt that it exercises a certain amount of attraction on many women. It is not only for fun that they talk about "having their own pitch in such-and-such a street" or whatever way they choose to joke about it. Even though many of them in reality never walk up and down a street to try picking up a man, the idea tickles their imaginations a little. (See also Fantasies, sexual). The real thing is not quite that exciting. Many years ago it was discovered that prostitutes were supposed to be less bright than average. Those who were examined, however, were those who were clumsy enough — or unlucky enough — to get picked up by the police.

All the girls who were careful enough and intelligent enough to avoid detection were naturally never put through any intelligence tests — and perhaps this applied to the majority? There are undoubtedly a number in luxury flats and who in due course end up with expensive businesses which they run with great efficiency.

Nevertheless, it is obvious that prostitution is far from being any sort of life in clover. There are humiliations and contempt, not only from customers, but also from within — from their bad consciences ·. We are all so dependent upon the society in which we live that we pay attention to other people's opinions, for this is also part of our 'personality' ·.

Quite a portion of spite is necessary in order to stand up against the accepted norms · of society.

These 'ladies of easy virtue' as they are also called, are thus not particularly happy or easy-going people. Nor are they particularly passionate girls combining the useful and profitable with the pleasurable — on the contrary, their share of erotic pleasure is particularly small and a number of them are moreover homosexual ·.

Nobody knows why some become prostitutes and others not. All we can observe is that some take the moral laws of society more lightly than others. Various theories have been put forth. One of them is to the effect that prostituted women are supposed to have felt themselves unwanted as children, and in their unhappy, distrustful and continuously disappointed yearning for warmth and love have slipped into letting money be a substitute.

At any rate it is quite definite that masses of girls, before, now and in the future, solely on account of their external attractions, will earn money, acquire influence and get married. They will get given big parts by going to bed with the director — or just because we like watch-

A lady of easy virtue...

ing them undress in a rather piquant way in front of everybody. No education or other qualifications are necessary. It is so easy to moralize. Let us leave it to those whose past entitles them to do so. Let us make do with admitting that if we men were able to get ourselves jobs as directors, professorships — or wherever our ambitions may lie — by being obliging to influential ladies (who have no need to be repulsive on that account) many a business concern and faculty would have a different leadership today.

Or perhaps a more extensive leadership.
s.h.

Prostitutes, male: This is what we call young men who, just like prostitute · women, try to pick up customers or interested persons by frequenting places where such persons are likely to be found and offering to satisfy their sexual urges against payment.

Various different sociological factors make themselves apparent in the whole question of male prostitutes. To start with, the law in Denmark is very strict. (The law was strict before, and recently it has been made even stricter). It is a law whose purpose is to ensure that ordinary, heterosexual · young men (and women) do not become seduced — are not abused. It is in a way an easy manner of making money. We know of many instances of elderly men who have fitted out young men and given them plenty of pocket money — out of infatuation. But many of the elderly men are only interested in young men. Suddenly the easy money stops. The way society regards homosexuality today, these young men have placed themselves beyond the pale; they have been anti-social by indulging in relationships of this kind.

Once stamped as anti-social, the jump is not so great to serious anti-sociality — to criminal things that also provide easy money. It is tempting for the disappointed young man to threaten to denounce his older, former friend for having seduced a minor — and thereby squeeze money out of him.

The older homosexual does not care to have his particular tastes talked about — even if the police promise him discretion — so he often pays. This is the reverse of the medal, namely that the law which is supposed to protect the young may be used for blackmail.

The lawmakers are afraid young people who might otherwise have developed heterosexual interests will acquire a taste for homosexuality if they let themselves be tempted during puberty or their youth.

(See also Seduction). The risk is probably slightly greater for women than it is for men. Women are to a greater extent made afraid of the dangers of ordinary marital relationships during their upbringing.

— — —

Much more can be written on this subject. Much more has been. Police-inspector Jens Jersild of the Danish *police de moeurs* (public morals police) has, for instance, written three books on the subject, among them "Barnet og det homosexuelle problem" (The Child and the Homosexual Problem) (Christtreus bogtrykkeri 1957) and "Den mandlige prostitution" (Male Prostitution) (Dansk Videnskabs Forlag 1953). Even though we are by no means in agreement with the police-inspector in all his suppositions, reasonings and conclusions, the books are the expression of a positive will to get to the bottom of the problems.   *i. & s.h.*

Prostitution: Is what we call it when a person places himself or herself at the disposal of another person in order that the said person can satisfy his or her sexual urges — and accepts payment for it.

We use the word prostitute in particular about girls who live by taking men home — or to a hotel room, etc. — and going to bed with them for a few pounds or so. This is what we call prostitution proper. It has been forbidden in Denmark for the past 50 years without its being possible to say that it is now non-existent or even rare. Prostitution is only permissible as a side-line.

Male prostitution also exists and consists of young men who place themselves at the disposal of homosexuals against payment. This is also forbidden.

Then comes semi-prostitution, which is far more difficult to define. It may be a question of indirect presents or payment.

Is a girl a semi-prostitute because she lets her lover pay her rent? Is a woman a semi-prostitute because she accepts gifts of expensive jewellery from several different men? Is a woman a semi-prostitute because she twice marries rich men — for the sake of their money? And how do we (or she) know that it was for the sake of money anyway?

A rich man is more efficient than a poor man — at any rate as far as earning money is concerned — and supposing she happens to admire efficiency? It has been said that the difference between the girl who marries rich twice and the ordinary prostitute is that the one sells herself wholesale and the other retail.

How many married women have not been a little more obliging the day they badly want a new hat? Just as with all the other fine and dandy words describing divergencies in sexual relationships we had probably better be a little careful not to draw too sharp a line between those of us who do the right thing — and all the others: the immoral, sinful, prostituted rest.

The fact that the line is generally drawn so sharply is because we human beings love our heroes on white horses and our villains on black ones — it makes things tidier.

But it is also because many believe that if the line is not drawn sharply, many will wander off the straight and narrow. They fail to realize that anyone already slightly off beforehand is thereby given a hefty shove.   *i. & s.h.*

Prudery: See Indignation.

Psychiatrists, psychiatry: Ordinary doctors learn, in the course of their studies, very little about the mind and mental illnesses — psychical sufferings.

But those interested can undertake an extra number of years of study and specialize in the science of the diseases of the mind — *psychiatry*. These specialists then become nerve specialists, or psychiatrists. But not even psychiatrists learn enough about the psychiatry and psychology of sex life. It is bound up with the fact that nobody *knows* enough about these things — likewise that it has never been regarded as really respectable, i.e. not quite 'done' to interest oneself in sex. There are for instance, psychiatrists who refuse to have anything to do with Freud · for the very reason that he took as much interest in the psychology of sex as he did. (See also Doctors).   *s.h.*

Psychoanalysis: A particular method of effecting a cure — a way of treating mental irregularities.

Neither psychiatrists · nor psychologists · receive training as psychoanalysts at university. Psychoanalysis is a subject on its own and requires — amongst other things — that the budding psychoanalyst be psychoanalysed himself.

Psychoanalysis is an expensive form of treatment because it takes such a long time. It demands a great deal of the patient — the person being analysed — because he himself has to do a great deal of work too. It takes the form of weekly (or more frequent) conversations each lasting an hour, and each hour costs upwards of 20 kr.

It may take years before the treatment helps, and some lose patience on the way.

The results of psychoanalysis are very difficult to evaluate because we never know how the patient would have developed without the protracted treatment.

Many people expect a person who has been psychoanalyzed to be a personality in complete harmony with himself and his surroundings — more or less an ideal being. Psychoanalysis cannot do this, but in the more fortunate instances it may liberate an inhibited personality ·, thereby enabling it to develop more (and to a more satisfying extent) and make relationships with other persons easier — or possibly guide an unfortunate development into more acceptable channels.

There are various schools and trends within the sphere of psychoanalysis, which was founded by the Austrian Sigmund Freud ·. There have also been doctors who believed that only doctors possessed the necessary faculties and knowledge for studying further and becoming psychoanalysts — the directly opposite opinion, incidentally, to Freud's. The truth probably is, however, that cure of mental illnesses can be effected in many different ways. A considerable part

224

of the curative effect of psychoanalysis consists in the fact of another person's taking, over a protracted period, a warm and positive interest in the person having the worries and the problems. The analyst, who at the same time is a neutral, disengaged person, makes up in this way for things not provided during upbringing, and helps to correct the mistakes from which the person being analysed suffered.

In Denmark anybody can set himself up as a psychoanalyst and get his name in the trades and professions section of the telephone book under Psychoanalysts.

This naturally means a risk of there being people with no, incomplete, or downright poor qualifications being allowed to receive patients and treat them.

On the other hand there may well be people without any letters after their name at all who are cleverer than some who have passed examinations as a doctor or psychologist first. *s.h.*

Psychologists: People who have knowledge of — or who intuitively use — the laws applying to the workings of the human mind. (See also Psychology).

There are undoubtedly people possessed of natural talents who are intuitively cleverer on the subject of human nature than many of those who have studied the subject at university — and among those who are studying or who have taken their examination there may well be those who are already what is called 'good psychologists'.

University training is thus no guarantee of the extent or quality of one's knowledge of human nature. On the other hand the theoretically schooled psychologist knows most of the pitfalls into which the amateur so easily falls.

There are reasons for stressing the fact that during the course of university studies in Denmark (and this applies to psychologists as well as to psychiatrists · and doctors ·) as good as nothing is learnt about normal and anomalous sexual relationships or the psychology of the subject.

This is the simple result of the taboo · we still drag round with us concerning all things sexual. It is not regarded as 'done' to concern onself with this sort of thing. *i. & s.h.*

Psychology: The science of the mind. As a rule this is taken to mean the fairly broad conception we call normal mental processes.

Psychology concerns itself with the mental life of the human being, and as we all have the apparatus at hand — and find it exciting to investigate it — the interest in psychology is large. There are countless books on the subject, both popular ones and others less popular. There are study groups, lectures and the Folk University — and finally it can be studied at Copenhagen University, where it is possible to take various degrees.
Students do not learn everything about human mental processes at university — it is far too big a subject. They learn a scientific approach, learn about various methods and experiences — and thereby acquire a foundation on which to build further. *s.h.*

Psychology of human sex life: The science concerning that part of our mental lives that belongs to our love lives and especially our sex lives. Many books on the subject exist, but not a fraction of the money has been spent that ought to have been spent on proper, scientific investigations capable of providing us with reliable information.

We are far from knowing enough about such things today, and the position is not improved by the fact that the little we do know is not taught to students of either medicine or psychology at Danish universities.

As we still know too little about sexual psychology, a great deal of superstition exists in the field. In 50 years or so, or perhaps less, others will be able (let us hope) to point out the majority of our mistakes and smile at our fumblings in mediaeval darkness.

Many books have been written on the psychology of sex, and Freud ·, in his works, has in particular made an enormous contribution to a greater understanding of the mechanisms which guide human actions on this score. *i. & s.h.*

Psychopathy: It may be worth while mentioning one or two things in connection with the concept of psychopathy — after all, it is something with which we operate in everyday speech in Denmark.

In order to understand things like psychopathy and neurosis we must refer to the model of the Personality · we used in the article under this heading.

A psychopath is a person who comes into conflict with his surroundings because his *super ego* is too weak. He does what he wants to do — without his conscience having sufficient strength to hold him back. Various comic strip cartoons feature some form of psychopath (e.g. "Kasketkarl" in Denmark, or "Andy Capp" in England) who delights and amuses us because he expresses our most secret wishes via displays of pure, uninhibited egoism.

However, we can also find psychopathic traits in people who are not, never have been, or never will come into conflict with their surroundings. And in order to make the whole thing just a bit more complicated, it can be said that it is the "adjusted psychopaths" who possibly stand the greatest chance of being harmonious persons. All of which is a bit of a play on words.

In the same way, people can live perfectly well with one or more neurotic traits in their character. Whilst the psychopath — the psychopath proper — has conflicts with his surroundings, but very few with himself, the neurotic person has his conflicts within himself — and with himself, i.e. with his conscience. In the neurotic person there is a question of a strong *super ego* continuously squabbling with the wishes and urges expressed by the *id*. In connection with neuroses we find anxiety ·, compulsive actions, hysteria · and much else besides.   *s.h.*

Puberty: The first sign of puberty in both boys and girls is hair growing round the genital organs ·. Boys have their first ejaculation (see Emissions, nocturnal) their voices break, their figures become more gangling — and much else besides. Girls have their first menstruation ·, their breasts and hips start rounding out — and much else happens to them too.

Added to these things come the mental factors, the feeling of uncertainty and the problems connected with taking leave of childhood and "stepping into the ranks of the grown-ups".

There are demands on the part of parents, and prohibitions too. And young people often have a violent struggle in order to tear themselves free and stand on their own, somewhat wobbly legs.

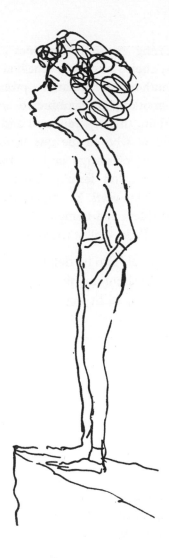

The sexual feelings become stronger without their really understanding what is happening to them. They are required to decide what they want to be in life, a choice they are nowhere near mature enough to make, yet they are forbidden to satisfy the sexual urges that arise in them and which may be far more ardent. According to Kinsey ·, a man's sexual urges reach their maximum during puberty before his 20th year. (See Masturbation; Titillation, sexual; and Orgasm).

Increasing growth, hormones ·, sexual urges, choice of career, rebellion against the authorities, demands, prohibitions and emotions all combine to create an uncertain, dreamy, confused and violent individual who on the one hand is full of masses of energy and on the other weary and 'off form'. Things happen during these years. Young people are raw and ruthless and tremendously sensitive and idealistic — all at the same time.

Puberty can also be defined as the time when all parents say to all young people: "You seem to be regarding your home more or less as a boarding-house—a place you merely come to eat and sleep in" and "I don't know what you've got in your head these days ... you always seem to be playing the giddy goat".

Generally speaking puberty is more or less over by the age of 20 but it is sometimes protracted, particularly in university students who live in a somewhat remote cloud of their own. In individual cases a form of protracted puberty can be evident up to an advanced age.

The fact that the idealism and revolutionary urges of youth are often kept up is not always to be regretted — on the contrary, it can often be particularly refreshing and have an inspiring effect on many of those who otherwise all too quickly switch over to a passive, conservative acceptance of anything and everything.

Talking to 22 and 23-year-olds one can discover that they already belong to "the older generation" that finds present-day youth irresponsible · and immoral. *i.h.*

In the original Danish edition, as well as in the Swedish and Norwegian, this space carried an illustration. Although it was allowed in Scandinavia legal opinion has warned us against its inclusion. We apologise to all readers for this omission and recognise that no intelligent adult would have regarded this particular illustration as being offensive.

The Editors.

Pubes: The hair growing round the genital organs ·.

Public decency, offences against: (See also Modesty): Offences against public decency are punishable by up to several years' imprisonment — at any rate in serious cases. The commonest 'violations' are things like baring one's genitals in public (see Exhibitionism) and the touching of children in a sexual manner. We can thus observe that children and women in particular are credited with feelings of modesty that can be offended. (See likewise Sexual Crimes).

If we try to look at these things objectively, we have to admit it is really rather strange why the sight of a man with his fly-buttons undone should have the effect of offending anyone. The explanation, of course, is that thanks to all the restrictions and veils of secrecy with which (despite all the small advances that have been made) we are still enveloped in our society, things of this sort are bound to have an alarming, threatening effect on the minds of women and children. If our general attitude and approach to sexual matters were more liberal and understanding it would be more difficult to offend anybody — and fewer would wish to try. *s.h.*

Pyrolagnia, pyromania: The yearning to see flames and play with fire is probably something very common and primitive in all of us. The yearning to see fire can become an obsession, a form of perversity in the sex lives of certain people, in the sense that they have to see fire, or set fire to something as a stage in the development of their sexual excitement, their sexual titillation ˙.

This special desire is called pyromania or pyrolagnia, and people who suffer from it are called pyromaniacs.

But the fact that one chooses to lie on a bearskin rug in front of the fireplace with one's lover and enjoy the flickering of the flames does not mean one is perverse. *i.h.*

R

Rape: To have sexual intercourse with a woman by force, i.e. against her will, is called rape. Most people will realize that it is impossible to force a woman to let one have sexual intercourse with her within a reasonable space of time by the mere use of strength — either she must be exhausted first or threats must be used. Women are therefore fairly well protected against the milder forms of compulsion. Rape generally requires privacy or very special means of compulsion. Serious instances of rape of this nature are naturally punishable by law. (See also Crimes, sexual).

Rationalization: A mental mechanism that consists in justifying by using reason.

If a man who has strong racial prejudices says, for instance: "Because I happen to advise my sister not to marry a negro it is not to say I have anything against negroes, but just that I think one should stick to one's own class . . ." — then he is making his motives sound more sensible and less emotional than they really are — in other words he is rationalizing.

It can be done very cleverly.

We all rationalize. We all try to doll up up our motives — not only for the benefit of others, but especially for our own benefit. We should therefore be on the watch-out and constantly suspect ourselves of having "less nice motives". *i.h.*

Reaction formation: Also a mental mechanism. A mother whose child really is a frightful strain will in many cases develop a bad conscience at having harboured unfriendly thoughts towards the said child. (See however Ambivalence).

Afterwards, she will react with a violent display of affection towards her child. The affectionate feelings caused in this fashion can be said to be a reaction formation.

A child that finds he or she has a kid brother or sister to share home with may react with an almost sickening display of delight on the surface — a reaction originating from deeper, negative emotions.

A girl who is unhappily in love with a man may, for instance, imagine to herself that all problems would be solved if he were run over. She has been brought up to suppress such feelings (for they are not acceptable) with the result that she may react by feeling even more intensely about him than before. *s.h.*

Rectum: The Latin word for the final section of the large intestine that terminates at the anus ·.

Reflex: See Pavlov.

Refusal to eat: Many mothers know what fights they sometimes have, meal after meal, to get their children to eat.

Children are dragged off to the doctors nowadays because their mothers are afraid their children will become undernourished. Children suffer from 'refusal to eat' it is said.

It would be more correct to say that mothers 'possess talents for provoking refusal to eat in children', for these 'sufferings' disappear like dew before the sun the moment one stops taking any interest in how much they eat.

Children can use refusal to eat in order to annoy their parents. The problem is not solved by asking mothers to stop worrying about whether their children eat enough — it is not that easy for them.

But all this is a digression. The important thing is that no child has ever died from refusing to eat. They get plenty to eat all right, at any rate enough to meet their minimum requirements. It is the same thing with sexual needs. Here too, circumstances can create a refusal to satisfy the sexual needs, and here too, the implicated parties are ready to swear that the sexual need is 'too small' or 'nonexistant' (see Frigidity).

But just as in the case of food, it has proved, time and again, that the individual will see to it that he or she gets his or her sexual needs met all right — at any rate the minimum requirements. Many couples have created a 'refusal to indulge in sex' in one of them, and often both are unhappy about it and think that everything is hopeless.

In such cases it is important not to force the other person, i.e. not to insist on sexual satisfaction in the other person. It is easier said than done — we know that — but we must learn from the example about refusal to eat: the hunger is there all right, just as the sexual urge is there, but neither can tolerate violent pressure.

There is a kind of psychological mechanism that somehow decrees that if two people have to get up together in the morning, and one of them leaps out in a fresh, breezy, bouncy good humour, the other one automatically becomes slightly sulky and unwilling. If the sulky and unwilling person then suddenly has to get up at the same time as somebody who is even more sulky and unwilling, the person who was sulky before suddenly becomes the breezily bouncy one.

In other words, it means that a person engaged in a sexual relationship with a partner who is on form ·, sexually, can become quite paralysed and obstinate; yet in a relationship with a person slightly less enthusiastic the same person can suddenly show plenty of life and spark — and in particular, desire.

Therefore it may well prove valuable not to press on too much, in other words that a man should be careful not to let his vanity · make him start demonstrating his enormous potency · (see Impotency) — or that the woman paralyse the man by making much too violent demands.

How one manages to get through these periods, how one manages to hold back, is basically speaking immaterial — it can be done by masturbation or by the man making do with concerning himself mainly with his own sexual satisfaction.

Nor should we forget that if we happen to be cheerful and bouncy in the morning, and the other person sour and sulky, we generally become even more cheerful and bouncy — whereas the other person becomes sourer than ever.   *i.h.*

Relativity: We so often chuck out the sentence: "Everything is relative." This relativity is probably a very important thing. One might develop a sort of psychology · of relativity.

The person that is hungry is happy to get a dry crust. The child that formerly fell asleep in its mother's lap gets unhappy the day it is made to sleep two feet from her. We find 'relativities' of the same sort within the sphere of the psychology of sex life. To the modest · young maiden, the sheer fact of allowing her lover to see her naked is a tremendously daring thing.

To the young man who has been brought up in more free-thinking circles it may well be a tremendous disappointment to find she is not directly active. Both are really right in their way — in view of their respective backgrounds.   *s.h.*

Relaxation, conscious: A special kind of muscle treatment — not massage, but a method of making a person conscious of each individual muscle. We use many of our muscles incorrectly, and manage to keep some of them in such a permanent state of tension that the result is unreasonable fatigue or actual pain. Women in particular find it an advantage to become more conscious of their pelvic muscles and thereby achieve more relaxation in their sex life (see Muscle Consciousness).

This is a bi-product sometimes resulting from muscle relaxation treatment. Such treatment is given by specially trained persons, (in Danish they are called *Afspændingspædagoger*, and may be found in the red telephone directory (Fagbogen) under this name), and is often given during the last 4 or 5 months before a birth ·. (See also Anxiety).

Relaxation of abdominal and leg muscles is naturally advantageous to a man's sex life too.   *i.h.*

Religion and Love Life: See Christianity.

Reliquiae: See Amulet and Fetishism.

Report: Here we are thinking in particular about Kinsey's two reports on the sex lives of white Americans, but sexuologists in several countries have been inspired to make similar investigations, e.g. Geoff. Gorer: "English Character" in England, and Kirsten Auken in Denmark.

The Danish investigations however, only involve 315 women.

There do exist, however, a number of reports prior to Kinsey's. One was made in Russia in 1904, another in Germany in 1910 and in Scandinavia during the 1940's, i.e. the Gottschalck report concerning 250 married couples in Denmark (1947).

Those interested should see Auken's survey in her book "Unge kvinders sexuelle adfærd" (The Sexual Behaviour of Young Women) published in Denmark by Rosenkilde and Bagger's Forlag, 1953, p. 25.   *s.h.*

Repression: See Personality.

Responsibility; also lack of: So much is written and said these days on the subject of young people and their sense of responsibility, particularly their lack of same. Young people of no more than 22—23 already start talking about how young people (i.e. younger than them-

A good position for resting or sleeping.

selves) have less sense of responsibility than they had themselves 'at that age'.

Older people are even worse and misuse statistics and much else to prove the decadence of the times. There is no reason for us to get upset. We can prove that young people of today are not particularly irresponsible. Seldom have so many young people got themselves an education as nowadays, and seldom has juvenile delinquency been lower. We can furthermore prove that even Socrates railed about the irresponsibility of youth; likewise that all generations are accused of being more irresponsible than their predecessors. This cannot be right — Adam and Eve cannot have been all *that* filled with a sense of responsibility, i.e. as they must have been if all the accusations were to be correct. The truth is quite simply that in a society in process of development, young people of necessity discard much of what is handed down to them, and this makes their elders uneasy. We know of human societies untramelled by such reproaches — societies that have stagnated, societies in which the sons make their vases precisely the same way as their grandfathers and greatgrandfathers before them. In such societies the children accept their parents' outlooks on everything uncritically.

In our society, progress is being made at a different pace. The Wright brothers flew a motor-propelled aircraft for the first time in history in 1903. Today we are photographing the reverse side of planets with sputniks and expecting any day to hear that the first human being has landed on the moon. Progress of this sort cannot take place without each generation's (and there are no more than four or five years between generations) discarding the work of their predecessors and improving on their inventions.

Whether we prefer a stagnant society and its tranquillity to a society undergoing constant revision is open to discussion. But we cannot expect meek youth *and* high-paced progress at one and the same time.

A society that has become stagnant is less inclined to correct its mistakes. On the other hand a society that permits changes — also for the worse — at least has a chance of rectifying its follies. What sort of responsibility is it we are so anxious for youth to assume? Is it political responsibility? No! Is it responsibility of starting a home? No! Is it responsibility for their sexual freedom? No, for society is not keen on giving them *that*.

One can only take on responsibility if one can be held responsible for something, i.e. run the risk of reprisals. But in that case one must also be given the chance of taking precautionary measures to counteract the risk involved in the responsible situation.

Responsibility implies something about having to recognize the obligations that are entailed when one starts doing something. As far as sex is concerned it means taking care not to have children, (see Birth Control), not to catch venereal diseases · and not to cause harm to others in any way.

But whose is the responsibility? As long as the pertinent facts of sex life are hushed up, enlightenment and contraceptives and venereal diseases merely become scare-value propaganda. Moralizing · and warnings merely frighten the young away, for after all we ourselves have taught them it is not done to talk about such things. Far too many young people become engaged and get married today without having even heard of the word *pessary* ·. Far too many parents rest satisfied with warning and frightening by means of loose, vague terms and phrases.

Of course it is difficult for them. Their parents told them even less. But it gives us no justification for evading the responsibility. "Mind out and be careful, you two!" or "You'd better not!" are still the most usual forms in which parental duty is fulfilled.

Many young people have little wish to talk to their parents about these matters — but is it their fault? Is it not because society still clings to romantic · shyness and modesty · and encourages a form of upbringing that completely bans such subjects? There is no reason to place the blame on parents — after all, they are merely the products of their times. We merely wish to stress that the young cannot be blamed either. Not until the day comes when we can justly state that we have given the young every chance of, and thoroughly equipped them for, assuming the responsibilities that go with a sex life — not until then can we start wagging admonishing fingers and reproach them for not having shown a sense of responsibility.

We too think that sexual relationships demand a sense of responsibility on the part of their practitioners (see also Personality). But in this case we must educate our young, not only to assume their responsibilities but likewise how to engage in sexual relationships. Parents who tell their children as much as they can, support them in their feelings, help them with their worries — such parents are on the road to the right sort of upbringing. But unfortunately our conscious upbringing is the least part of upbringing. Many parents have consciously tried to help and talk, but discovered that their children have lost confidence in them. One cannot reproach such parents and say they have failed to face up to their responsibilities, but on the other hand one cannot reproach their children for the same thing either.

We must give up believing that never has sex been discussed so much and so frankly and that never have human beings led happier sexual lives than now. It is not true. There is still a long way to go. But progress is being made. (See also Sexual Enlightenment). *i. & s.h.*

Revulsion: Is a sensation we all know, being a strong dislike for something or other, be it food, or something to do with sex, or something else. These emotions can be experienced in such a genuine fashion we feel them to be natural · and that we were born with them. But this is far from being the case. There are not many dishes, for instance, which, while regarded as delicacies in one part of the world, are regarded as uneatable somewhere else. Many women think the male body — and the male sexual organs in particular—ugly or downright repulsive.

But there are many other peoples in the world who look at things differently — and we are familiar with the cult of phallos worship from all over the world.

The Chinese cannot understand how we can eat cheese seeing that it stinks the way it does, and it is actually a riddle to them that we (with all our snobbish feelings) should have ever thought of doing so.

The Americans refuse to eat fried "snakes"—which is the way they refer to the dish we Danes call "fried eel". The French have eaten snails and frogs' legs for a long time — we are only just starting to dare. In the olden days we used to eat masses of horsemeat in Denmark.

Many women experience deep terror and revulsion at the sight of mice, snakes or spiders. (See Anxiety). Little boys and girls play happily with these animals — the anxiety is an acquired emotion, and the revulsion does not develop until later.

And then the distance from the revolting to the very exciting is not so very great. We should be very careful before classifying anything as "dreadful", "disgusting", "revolting" etc., etc. (See also Words, naughty).

It is more correct to say: "I don't think it tastes nice" or, even more correctly: "Just at this moment I think it is revolting or dreadful". For the judgements we pass in this way are extremely subjective, and our attitude may well change.

In the course of time, many women have entered marriage with the firm conviction that sex was a dirty business and a beastly demand on the part of the man. A few have discovered that they were on the wrong trail, and that love life can be a great pleasure to both parties.

But there is still a long way to go, for new generations are continually growing up and being brought up with anxiety and revulsion towards this side of life — not an inherent anxiety and revulsion, but an acquired attitude produced by the wrong kind of sexual enlightenment and a public code of morals hostile towards sexual matters. (See Morals).

Revulsion is an honest feeling, but it is something imposed, something acquired.

A number of these imposed feelings can be somewhat impractical. Since they are learnt there is some hope that they can also be removed or weakened, even though it requires time, patience and understanding in both parties. (See Pavlov). Sex is lovely, but at the same time it is allied to nature — and nature is neither particularly well-bred (see Breeding, good), nor cultured.   i. & s.h.

Romance: Sensible and otherwise free-thinking people often argue against sexual enlightenment. They are of the opinion that enlightenment kills the romance and charming mystery of love.

Romance created against the background of the sum of human problems which ignorance (and its resultant prejudices·) cost is a very expensive article. Let us rather be a little less romantic.

We by no means underestimate the spiritual values of sexual relationships, the mental side of love. We do not merely aim at physical satisfaction, sexuality. It would be like trying to quench one's thirst in expensive vintage wines.

Who, by the way, has ever proved that enlightenment killed romance? After all, we do not enjoy a lobster salad any the less because we learn that it contains 10% carbohydrates, 55% fats, 8% proteins and 270 calories — unless it makes one too fat, in which case it is useful information. ·

Similes are always dangerous things to use — they prove nothing. But those who profess sentimentality are under an obligation to us to prove that enlightenment takes the romance out of love. On the other hand it has been made overwhelmingly evident that a lack of enlightenment has been responsible for tragedies.

i. & s.h.

Rubber: See Condom.

Rubber Goods Shops: Shops that sell condoms ·, pessaries ·, pessary ointment, irrigators, other contraceptive aids, etc.

There are some 20 or 30 of these shops in Copenhagen. Everything is done to make the customer feel at his or her ease.

Some even feature small cubicles where each customer can be served privately.

Others have separate departments for men and women.

We have conducted an investigation — on a small scale — concerning the way these shops treat their customers (likewise of the service they provide) and we found one firm that is distinctly superior to the rest, even though many other firms are excellent enough in their way.

Even at the risk of being accused of unfair advertising we have decided in the interests of the public, to give the name of this firm.

Anybody who cares to can check for himself — or herself — and see whether they agree when we say that *Abis* is the firm which in many ways provides its customers with the best service at the moment.

The trade section of the Copenhagen telephone directory carries advertisements by rubber goods firms, likewise the daily papers. (See under *Gummivarer*).

i. & s.h.

Rhythm method: See Knaus and Menstruation chart.

S

It is impossible to tell by looking at a man whether his sex life differs from the normal.

Sac, scrotal: The scrotum · (see Genital Organs, male).

Sade, Marquis de: A French nobleman who lived during the period prior to, during, and after the French Revolution.

He has given his name to the term sadism · on account of his books about sexual stimulation derived from torturing others. The French noblemen of the time were in many cases little better than de Sade, but for one thing they never wrote about it and for another they avoided annoying those in political power at the time the way the marquis did on top of everything else.

His sex life did not consist of sadism only — on the contrary, for he practised sex life in all its forms. His wife and two of his many girl-friends were astonishingly faithful to him even during the years (27 in all) he was in prison.

The Marquis de Sade has scarcely been the kind of a man who, after excessive normal sexual satisfaction, set about discovering new ways of satisfying his desires — the way he has often been portrayed.

On the contrary, he was, if anything, more of a mentally dissatisfied and inhibited erotomaniac who tried time and again to find satisfaction in one way or another. It is important to understand the mechanism behind his mental derailment and the causes of it; not so much in order to excuse him, but to teach us how to avoid similar derailments. (See also Dippoldism and Governess).   *s.h.*

Sadism: Satisfaction derived from torturing others. Generally it is imagined that a sadist obtains sexual satisfaction — an actual orgasm — from torturing others, but this is highly unlikely — if possible at all. There is more frequently talk of the practice having a sexually stimulating effect, and from here we are practically into the realm of normal sex life, in which hard squeezing and biting often occur. (See also Deformity Fetishism).

But of course we can employ the words as we like and say that we are all sadists, but in general we only use them to describe persons who harm others seriously — or harm them against their will.

The dividing line between the normal and the pathological is not a clearly demarcated one. Is the man who comes home drunk every pay-day and starts by beating his wife and ends by going to bed with her a sadist? Even if she would never dream of having a divorce?

Is the woman who enjoys humiliating her husband at every opportunity a sadist? As long as there are people who happily submit to such rough treatment we had better be cautious before passing judgement. (See also Masochism and Governess). They are probably sadists according to the definition, but within the bounds of normalcy.

At the same time it must be stressed that in the sphere of child upbringing we find, in a number of people responsible for such bringing up, perverse examples of Dippoldism ·, a sexually prompted and therefore sadistic desire to punish children. Masters and older pupils at English boarding schools have, in the course of time, demonstrated marked forms of sadism.

The fact that one gives one's children a thick ear if they are cheeky is not only understandable but far less harmful than many other kinds of mental cruelty. Nor has it got anything to do with sadism. But when the punishment is systematized with rituals and traditions and sober, regretful piety — then there is reason to be on one's guard. The person administering the punishment will always deny deriving any pleasure from his role as the executioner.

The dangerous thing about systematized punishment — and this is the reason why the former practice of flogging has been opposed so strongly in psychological circles — is that sadism possibly produces masochists, i.e. that flogging results in enjoyment — in the person flogged as well as in the flogger. The really sadistic teacher gradually starts using the slightest excuse, the most ridiculous little misdemeanours, for meting out his punishments, and the person so punished gradually starts committing the misdemeanours in order to enjoy the pleasure of being punished. (See Governess).

There are also grounds for stressing that it is the inhibited, unsatisfied sexual relationships that result in sadism and masochism. Basically speaking both are inhibited aggressiveness ·. It is very easy to combine sadism with a strict moral code the way we have seen it done in Nazi Germany, amongst religious fanatics and amongst strict schoolteachers and educationalists. *i. & s.h.*

Sati: The name given to the Indian custom of widow-burning. Right up to the days of our grandparents the custom of burning a widow together with the corpse of her husband has been kept up.

It seems to us to be a barbaric custom, but many societies · — ours included — are barbaric in their demands on their members. In this case the influence brought to bear was so powerful many of the widows went up to the stakes and let themselves be burnt voluntarily.

Customs are stronger things than external force.

It was their consciences · that demanded of them that they should conform to the demands of tradition. In our society, young men voluntarily let themselves be shot in the defence of their country. This is another type of custom, and the explanation is a different one. We believe in our bounden duty to defend democracy and freedom. In India, widows likewise obediently followed the demands of duty.

s.h.

Satisfaction: When we have eaten and are full, we have satisfied our hunger.

Like all other needs or urges, we start by being a little hungry. Perhaps we hardly even notice it. We may realize it upon smelling a steak sizzling in a frying-pan. It would be wrong to say that hunger is created by the smell of the steak, for if we are thoroughly stuffed already, the smell of food certainly does not arouse our hunger — on the contrary.

It is exactly the same with sexual needs. Here too, a suggestion, a glimpse, can make us aware of our sexual needs. It is not the suggestion or glimpse that creates the urge — it is merely that they remind us of the presence of an urge already there. If we are thirsty, we start by being a little thirsty. Perhaps we notice it, and the thought of drinking will occur to us now and again, but gradually more and more as our thirst increases. Finally we can think of nothing else but water or having something to drink.

The sexual urge likewise increases in strength, but our moral · code does not permit us to acknowledge this need in the same honest way as we can say to ourselves or to others: "Heavens, I'm hungry!" or "Heavens, I'm thirsty!"

The consequence is likewise that satisfaction of the sexual urge can take on grotesque and warped forms.

There is a psychological mechanism that causes us humans to seek out, again and again, something which has at some time given us some form of satisfaction.

There is nothing surprising in the fact that we go back, time and again, to that little hotel on the left bank of the Seine where we once spent that lovely honeymoon with our wife.

Correspondingly, we avoid anything that on a single, or repeated occasions, has disappointed us.

Like all other laws, this one is not without its exceptions either, but it applies, broadly speaking, to our choice of brand of cigarette, place to eat, petrol station and lots of other things. In other words we are faithful to whatever has satisfied us and fight shy of anything or any place that has disappointed us. This applies to a high degree to sexual relationships too. Thus one cannot cure people who have had homosexual experiences in such a way as to cause them to have the same exaggerated, fear-ridden revulsion for homosexuality that the majority of heterosexuals have.

They can, if they personally wish, and if the treatment is successful, get as far as being able to experience heterosexual love *too* — so that they can choose for themselves. And this is perhaps a more natural attitude than our fanatical one.

And when we speak about seduction · to homosexuality we must realize that there is a question of a person having homosexuality revealed to him or her as a means of obtaining satisfaction. We see, in the majority of cases (see Kinsey) that the person concerned nevertheless will prefer heterosexuality.   *s.h.*

Satyriasis: Comes from the word satyr, which was the name for a kind of demigod, half human and half horse, that had a great weakness for wine and women.

Satyriasis means violently uncontrollable sexual urges in men, i.e. erotomania ·.

Scabies: A skin disease caused by little mites that bore their way beneath the skin and lay eggs. Just as with crab-lice · and venereal diseases ·, the cause of the trouble cannot live for very long away from a human being, and can therefore only be transferred in the course of intimate relationships, e.g. sexual intercourse, but also by holding hands for a long time, etc. Scabies is fairly rare nowadays and easy to cure. There is no need to go to hospital; a doctor can treat it during normal consultation hours.

s.h.

Science of sex: Our entire accumulated knowledge about sex. See also Sexuology.

Scopophilia: Another instance of a Latin name for a completely normal thing in ordinary sex life. This time it is the pleasure of seeing other people naked. And just as in the case of all the other isms it can, in rare instances, develop into a person's sole sexual pleasure; and when it becomes a sad kind of one-sidedness of this type we call it perverse ·. When young boys row close past a ladies' bathing establishment it is not for the purpose of admiring the architecture, but the anatomy; but this does not mean to say they are perverse. (See also Peeping Tom).   *s.h.*

Seduction: An abuse of power in which the seducer takes advantages of his superiority in order to reap benefits he would not otherwise have had. It is used in particular about mature, experienced people who succeed in having sexual intercourse or obtaining some other form of sexual satisfaction with younger persons. It may also be a superior taking advantage of his rank or position over an inferior, or a man who tempts young men with money. (See also Prostitutes male). But we also talk of seduction when it is a case of a person who attempts to persuade another without using any particular power or superiority. Clear cases of abuse of power of this nature can be punished by law, but there are naturally borderline cases here as everywhere else. Of particular interest in this connection is the seduction by homosexuals · of young men. The years during and just

Scopofiles out sculling.

after puberty ·, when sexual urges are beginning to make themselves felt, is a sensitive period. Acquaintanceship, friendship, falling in love, love, are not independent things, but steps on a ladder.

It is therefore possible for many homosexuals to seduce young men into practising homosexuality. It happens quite often too, but it does not mean that these young men will necessarily continue homosexual activity for ever after.

The fact that boys, in the course of their friendship and enthusiasm, can fall in love with other boys, is not commonly accepted as a natural · and normal thing.

If two boys therefore engage in sexual activity together, they may easily feel that they have been behaving abnormally, and the same applies if an older man seduces a younger man. (The same thing applies to girls, who, however, enjoy somewhat greater latitude).

Such young men easily find themselves elbowed out of the circle of 'normal' persons their own age; they become anti-social · in the sense that they feel they have placed themselves outside the official norms and rules of society — that they have been expelled.

It is possible that feelings of this nature

can assist in causing a perfectly normal boy to turn definitively to homosexuality.

And this is the basic factor in the concern that is felt on the subject of homosexual seduction: that a boy should turn homosexual and that this should leave its mark on his sex life in the future.

It seems as though the commonest form of sex life, the heterosexual·, is a particularly persistent kind of thing. There are, for instance, countless examples of boy prostitutes who have given up all homosexual activity, married and had children.

We know too, that a number would have become homosexual anyway, i.e. without seduction. The difficulty lies in the fact that an intermediary group becomes homosexual or bisexual ·, and we have no idea how their sex lives might have developed if they had not been seduced in the first instance.

The main error lies in the anxiety displayed by our society towards the whole subject of homosexuality. Just because a young man happens to have had one or several homosexual experiences we immediately think he is a lost case. We make him believe it as well. Thus when we so fanatically try to protect young people against experiences of this sort we are

241

really trying to maintain what is rather an artificial situation. If the fear and the prejudices were removed, the results would in all probability be less dangerous than artificial and fanatical opposition.

Apart from the ancient Greeks we know a number of modern societies where no fear of seduction exists, societies where all the boys have homosexual relations with the grown men in the tribe as a part of their puberty ceremonies; in other words, just at the age when we believe the 'danger' is greatest. These societies still exist, for the young men previously so seduced marry and have children just as in other societies.

The study of sex life and the history of sex, likewise of nature · itself, must of necessity make us less censorious and unsympathetic towards nature's multiplicity. It is our emotions · and prejudices · that prevent us from regarding infatuation for a person of the same sex calmly.   *i. & s.h.*

Self-abuse: See Masturbation.

Self-mutilation: A practice known during the Middle Ages, when it became fashionable to whip oneself (see Flagellant) and even castrate · oneself. Right up to modern times we come across cases of very young men attempting to castrate themselves as a result of desperation or bad consciences.

Self-satisfaction: Being satisfied with oneself — being complacent — is unfortunately regarded as scandalous, but in reality it is a prerequisite if we want to be in harmony with ourselves. If one is not satisfied with oneself, i.e. able to accept oneself — how can one expect anyone else to be?

In that case, would we only be supposed to love those who were sufficiently gifted to discern how little we could really claim to be charming people? Would we have to despise those who thought we were wonderful? This cannot be right.

On the contrary, the goal must be that we should like ourselves as we are. (See also Inferiority).   *i. & s.h.*

Semen: See Sperm.

Sense, common: Everybody talks about using common sense. Many believe that we are all basically imbued with common sense. It is said that women are creatures of emotion, but that men use their common sense. Nonsense. We are all extremely prone to be guided by our emotions in our choices, actions, judgements, etc. All girls declare they hate to have their skirts flying above their knees when cycling, and that they would be very interested in any smart little device to prevent this happening. Such devices actually exist, but they cannot be sold.

All men talk about their car as a practical object of necessity — but what car manufacturers sell most of are nevertheless impractical chromium-plated monsters that are extraordinarily difficult to crawl in and out of. Shoe shops quite seriously try to attract customers with the slogan:

"We also have shoes that are comfortable to walk in."

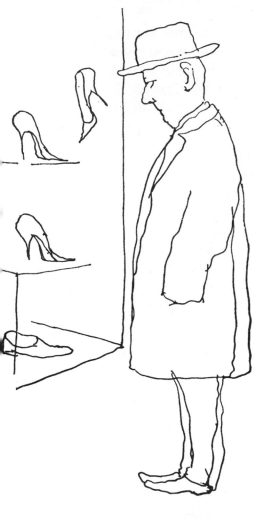

So there are two paths we can take: one is try to deny and suppress our emotions and force ourselves to think sensibly. In this way we run the risk of fooling ourselves. (See also Morals).

The other way is to admit to our emotions, accept our feelings and let them come out into the daylight. By being suspicious of all the judgements we pass on the basis of what we feel (and not until then) we shall have taken a step towards becoming practitioners of common sense.   *s.h.*

Sensitivity: See Erogenous; Fantasies, sexual; Petting, Masturbation; and Titillation, sexual.

Serving: See Mating.

Sex determination: Can mean two things, firstly a decision by the parents whether they want to have a boy or a girl. There are any number of methods and tips said to be of help in deciding this matter.

If we ask our acquaintances why they brush their teeth, most of them answer: "In order to remove particles of food from the mouth and keep our teeth looking as nice as possible." Any dentist can tell us that we should brush our teeth after each meal. When do we — and the dentists — brush our teeth? After every meal? No! Most people brush their teeth in the mornings.

Those are just a couple of minor examples. There are thousands more. We are none of us so full of common sense as we would like to think ourselves.

No certain method is known today, even though we know quite a lot about how the matter is decided. A man's sperm cells contain either an x-chromosome or a y-chromosome. If an x sperm cell fertilizes the ovum, the child will be a girl. If it is a y sperm cell it will be a boy. If we were now able to discover that x sperm cells lived further inside the vagina than y sperm cells, or that they were heavier, it would perhaps give us a chance of influencing the sex of the child, and this would be of great importance, e.g. from a hereditary viewpoint.

A lot of experimenting is being done, but so far we still have no idea what we are supposed to do to be certain — or even to provide a reasonable chance — of determining the result.

The other kind of sex determination is that of deciding whether the actual foetus is a boy or a girl. After all, it would be quite interesting to know at an early stage, i.e. during the mother's pregnancy, whether the child was going to be a boy or a girl. It can, for instance, be of importance in the case of certain hereditary diseases that can only be transferred through one sex or the other.

It *is* possible to go in and extract a sample of the liquid enveloping the child during pregnancy and predetermine the child's sex with a fairly large degree of certainty.

But an intervention of this sort is only carried out when there are serious reasons for wishing to do so — for it is risky.

In the case of hermaphrodite · births it is likewise possible to determine the true sex of the child by observing certain cells under a microscope. (See also Bisexuality).

Sex life under special conditions: What we are thinking of here is sex life in prisons, during wartime, on expeditions to the North Pole, at boarding schools, etc. In other words under conditions during which the opportunity of being together with a member of the other sex is hindered or reduced.

It is generally realized that sexual urges in prisoners are often somewhat reduced.

The result is that they believe they have been given special medicine in their food — medicine to reduce their sexual urges. It would appear that such medicaments do not exist — at any rate, certain experts deny it.

These and other prisoners as a rule manage with the help of masturbation ·, but a few take up relationships with other prisoners of the same sex, i.e. homosexual relationships. The interesting thing about these homosexual relationships is that they seldom last, in other words when the prisoner is set free, heterosexual relationships are generally resumed.

We are also aware that wars, expeditions and boarding-schools can result in temporary homosexual behaviour.

There is nothing really surprising about it — except for people who believe that permanent homosexuality arises as a result of seduction ·. (See also Satisfaction, sexual.)   *i.h.*

Sexual clinics: For years we have talked about the need of places where people can go and obtain advice and guidance on sexual matters. One may call them Family Counsel Offices, Sexual Clinics, Family Planning Institutions, Unmarried Mothers Offices and lots of other things.

It is all a question of helping to solve the difficulties of living together.

It is therefore pleasant to find that the town of Aarhus has a sexual clinic that has been set up by the town council — a clinic where those with means as well as those without can apply for help.

In Copenhagen, an association of women doctors has set up a similar clinic for Family Planning ·.

The Danish Women's Society (Dansk Kvindesamfund) has a clinic in Kolding.

Mødrehjælpen's · offices all over the country also provide some guidance.

Finally, the Association for Mental Hygiene (Landsforeningen for Mental-hygiejne) has its advisory clinics in Copenhagen, Horsens, Odense, Randers, Næstved, Aabenraa, Aalborg and Esbjerg — admittedly advice on all human problems, but this means including the sexual ones.

However, we are still short of clinics. We are short of knowledge about sex life — in other words we need money for research and support in general.

What we are more short of than anything else, however, is general acceptance of the fact that sex life involves great difficulties. Young people should be given information, not scared out of their wits.

It should be just as acceptable a thing to concern oneself with sex as with atoms — both in theory and in practice.

Professorships in the most peculiar subjects exist. Is it only sex-missionaries like us who find it strange that no professorship in sexuology exists?   *i. & s.h.*

Sexual Derailment: See Perversity.

Sexual differences, sexual character: Here we can differentiate between the bodily and mentally different factors between men and women, between the physical and the psychical.

The physical differences are fairly clear.

Apart from the difference in genital organs · a man has a deeper voice, a beard, other hair growth, a more powerful and larger body, narrower hips and greater strength than a woman, who, however, has breasts.

When we go over to the mental differences it immediately becomes more difficult. We talk about passive girls and aggressive · men, about a woman's greater mental sensitivity, her interest in feminine occupations and lack of practical talents, etc.; but the study of other peoples reveals that not many of these characteristics are to be found among all of them. On the contrary — now and again we find the parts played to be in direct opposition. We can find tribes whose women become chiefs and take decisions and sit on the council while the men run the homes, doll themselves up and generally fool around.

It is on the island of Bali — so one hears — that they say: "Never confide a secret to a man — he can't keep it!"

In certain African tribes — and in guereza monkeys — it is felt unwise to entrust the difficult job of looking after the young to the females. They are allowed to give their children milk, but the men look after them.

As far as can be seen, society · has decreed — without asking and without investigating the matter — that women must kindly toe the line and behave in this, that and the other way. And men had better see to it that they are brave, active, practical and efficient. And just as happens in so many other spheres of activity, we human beings submit obediently and permit ourselves to be brought up to play the part fortune happens to have allocated to us — according to the society we are born into. The human mind permits itself to be moulded quite easily — it is plastic — and the majority of us play our roles so well we manage to believe them without much difficulty. We actually feel we are like this, that we were born like this. But then we so often let ourselves be fooled by our emotions. So we cannot really trust in them.

— — —

We shall probably never find out exactly which common, innate qualities can be called masculine and which can be called feminine — if such exist at all. We must accept the conditions imposed upon us, but at the same time realize how easy it is for us to make mistakes and how careful we should be about believing in what is innate and irrevocable in the human mind.

Putting human beings in different booths haphazardly like this can naturally make for extraordinarily great human adjustment problems. It is remarkable that things have not gone worse than they have. One of the most fascinating and famous books containing these deliberations is Margaret Mead's *Sex and Temperament in Three Primitive Societies*.

(See also Aggression Inversion, Homosexuality and Hermaphroditism).

i. & s.h.

Sexual dreams and symbols: See Freud, Psychoanalysis, Dreams; Fantasies, sexual; and Symbol.

Sexual education: See Education, sexual.

Sexual enlightenment: See Enlightenment, sexual.

Sexual ethics: See Morals.

Sexual excitement: See Titillation, sexual.

Sexual fantasies: See Dreams; Fantasies, sexual; and Masturbation Technique.

Sexual glands: The gonads. In a woman these are the ovaries, which produce the ova, or eggs, and in a man the testicles, which produce sperm. (See Genital Organs and Fertilization).

Sexual Gymnastics: Really a derisive term for all the different positions that have been recommended in the course of time for sexual intercourse. It is really a thoughtless way of putting it, and it is pointless to throw a touch of ridicule over all the genuine attempts that are made to help people get on better in a sphere that has been encumbered with so many taboos ·. It is the result of ignorance to believe that only one position or one method of having sexual intercourse is the right one. Neither nature, the history of civilization nor anthropological research would appear to indicate anything to this effect.

246

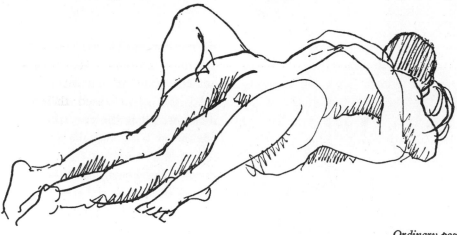

Ordinary position.

It must also be mentioned that all these taboos render us less conscious of the muscles on the floor of the pelvis. In this connection various gymnastic exercises can make us more conscious of them and help us to use them to greater advantage. Many women who have learnt to relax properly for entirely different reasons, for instance birth relaxation, know about the pleasant sensations that may result as a bi-product of training in conscious relaxation ·.   *i. & s.h.*

Sexual hormones: See Hormones.

Sexual hygiene: All the things which make us mentally and physically healthier in our sex-life.

Sexual intercourse, also technique involved: By sexual intercourse we as a rule understand the situation whereby a man has his penis · inside a woman's vagina (see Genital Organs, female).

Furthermore we talk about 'the ordinary form of sexual intercourse' which means the position and technique commonest in the western world — in Europe and the USA.

But the fact that it happens to be the commonest in some societies · does not necessarily mean that it is the right one, the only right one, or even the most suitable. It only means that it happens to be the form of sexual intercourse we in our society have chosen to adopt and authorize.

The ordinary form of sexual intercourse is when the woman lies stretched out on her back with her legs more or less spread apart and the man lies on top of her. They are facing each other, and the man can support himself on his knees and elbows. Sometimes the woman may have a pillow under the small of her back — not under her bottom but a little further up the back. (See also Bed).

As already stated, this position is used a good deal and many are happy and satisfied with it. But, as we are able to learn from nature's · multiplicity, it is one-sidedness that is perverse ·. And this position has been recommended — insisted upon, in fact — with a display of fanaticism which was very one-sided.

The harmonious person, however, has several possibilities.

The sensation of the penis inside the vagina is of great importance to the man's orgasm ·. In sexual relationships there are other things besides actual intercourse that have an effect on the woman's orgasm. (See also Titillation, sexual; and Petting).

Variety is the spice of life. It is not the person who knows how to vary his life that is perverse, but the person who is only able to satisfy his hunger on watery porridge.

There is good reason to stress this point strongly because there are still people who believe it is impudent and somewhat immoral if anybody suggests that they might like to try making love differently.

In the sphere of food we have, fortunately, got as far as accepting the fact that it is possible to satisfy one's hunger on other things besides meat-balls and gravy.

We can also learn from the sexual habits of other peoples. In the East they have a wide selection of positions for sexual intercourse, and statues of men and women entwined in the most imaginative positions decorate their temples. The ancient Romans and Greeks probably used the so-called straddling position most, which is the one where the man lies on his back and the woman sits on top of him with her legs apart. In this position the woman has a slightly greater chance of moving and thereby the better possibility of direct titillation · of the clitoris.

In another position, both partners lie on their sides. The woman can kneel with her back towards the man. They can stand up and sit down, etc., etc. There is no particular reason for describing all the endless different variations and their advantages and disadvantages. They can be looked up in the majority of books on sexual enlightenment for grown-ups, e.g. van de Velde: "The Perfect Marriage", the Danish doctor, Fabricius-Møller's books on sexual relationships, Hoffmeyer's *Samliv og Samfund* (Sex Life and Society), in Axel Tofte's books, etc.

The important thing is that both partners should give themselves (and each other) permission to experiment — that they do not, as a result of misplaced modesty · and shyness, spoil their relationship entirely for each other by not daring to experiment their way to something new and possibly more exciting.

The way (or ways) they discover mutually is something they should also be fully entitled to use without small-minded moralizing · on the part of anybody else.

Furthermore, it is important to realize that even though some women can have

*The woman should use the man as **a** means . . .*

an orgasm from the sheer fact of the presence of the penis inside their vagina during intercourse, this is not the usual thing. Even though some women enjoy the feeling of a penis inside their vagina, it is not the vagina itself that is the focal point for their physical titillation, nor does it liberate their feelings of erotic pleasure. It is the clitoris (see Genital Organs, female) that arouses the erotic feeling of pleasure in a woman in the same way that the penis — in particular the tip of the penis — that arouses erotic pleasure in the man.

Whilst a man as a rule can easily tolerate interruptions and disturbances during intercourse, it would appear that many women prefer a more constant, uninter-rupted, undistracted influence — direct or indirect — being brought to bear on the clitoris itself, the tip of the clitoris, the whole clitoris, or the area round the clitoris.

There is an old, widespread superstition to the effect that it should be the common and normal thing for both partners to obtain orgasm · simultaneously. This mis-understanding has resulted in many couples erroneously believing themselves to be abnormal and 'all wrong'.

It is not common for both the man and the woman to obtain sexual satisfaction, i.e. orgasm, simultaneously.

It can be said that simultaneous orgasm is lovely when it occasionally happens.

The commonest thing in instances where sexual intercourse results in both partners having an orgasm is that the woman first obtains hers in one way or another, after which the man has his. And as far as the man is concerned, the sensation of having his penis inside the woman's vagina will often be of great importance to his orgasm.

249

— — —

As already mentioned, it is important that the woman should use the man as a means of obtaining her orgasm. It is not the man who is supposed to give her an orgasm. He is merely to offer himself as an implement, a means for her to employ if she wishes to do so. Her orgasm is not a present she makes him, nor is it a feather in his cap, nor a scalp in the belt of his vanity.

In exactly the same way she should not give him his satisfaction as a present, but offer him the possibility of sexual satisfaction.

The words 'Thou shalt love thy neighbour as thyself' are the direct progenitors of misplaced consideration · in love-making.

We believe, on the contrary, that we should love ourselves just a little bit more than the other person. We should show ourselves a little more consideration — think a little more about ourselves.

It is only in this way that both partners can achieve a healthy balance in their relationship together.

— — —

There are people who have sexual intercourse once a month and others who have it several times a day. Thus nobody can say how often one must, should or may have intercourse. One can only use oneself and the other person as a yardstick — with confidence in oneself. One must adapt oneself a little to the other person, and here as a rule it is the woman who has to adapt herself a bit to the man.

A woman is generally always able to have intercourse, i.e. is always potent ·. And a man has many opportunities of making himself independent of his potency.

If the man wants to have intercourse more frequently that the woman it is important that he does not demand of her that she should join in fully too, i.e. demand that she should have an orgasm every time too.

On the other hand women should not be stingy either — even though they may not be madly interested in placing themselves at his disposal. It is a little more difficult if it is the woman who wants to have intercourse more often than the man, but in this case it is important that they select — as already mentioned — a technique that makes them independent of his erection ·. Perhaps one should call it a 'togetherness technique'. (See also Petting).

It must also be mentioned that masturbation · in marriage is not a fiasco or in any way unworthy, but an entirely reasonable and natural way of satisfying one's sexual desires. One cannot expect two different people to have precisely the same sexual needs. In particularly strained situations — when reading up for exams, for instance — masturbation will often be a reasonable way of obtaining orgasm.

As regards intercourse during menstruation and pregnancy, a good deal of superstition exists too, and many seize happily every opportunity to forbid and warn. (See also Abstinence).

Sometimes we ought to have a little more confidence in our desires and a little less confidence in the various authorities who are so eager to forbid one thing and another — authorities who have made such appalling errors before, for instance in their unreasonable fight against masturbation.

In any case it should be repeated that forms of togetherness also exist in which the penis is not inserted into the vagina — and that these forms can also be made use of in cases when one may feel ordinary intercourse unpleasant for one reason or another.   *i. & s.h.*

Sexual urges: See Sexual need.

Sexual need: Can be briefly defined as the sum of all the powers within a human being that work together with the object of obtaining sexual satisfaction, or orgasm ·. They represent a vital human need of the same intensity as the need to eat or drink, but in our society we do not allow this fact prominence.

— — —

We give sexual urges a place in the corner, in the doghouse, and suppress them with difficulty. In by far the majority of human beings sexual urges are so strong we cannot permit ourselves to neglect their existence. (See also Kinsey). It is not so very many generations ago that it was asserted that normal women had no sexual urges (see also Frigidity) and what was worse, many believed it. It was not until Kinsey gave us his reports that we at long last obtained a measure of clarity concerning the extent of human sexual urges and the many different ways in which they can manifest themselves.

— — —

Many have realized this, including Freud ·, whose theories concerning the mental lives of human beings have been of very great importance. It was a remark made by the famous French psychiatrist Charcot that put Freud on the trail: "It's always something to do with sex"

C'est toujours la chose genitale, said Charcot, speaking of the causes of mental sufferings.

— — —

Freud was not quite so dogmatic about it as Charcot — and as Freud's opponents like to claim. But he certainly dragged sex out of its place of disgrace in the corner and presented it to our unwilling eyes.

And he had to shout very loudly, because nobody wanted to look.

— — —

People have wondered why so many mental troubles always have perforce to be traced back to sexual urges. But it is not so very strange.

Let us try a hypothetical experiment. Let us imagine that sexual urges had become just as frank and natural a need as thirst, but that the same violent taboo with which sexual urges are now saddled had been imposed upon hunger for food instead — with the result that our mental troubles were no longer the result of problems connected with our sexual urges, but that instead we found ourselves plagued by serious neuroses on account of conflicts arising concerning the forbidden need for food.

We would go round with permanently bad consciences. We would fight against our hunger and have to give in to it every day. We would eat on the sly, and when we were full we would promise ourselves never to do it again. We would be deeply shocked if anybody started eating in public. With gentle horror we would tell each other about people who had been caught indulging in perverse eating habits such as chicken roasted on a spit or Malayan Curry. We would giggle at dirty food recipes in pornographic cookery books.

In time, however, liberality of thought would triumph. People would be allowed to survive on watery porridge every day provided they did so with moderation.

In fact they would even be allowed to *enjoy* their watery porridge as long as they promised never to tell anybody else about it — and in particular never admitted it to their children. Apart from which it would naturally only be permitted for the purpose of staying alive.

But we are of course saddled with our taboo on sexual urges and must therefore try and make the best of things the way they are. But we none the less have the right to criticize and attempt to revise the worst consequences of the present lop-sided state of affairs whereby such a lovely thing has become the black sheep of the need-family. (See also Epicurean and Erotomania).   *i. & s.h.*

Sexual neuroses: See Neuroses, sexual.

Sexual organs: See Genital Organs.

Sexual similarities: In order to understand the article on titillation it is important for a man to realize that a woman's sexual organs anatomically resemble his own on many points.

It has often been mentioned that the tip of the penis · is the centre of a man's feelings of sexual pleasure, and that the clitoris is the corresponding centre in a woman. It is rhythmical stimulation stroking or other form of irritation that produces the height of sexual pleasure, the orgasm ·. It is the glans · in particular that is furnished with many nerves in both the man and the woman.

The three diagrams illustrating this article are all very schematic. The clitoris has intentionally been drawn a little larger and the penis slightly smaller than in reality in order to stress the points of similarity.

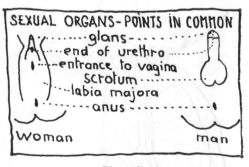

Figure 1.

Diagram No. 1. is thus a schematic illustration of the male and female genital organs seen from outside and from below.

The entire clitoris in a woman correspond to the tip of the penis in a man.

The larger vaginal lips (*labia majora*) in a woman correspond to the scrotum in a man. Rhytmical pulls at the skin of the larger lips or at the skin of the scrotum will cause the skin on the clitoris or round the tip of the penis to glide over the sensitive tip, or glans. Excitation of this kind may in some instances even result in orgasm. One might call such an orgasm a 'labial orgasm' in the case of a woman or a 'scrotal orgasm' in the case of a man, but in actual fact they are merely an indirect 'penis-head orgasm' and an indirect 'clitoral orgasm'.

Diagram 2 (a and b) shows some of the muscles on the floor of the pelvis seen from below, namely the muscles forming part of the sexual 'limb' in both the man and the woman. It so happens that the muscles in both the clitoris and the penis

continue backwards in the muscles of the floor of the pelvis and thus produce one long 'limb' in both sexes.

We can see that there are two essential differences:

(a). The man's urinary canal terminates at the very tip of the penis, while the woman's urinary canal ends just below and behind the tip.

(b). In the woman, the muscle fibres in the limb are forced apart in order to make room for an opening. The 'limb' has — so to speak — a hole bored in it slightly larger than the anus ·.

The muscle fibres in the 'limb' in both the man and the woman extend from the tip of the limb all the way past the anus and end behind it.

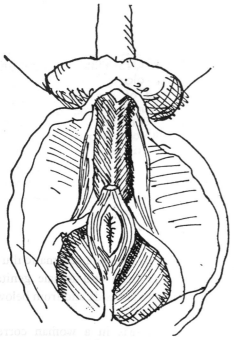

Figure 2 a.
Muscles on floor of pelvis. Man.

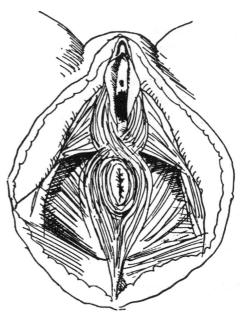

Figure 2 b.
Muscles on floor of pelvis. Woman.

If any fibre anywhere at all on either the male or the female 'limb' is touched, the sensation will be transferred through the muscular tissue and out to the very tip of the clitoris or penis.

Thus, theoretically speaking, titillation or stimulation even right back in the region of the anus would be able to result in an orgasm by reason of the indirect effect on the sensitive parts in front. But in practice this would be very rare.

Thus rhythmical movements inside the vagina can be transplanted through the walls of the vagina to the musculature at the entrance to the vagina and from here out to the tip of the 'limb', i.e. the clitoris.

This meticulous and yet schematic explanation will serve to support the information given concerning indirect and direct clitoral orgasms · and the superstition about a 'deep vaginal orgasm', which is described in greater detail in the article on titillation.

In the majority of cases it is a question of years of training before a woman can become capable of deriving benefit from these indirect forms of clitoral excitation to the extent of obtaining an orgasm from them. (See also Practice). A few women, however, are able to take advantage of these indirect, diffuse forms of stimulation fairly quickly, whilst others — and this is to say the majority — although able in time to derive pleasure from them, seldom get an actual orgasm from them.

The orgasms all these women have are by no means inferior, less satisfying or more immature — as has been claimed formerly. The fact is quite simply that it is the direct, more straightforward form of clitoris tickling that generally leads to an orgasm. *i. & s.h.*

Sexuality: Means being in possession of sexual urges ·.

Sexuology, sexuologists: The science and the scientists who concern themselves with sex — attempting to increase our knowledge about sex life.

We all have a curious as well as a personal interest in this side of life. The fact that Kinsey's · two reports on sex life in the USA became best-sellers despite their heavy weight of tables proved that people bought them not so much on account of any sober, professional interest in the subject, but because of a warm, subjective interest: "What are other people like? What can I learn about myself?"

If only we could get as far as recognizing the naturalness · of this subjective curiosity! Far too many people buy books with exciting pictures and interesting information on the sly — but officially declare their disapproval of pornography ·.

Kinsey speaks about closed and open cultures — what we really do and what we say we do. Our object must be to reduce the distance between the two. *i.h.*

Shoes: Just ordinary shoes — the kind we wear on our feet. If anybody should be in any doubt as to whether a society can make the most unreasonable demands on its members — and have them obediently fulfilled — just take a look at our shoes.

It applies to men's shoes, but in particular to women's shoes, that a state of dictatorship exists — a relentless demand that we adapt ourselves. (See Morals). One cannot draw a picture of a soul (though see Personality). But shall we pretend that we have drawn three symbols for souls? Shall we pretend that the three pairs of feet are human souls from three different societies instead?

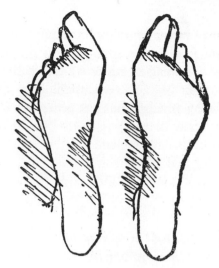

Mild, almost unnoticeable tyranny has resulted in conformity.

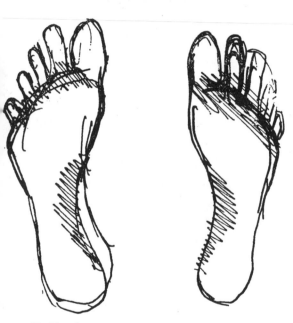

Nothing has attempted to transform or subjugate these feet.

First, then, we have a soul that has been allowed to develop with the least possible external pressure, in harmony with itself.

The next soul has been locked up a little ever since infancy. It has not been tor- tured and pestered, but it has become slightly deformed over such a long period of time that it has hardly noticed it. This soul has, let us note, grown up in our own society.

The last soul has been through very rough treatment. It has submitted to it because it was the custom of the times in that part of the world — and it was allowed a number of years to grow accustomed to it too. This little soul will probably never learn to stand on its own little legs.

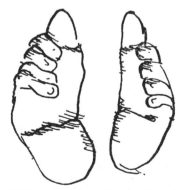

In the Chinese nurseries of former times, feet like these were only produced with tears.

It may sound a little sentimental to talk about foot-shaped souls, but we should bear one thing in mind: we are sharing the right — the responsibility — of deciding whether the next generation of little souls is to approach the first little soul in its development, whether it is to be crippled like the last little soul, or merely like our own little souls. (See also Suicide).   *i. & s.h.*

Shy, shyness: It is very unpleasant to be shy. It is something from which young people suffer, especially during puberty, but many go on being shy later in life.

One of the ways of getting over shyness is to get to know oneself and accept oneself, but it sounds easier than it is. Some find it helps if they discover there is some subject or accomplishment at which they are expert; in this way they establish firm ground on which they can stand, a point of departure. Others go to elocution classes in order to overcome the fear of speaking to an audience. But behind shyness there lies a tremendous desire to show off, to be the centre of attraction, (see Exhibitionism) — a very natural, but unsatisfied desire to please.

Little children are not shy — on the contrary. They can walk up and down a dining-table stark naked at a banquet while all the guests laugh and titter. (See Modesty and Vanity).   *i.h.*

Simulate: Means to pretend, which in the sphere of sexual relationships can be a serious and dangerous thing. Far too many women pretend to their husbands that they have orgasms — far, far more than men would ever dream. They groan and twist and sigh — without feeling anything at all, or without feeling enough.

In so doing, they lock themselves up in a kind of loneliness that puts them at an ever-increasing distance from the man.

It is a dangerous habit to get into, because it is something they do in order to be left in peace (see also Lie); to be spared the man's relentless demand that they should have an orgasm. (See Consideration).

All human beings — including women — would like to have orgasms, would like to satisfy the sexual need common to all.

It is therefore important that a man should offer a woman many chances of obtaining sexual satisfaction so that she may — for her own sake — achieve this end.

It is reasonable that a man should make demands concerning his own sexual satisfaction · at intervals, and it should not cost a woman too much sacrifice to allow him to have such demands met. But it may irritate her, and she may use it as a weapon against him in the course of some squabble about something else.

It is obvious that it is not much fun for her to have to place her body at his disposal, especially if she perhaps would gladly join in the pleasures too, but cannot for one reason or another. On the other hand, as already mentioned, it is not entirely unreasonable on the part of the man — and she can probably persuade herself to let him have what he wants, just as one can make food for somebody else without necessarily being hungry oneself. It should be possible for a woman to go this far now and again.

But if the man, in his vanity, demands that she should stuff herself with food too, i.e. that she should also obtain sexual satisfaction, a store of anger, or aggressiveness, is built up — one that can start things off on a vicious circle and have unforeseeable consequences.

Unfortunately we men are very vain · on this score. We take it as a personal affront to our manliness if we are unable to satisfy her. We become insulted, bad-humoured and stubborn; we make demands, and demands can have an utterly paralysing effect.

What easily happens next is that she does everything she thinks he likes — and he does everything he thinks she likes. Then we are back to Jack Spratt and his wife again, and the jokes about how a wife and a husband have done some nonsensical, distasteful thing for 25 years because they thought (mistakenly) that the other party would like it. But from a psychological viewpoint such stories are tragedies, for the result is that they are both left with an enormous bill which the other can never pay.

To be an egoist · in the wrong way can have disastrous effects on mutual sexual relationships. Consideration · and good breeding· are concepts we are accustomed to praise and encourage. But they can be fatal things to introduce into a couple's love life unless handled with the greatest care — and combined with healthy egoism.

Unfortunately it can be highly dangerous to a relationship if the woman suddenly admits she has been simulating. Very few men will be able to take it calmly. Perhaps she can suggest instead that she is having difficulties with her orgasm. She may possibly suggest changes, a little experimentation · — but without making greater demands on the man's powers of endurance. (See Potency, and Titillation, sexual).

Vanity· and potency worship·, misplaced consideration· — all these can cause us to make these mistakes and more besides. Unfortunately it is probably not enough to explain the pitfalls. We must make do with hoping that if we become intellectually conscious of the mistakes we make it will mean we have made a little progress. Perhaps the emotional part will follow on after the intellectual understanding of the problems. It is conceivable that in this way women might obtain the support and encouragement they need to put us men in our places with a few well-chosen words now and again. (See also Potency, Ejaculation, Impotency; Titillation, sexual). *s.h.*

Sissy: If a boy or a man is very sensitive or 'soft' he is called a sissy. In other words, girls and women are suspected of being particularly weak. There are, however, societies who believe that the female sex is the stronger of the two — perhaps they are right.

Is it women who faint flat on their backs when they are vaccinated? How many men could stand having to feed an infant all round the clock as well as look after a house? How many men would be able to stick all the trouble involved in having a baby at all? How many men would use condoms, one cannot help wondering, if they had to go and see a doctor and have their measurements taken first?   *s.h.*

Slave: The expression 'humble slave' is an expression often used in heterosexual · as well as homosexual · sado-masochistic relationships (see Governess).

Slave trade, white: A favourite film theme because it provides an opportunity of showing women being subjected to "a fate worse than death". As a rule the accounts are romanticized, but white slave trade still exists.

Young girls are lured into signing contracts to perform in various capacities in foreign countries. In this branch, as in so many other branches, it is not unusual for the girls to find things much easier if they are a little obliging and sexually charming towards the people with whom they sign contracts. Later on it may transpire that their performance also includes having a drink or two with the male guests.

The customer has certain rights, and one likes to be polite too, so a logical path leads straight to prostitution ·. It is lovely to be admired by many (see also Exhibitionism). There are probably no men or women who will not admit it. For this reason the careers of film stars, mannequins, advertising models and dancers are envied by other young women. It is the road to fame and worship.

— — —

It is a hard road. If the well-known, envied and famous men and women would speak, they would be able to tell of many humiliations and of the price they have had to pay. Some are also willing to pay the price in the form of proper (or semi) prostitution. Many men would probably also be glad to pay if it would secure them the career they dream about. Let us not explode with indignation.

The sad thing, however, is that in most cases the road does not lead to fame and worship, but the other way, to a life that is nowhere near so romantic, involving drink, self-reproach, loneliness and the contempt of society. The reverse side of the medal is far larger than the front.

Many married women have dreamt at intervals of being stewardesses, singers, etc., etc. But it is a bargain one is obliged to strike and keep. It is a matter of adding up the cost. One cannot have a husband and children and a chummy life at home and at the same time charge round the length and breadth of the country in order to perform at village hall social evenings. And one cannot start appearing in films, on the radio or TV straight from one's armchair. At one point or other in a career of this nature one has to ask oneself frankly: Which ambition is the stronger? Which dream would one rather have come true?

What has been said about a woman's path to praise and power applies to businessmen and politicians too. Men, too, must find a way of realizing as many of their dreams as possible. They, too, have to draw up their accounts: what do I want most? Ensconced in the lap of the family,

the other role may appear the most attractive. The politician sighs on the other hand: "If only I had chosen a more peaceful existence!"

We cannot expect to find what would make us most satisfied. We can only hope to select the sphere of activity in which we can be least dissatisfied.   *i. & s.h.*

Sleep: It is said one cannot sin when sleeping or half-sleeping. Therefore there are some people whose sex lives take place in the form of masturbation or in the company of their loved one when in this state of irresponsibility. It can be quite a charming way of making a start. Others can be terribly frightened by the slightest approach · made to them when they are sleeping. Sleep-walking and other acts while asleep are fairly rare, though perhaps a little more frequent in children.

During the last century a lady woke up one night feeling she was being pushed.

Somebody went in and out and hands touched her every now and again. As she was not expecting anybody and had fallen asleep alone, she was so terrified she fainted.

Much later on she came to her senses and by the light of the dawning day saw that her butler (who, incidentally, was a genuine sleep-walker) had laid dinner for fourteen people on her bed.

But of course this sort of thing is rather unsusual, especially nowadays when so few people have servants.

Talking during sleep on the other hand is quite common — again, especially in children. (See also Bed).   *s.h.*

Smells: We all know the value of perfume in arousing erotic feelings. Less attention is probably paid to the part played in our sex lives by our own body smells — or those of our partner. We all smell very differently—and different parts of us smell differently too. Our armpits have one particular smell, our genital organs another. The hair on our heads has its own special smell. All these particular smell sensations are by no means as pronounced as the impressions we receive via sight or sound, but they nevertheless contribute to our total impression of another person. When kissing, the smell of the skin of the face of the person we are kissing plays a greater part than we notice.

These smells are very personal things.

While we get on fine with our own various smells, we are often extremely intolerant towards those of others.   *i.h.*

Snake: A very common fertility and sex symbol (see Symbol) as a rule for the man's penis ·.

Sneeze, sneezing: It has been contended that there must be a direct connection between a person's ability to have a thoroughly good sneeze and the ability to have a satisfying orgasm ·.

There is probably little likelihood of a direct connection — but possibly an indirect one. It is not improbable that there are people who are equally inhibited · in both spheres. We cannot assume that the lady who is only able to let out a feeble "Atishoo!" must also be inhibited in her sex life, but it is possible. Letting off a thoroughly good sneeze is a natural, spontaneous, frank action of which some people really are a little afraid in the same way that they are afraid of being spontaneous and letting themselves go in their sex life.

There really are people who believe it is better manners, more cultivated and well-brought-up to press sneeze, mucus and bacteria into the various sinus channels and cavities of the head by holding their sneeze back. There are many well-brought-up and inhibited ladies and gentlemen of this type who, rather than sneeze calmly, vigorously and frankly, let off a series of splutters and sputters that cause everybody around them to put down their knife and fork and look at them. These people often say they prefer not to arouse attention by letting out a single violent sneeze. Naturally there is no need to trumpet a shower-bath out over one's surroundings. If there is no time to get out a handkerchief one can always bend down towards the ground so as not to be a nuisance to other people.

Most of those who splutter instead of sneezing properly have more or less lost their ability to sneeze — they cannot even do so when they are alone out in the open air. But it can be re-learnt — bless you!

s.h.

Soap-and-water passion: A good example of the more or less ingenious way a need can be satisfied (see also Eroto-graphomania). A clear-cut mania for house-cleaning or the like may well often turn out to be a desire to busy oneself with dirt — a sort of pleasure derived from handling dirt. It is a kind of ration-alization · of this motive, for the clean-ing fanatic, who declares he hates dirt, is given an opportunity of dealing with dirt by the very process of cleaning.

— — —

There are also women who give them-selves vaginal douches several times a day. This provides them with an opportunity of handling their genital organs in an entirely permissible manner at which even the most pronounced moralist cannot take offence.

i.h.

Society: A group of people living in a community with the same habits, with the same culture in an extensive series of spheres. If the differences between neigh-bouring societies are very small we can speak of a cultural sphere. Thus we speak of the western cultural sphere, or western civilization, which comprises Europe and the USA.

In other words there has to be some dif-ference in living habits before one can speak of two different societies.

We reckon on there being some three to four thousand different societies today.

By comparing their habits and attitudes to life — their sexual habits, for instance — we obtain a small notion of what we can really permit ourselves to call universal human behaviour.

"Women are born impractical" we say, because we really do see a lot of women who fumble rather helplessly with a hammer or a pair of pincers. But when we hear that there are societies in which the women go out to work, go fishing, hunting and to market to do their bargaining while their husbands sit at home and decorate their persons, our theories about inherent female clumsiness and masculine disdain for feathers and finery get thoroughly scuppered.

We can learn by observing other societies and their habits.

First and foremost we can learn to be careful. We learn to be much more careful about stamping things as right and wrong, natural · und unnatural, normal · and abnormal, perverse · and all the other stamps we are so ready to apply. (See also Minority, Personality and "One").

It is also easier for us to see that the other societies are silly when they believe that their habits are the only right ones, that their code of morals is the result of divine intervention and cannot be revised, or that fat women with laced-up feet are the most beautiful.

But of course it is much more difficult for us to see the foolish side to the shoes · we wear and put up with. Perhaps we may

This shows a pair of lady's shoes — not that men's shoes are so very roomy or healthy either.

just reach the brink of understanding, just vaguely realize that perhaps we after all have not taken out a patent on the one and only right thing that can make human beings happy.

With a spot of luck we can advance so far as to feel a little healthy uncertainty with regard to what we feel. When we see that other peoples can tolerate, in fact even make demands concerning homosexual · behaviour in respect of all the boys in the throes of puberty without such societies perishing on this account and without the said boys acquiring a lasting taste for homosexuality, then our own fears for the homosexual seduction of our own young people must of necessity be decreased somewhat.

When it is complained that young Danish girls are led into sexual activity by their boy-friends, not because they have any particular wish, but because they are afraid of losing the boy-friend in question — then we cannot accept this concern too seriously either, considering the fact that we know of societies in which all the 10-year-old girls personally select which boy they would like to take into their hut and sleep with.

Of course this does not mean that we should adopt all the practices we observe in other societies indiscriminately. But we can learn something from their way of life and study how this custom or the other works in this or that connection.

We smile a little at the American demand that each family must 'keep up with the Joneses'. The study of other societies can also teach us that all societies at all times make colossal demands — but unnoticeable ones — concerning conformity.

"Look," says society gently to us, "with a few small alterations your backside would be able to fit beautifully into just the very same chair all the others are sitting in!"

And so dutifully we carve a hunk off one buttock and squeeze our thighs together in order to be allowed to exist. *i. & s.h.*

Sodomy: See Bestiality and Homosexuality.

Soixante-neuf: French for sixty-nine. An expression — a symbolic one — meaning the position for sexual intercourse in which the two partners lie next to each other with their heads at opposite ends — as in the figures 6 and 9 when placed together. (See also Cunnilingus and Fellatio).

Song: "He who sings in the morning will weep before night". Morning sourpusses have used proverbs like this for generations with the object of dampening good humour in others.

In a way it is a piece of abuse, but after all it originates from a human superstition to the effect that one is asking for trouble from the evil spirits if one is too cheerful about life. (See Epicurean). The proverb is thus the expression of a magic feeling in *us* completely on a par with the kind we smile at in primitive societies. (See also Words, naughty). *i.h.*

Sounds: See Noises.

Spectrophilia: Sexual intercourse with spirits, ghosts and other supernatural beings. It is not only the prosecutors of the Inquisition (see Witch Trials) who contended that others had had intercourse with the devil in the shape of a man or a woman (see Incubus and Succubus) — there have also been many unhinged persons who have believed the same thing.

There have furthermore been nuns who believed they had had intercourse with Jesus, and monks with Maria. In our day too, there are people who think supernatural beings are after them — or who believe they have seduced such beings themselves. When people behave in a manner incomprehensible to us we call them insane, but this is no explanation. The reason for these obsessions may in some cases be strict abstinence· and/or religious scruples. *i.h.*

Sperm, sperm cells: Also called sperm-atozoa, or semen. Sperm comes from the Greek word for seed, *sperma*, while *semen* is the Latin word for seed.

Sperm contains sperm cells as well as seminal fluid. The sperm is a slightly milky, smooth, likewise sticky liquid. As a rule a couple of cubic centimetres are ejaculated, and these contain several hundred million sperm cells. Sperm does not tolerate heat or acid very well, but can be deep-frozen, packed up and posted for artifical insemination·. Sperm spots are easiest to wash off with a little cold or lukewarm water — boiling water only makes them more difficult to get off.

They are also easy to remove when dry.

There are scientists who contend that sperm is supposed to have the same effect as penicillin, i.e. the power of killing bacteria, but not all are convinced as to the accuracy of this. *s.h.*

Sterility: A person who has been steri-lized· is then *sterile*.

Sterility can occur in other ways apart from sterilization. It may be the after-effects of a venereal · disease not cured in time. It may be an inflammation of the abdomen in a woman and, in rarer instances, chryptorchism in a man.

But in the majority of cases venereal diseases, inflammations of the abdomen and chryptorchism do not produce sterility.

There can be many other causes of sterility, and sterility can last for varying lengths of time — some short, some longer.

In many cases sterility can be treated with favourable results. Doctors are getting cleverer and cleverer. Some cases cure themselves. Much in connection with fertilization still needs clarifying.

Sterilize: Means to make unfertile, and is often used to mean the destruction of infectious matter. Used about people it means to operate them so as to prevent them from having children.

In men it can be done by closing off the tubes that conduct the sperm cells to the penis; in women by closing off the tubes that lead from the ovaries to the womb (see Genital Organs, female).

It is done as a rule in order to pacify, or to put an end to a risk. It may be to calm a person who is afraid of producing un-fortunate children for hereditary, genetic reasons — or because society believes that a certain risk of unfortunate children resulting from the person in question exists.

But sterilization does not only have a calming effect — does not only reduce the risks.

Sterilization does not render a person's sexual capacity any the less nor his sexual activities less frequent. But it can have a mentally paralysing effect.

Both men and women can feel themselves seriously stilted, i.e. mentally impotent, when they no longer have the possibility of having children — even though they might not have the slightest wish to avail themselves of the possibility. *i.h.*

264

At the Stork Fountain, in the centre of Copenhagen, we can still find traces of ancient Greek worship of the penis, the cult of the phallos.

Stimulance, stimulation: See Titillation, sexual; Aphrodisiacs, Alcohol.

Stories, naughty: See Jokes.

Stork, Stork Fountain in Copenhagen: In former times it was a common thing to tell children the stork had brought them into the world. Originally — or at any rate in other parts of the world — they were told it was a pelican.

In this way children were indirectly told that their parents were ashamed of the truth and that they were loath to talk about the facts of life. The stork appears in the form of a fertility symbol at the Stork Fountain in Amagertorv, Copenhagen. Around the fountain are, moreover, some small pillars inspired by Greek phallic worship. (See also Symbol).

s.h.

265

Sublimation: An expression taken from Freud's writings on psychoanalysis. Sublimation means to transfer mental energy from one area to another, as a rule from a less accepted area to more accepted.

If a man is so furious with another man that he feels he wants to strangle that man with his bare hands, his anger is this kind of mental energy. If he then, instead of choking the man, shatters an empty flower-pot with a sledge-hammer, he is changing the direction of his mental energy, i.e. his desire to choke the man, and applies it to the flower-pot instead.

This can give him a certain satisfaction ·, a certain outlet for his mental energy. And it is more acceptable to shatter a flower-pot than to choke a man.

Instead of the flower-pot he can transfer his energy even further away from his original anger. Perhaps he will sit down at the piano and play the "Apassionata" with his foot on the loud pedal.

Or — if he possesses even greater artistic talents — he may paint a picture of a thunderstorm.

In such cases we speak of his sublimating his anger, of his transferring his mental energy to another area where it is easier for him to get rid of it. There is no doubt that if none of us needed to sublimate anything, if we were all able to satisfy any and every desire directly, the world would be a dull and colourless place.

To think means to solve problems. To live is to think. We would not want to live in a world without problems, in a world where all wishes were immediately fulfilled.

Nor is it possible to do so. Every society, every human relationship, involves restrictions in man's possibilities of immediate and direct satisfaction.

So we should not be so unhappy about having to sublimate the odd wish now and again. Our sex life is one of the spheres where we particularly have to sublimate our desires. Here we are not talking about complete sexual abstinence ·, but about the various restrictions we must impose upon ourselves for various reasons. But sublimation is thus a different process from subjugation, or inhibition.

Even in the most ideal society with the really ideal code of morals, the human being will have a certain portion of sexual feelings, a certain sexual need ·, that cannot obtain a direct outlet. Here, the harmonious human being will direct his sexual energy into other channels such as a little sport, some form of excitement, or direct artistic means of expression.

Conversely it will be possible to observe that great artistic or scientific effort, including intense preparation for examinations, will often reduce the sexual urges for a time. A concentrated effort draws on the energy it requires from other spheres.   *s.h.*

Submission: (See also Giving). When Elvis Presley sings to the girl: "Be mine to-night!" the idea is that she should submit to him, give herself to him, become his. He never becomes hers.

To submit to, or give oneself to a man, is somehow reminiscent of a cow piously allowing itself to be led to the slaughter-house. This is not in the interests of either party. (See also Defeat). *i.h.*

Suck, suck-marks: Suck-marks are the blue or reddish marks that appear beneath the skin after a sucking kiss or bite.

These tongue kisses are perfectly common. There is nothing extraordinary in choosing to kiss one another all over the body, nor in the fact that one may bite or scratch a little in the process — this is no reason to be afraid of having sunk to perverse behaviour or anything abnormal in sexual relations. (See also Anilinctio). *s.h.*

Suicide: There have been countless instances of people who have committed suicide on account of sexual · problems, in other words as a rule because an over-strict society has attempted to lace them up inside a strait-jacket which they found impossible to wear.

Every society puts its members into a strait-jacket. And the majority of people can probably get used to living in their strait-jacket providing it not too tight. They believe they were born wearing it — that it forms part of their body and soul. But it should be possible to create a way of living that permits even more people to develop in harmony. *i.h.*

Superiority, struggle for: In many marriages — and many other relationships between men and women — a constant struggle for superiority goes on — a continual fight to get the upper hand.

In far too many cases only one of the partners wins time after time. In our patriarchal society it is more 'acceptable' that it should be the man who wins every time — rather than the woman — although happy couples do exist in which both partners are content that the woman should dominate.

As a rule it is better if both partners find they both win every now and again — and that the man perhaps wins just a little oftener than the woman.

Things become particularly complicated in the case of many women who fight like lions and tigers to win every time — and hate their victories. They despise the man they conquer and wish passionately that he would win — but the fellow never gets a chance.

The latter attitude occurs particularly in women who are dissatisfied with their sex, who envy their husband the fact of his being a man. In psychoanalysis the term *penisneid*, or penis-envy, is used.

It is hardly surprising that the suppressed members of a society should rebel to a certain extent against the more privileged, that they should be to a certain degree envious of them. And after all we men are privileged in many ways, even though responsibilities and duties are involved in the process. (See also Intolerance, Penis, Defeat, and Sexual Similarities). *s.h.*

Superstition: We modern people like to praise ourselves and say we are not superstitious. It is certainly true that in a number of spheres superstition has been replaced by knowledge. We no longer believe that storms and bad weather are the work of the gods; that the sun revolves round the earth, that cattle disease, blight and syphilis (see Venereal Diseases) are punishments meted out by the gods.

But there have been times when these things were officially believed. In those days they burnt scientists at the stake.

Women were not allowed to receive anaesthetics when giving birth — it was an interference with the intentions of the gods.

Queen Victoria of England, who gave her name to a very anti-sex epoch — Victorianism — has acquired eternal honour for being one of the first to let herself be given an anaesthetic during a birth. In this way she broke with the prejudiced opposition holding sway at the time.

The Catholic Church still forbids — and actively opposes — the use of contraceptives (except for the Knaus method) because they constitute intervention with the course of nature.

The use of forks was likewise actively opposed in religious quarters under the pretext that it was "God's intention that we should pick up our food with our fingers".

The Protestant Church used to oppose birth control but now no longer does so.

But the conduct of scientific research on human sex life — sexuology — is still actively opposed in many quarters. It took a professor of zoology — Kinsey — to conduct one of the investigations we have been waiting for all too long.

Modern people in the age of technique and enlightenment. Nevertheless, their daily lives are filled with superstition and likewise with problems that cannot be solved because there is still so much we do not know.

The same thing applies to superstition as to lack of knowledge, namely that we find it very difficult to acknowledge in ourselves.

A good deal of superstition still lingers in all of us. Particularly on all the subjects we know too little about, but also in daily life. (See also Epicurean and Excess).

Fortune-tellers still attract. The newspapers print our horoscopes — and we read them. We 'touch wood' for 'fun', but we remember to do so, just the same as we have our children christened without being believers ourselves, because "there might be something to it after all". We think that a tremendous amount of superstition existed in the olden days, particularly on the subject of sex. Not until the year 2000 (or perhaps later) will we be able to see how superstitious we were in the nineteen-sixties. *i. & s.h.*

Suppositories: Small 'cartridges' or cones that can be inserted into the vagina (see Genital Organs, female). Suppositories can contain sperm-destroying chemicals for birth control· purposes, or prophylactic medicaments against diseases of the vagina.

Contraceptive suppositories of this type can be used on their own by those who are not too terrified of a possible pregnancy. But they can also be used as an extra form of protection, for instance in combination with a pessary · or a condom ·. (Sperm-destroying creams also exist). *s.h.*

Surgery, plastic: See Plastic Surgery.

Sybarite: Somebody who enjoys life — something which unfortunately is often frowned upon. (See Epicurean).

Symbol: Something which can be used to represent something else.

Strictly speaking all *words* are symbols. All letters are symbols for sounds, all pictures symbols of reality. Thus we are very much accustomed to using symbols. Symbols are synonymous with culture, the foundation of all culture. We define primitive peoples as *peoples without a written language*. But primitive peoples still have a language that consists exclusively of symbols.

So the fact that there should be such great opposition to believing that in dreams, for instance, we make use of a symbol language, is really strange. It was Freud · who, in his psychoanalytical teachings, tried to tidy up the symbol language of dreams.

As our less acceptable wishes take place in particular within the sphere of our sex lives (because it is there we have our strongest taboos) it is hardly surprising that a complicated symbol language should be used especially to express sexual wishes.

But it is not only in dreams that we use symbols of a more complicated nature. We do not say in so-called polite company: "I want to go and piddle" but instead use a more complicated form of symbolism: "Would you show me the geography of your house, old boy?" — "Where can I spend a penny?" and similar subterfuges. Nor do we always say "Do you want to piddle or do big things?" which are also symbols, but perhaps "Do you want to do big business or little business?" — in other words an even more camouflaged form.

A snake is often a symbol for the penis, e.g. in dreams.

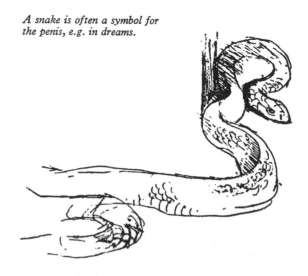

269

And of course in poetry: ".... As the lily among thorns, so is my love among the daughters ... thy teeth are as a flock of sheep that are even shorn, which came up from the washing, whereof every one bear twins, and none is barren among them ... thy two breasts are like two young roes that are twins, which feed among the lilies ... a garden inclosed is my sister, my spouse; a spring shut up, a fountain sealed ..."

Thus does the poet sing of 'his undefiled one' (see Hymen, Virginity worship). And he lets the girl sing about her friend: "Let my beloved come into his garden, and eat his pleasant fruits! ... his belly is as bright ivory overlaid with sapphires, his legs are as pillars of marble, set up on sockets of fine gold ..."

And he answers: "Thy navel is like a round goblet, which wanteth not liquor ..." She sings: "Until the day break and the shadows flee away, turn, my beloved, and be thou like a roe or a hart upon the mountains of Bether."

In spite of the somewhat involved symbolism, nobody can be in any doubt as to the meaning. Precisely the same symbols are used as those we are familiar with in dreams with sexual wishes.

The above quotations have been plucked at random from The Song of Solomon in the Old Testament. *s.h.*

Syphilis: See Venereal Diseases.

Syringe, vaginal: See Irrigator.

T

Taboos and traditions: These are what we call rules and restrictions that have no practical foundation but which are the result of custom or religious teaching.

We must not steal from each other. We must not attack each other. These are rules that have practical considerations. We are accustomed to regarding taboos as forms of prohibition existing amongst ignorant, superstitious, primitive peoples. We smile in a superior fashion when natives throw themselves on the ground and dare not look up for fear that something dreadful will happen to them if they gaze upon their king's countenance.

If we were to explain to a man from Mars why the statues in the parks wear fig-leaves, and why men and women on the beach have to wear little pieces of clothing that hide a little bit on men and a little bit more on women — we would find it very difficult to explain the difference between us and primitive peoples to him.

It is terribly difficult to see all one's own taboo rules. Just like morals and tastes, they have a tendency to become part of our mental make-up from birth. If one has worn a not-too-uncomfortable strait-jacket ever since birth, and then somebody comes along and says, "What's that you've got on?" one would answer,

"Got on? *I* haven't got anything on!"

And if he then points at the strait-jacket, we would say: "Oh, that! I'm not wearing that, old boy. I was born with it!" This is the way things are with customs, morals and taboos.

Of course there is nobody who can just take off his strait-jacket and throw it away. It has actually grown on fairly permanently and become part of the body.

We can loosen the straps a little here and there so that we can move a little more easily, and above all we can make it quite clear to ourselves that it *is* a strait-jacket into which we were laced after birth; that it is not natural ·; that it is not something entirely unchangeable; and that it is not exactly a product of common sense, but that it is something which has allied itself with our emotions.

It is easier for us to see a taboo that has been discarded. Today we can all see that it was not masturbation at all but the taboo that was dangerous to people's health.

When we have to decide whether a rule is practical or merely rests on tradition, we have the possibility of observing all other societies collectively. There are such great differences in the customs upheld all over the world that the rules we find in *all* societies must surely be more strongly founded than on mere custom and tradition — they must be common to all mankind.

There are also a number of relatively harmless and pointless taboos — for instance that fresh hot, gooey white bread is supposed to be unhealthy. Of course a number of very charming traditions exist too — but there are good grounds for taking up taboos and traditions for the purpose of thorough revision. We still have taboos that result in mental sufferings and tragedies. Our strait-jacket is not equally easy to wear for everybody. There is nobody whom it fits exactly.

i. & s.h.

Tampon: The term is used as a rule about a cotton wool tampon designed to absorb menstrual blood when it flows out through the vagina (see Genital Organs, female) during menstruation. Broadly speaking there are three forms of absorbent apparatus for use during menstruation.

1. A pad of cotton wool wrapped in gauze and worn outside the genital organs.

2. An ordinary piece of absorbent cotton wool that is placed between the large vaginal lips (see Genital Organs, female).

3. An ordinary piece of cotton wool, or a compressed cotton wool tampon. This is inserted inside the actual vagina.

All three forms are used, and all three are popular. *i.h.*

Taste: Tastes differ, we say, generously, without always respecting them anyway.

We find it confoundedly difficult to understand anybody who fails to like chocolate or roast chicken. We demand of others that they should think the same way as we do.

An Englishman once pointed at a dish of honest Danish beer-and-bread soup and asked "Have you had it, or are you going to?" On occasions like these we catch a glimpse of the fact that other people have different tastes.

In the sphere of sexual relationships we are just as eager to chivvy others into the fold in order to make them as 'normal' as we believe ourselves to be. Normality is a much wider concept than many would have it to be. (See also Smells, Fashion, Natural and Society).   *s.h.*

Temple prostitution: Is what we very firmly call the temple duties women in many civilizations and in many nations have performed. The men were able to go to the church, temple or house of God and have sexual intercourse with the women. Within the bounds of Christianity there have also been sects in which sex and sexual urges were regarded as something divine.

Just after Jesus people expected the end of the world to come, and this was not exactly inspiring to sexual activity. But during the first century A.D. it was not uncommon to regard actual orgasm as the moment when one came closest to the divine. It is a beautiful and attractive thought, and one which Christianity ought to have kept up instead of thrusting sex life away from it.

Testicle, testis: Corresponds to the ovary · in a woman. The testicles are the man's sexual glands, where sperm cells are manufactured in the same way that egg cells are manufactured in the

woman's ovaries. (See Genital Organs, female; and Fertilization). The testicles hang in the bag called the scrotum · behind the penis · and are somewhat vulnerable and unprotected. Blows or pressure on the testicles can result in nausea and loss of consciousness.

Cannibals have regarded the testicles of the enemy as a great delicacy because it was felt that they represented power, strength, potency. (See also Castration).

The testicles are originally placed up inside the abdominal cavity in the place corresponding to where the ovaries are in the woman. Just before a boy is born the testicles begin to slide down towards the scrotum, and just before actual birth they slip out through the abdominal muscles and down into the scrotum. (See Cryptorchism).   *s.h.*

Testicles, descent of: See Genital Organs, male; and Cryptorchism.

Tickling: Tickling — being tickled — is something very much akin to feelings of sexual pleasure. Whether one cares to say that tickling is sexual, or that sexuality is a kind of tickling, is immaterial. (See Titillation, sexual).

Time: Is another of the prerequisites to a happy sex life (see also Housing Shortage). Time is not always something one has. It may be something one has to take.   *s.h.*

Titillatio clitoridis: Latin for titillation · or tickling of the clitoris ·. The story is told that the Empress of Austria,

Maria Theresa, failed to get the satisfaction out of her sex life she had hoped, and that her court medical adviser drew her attention, discreetly but judiciously, to the possibilities attainable through a spot of titillation in the right place.

The same story, curiously enough, has versed in respect of Queen Victoria and a few other famous royal ladies. In each case the advice is said to have done the trick.   *i.h.*

Titillation, sexual: We can differentiate between two forms of sexual excitement or titillation: mental and physical.

Mental titillation is apparently different in men and women. We know from many other things that upbringing · plays a tremendous part in forming our subsequent attitude to things. Thus we generally believe that men are more polygamous · by nature · — and that women are more monogamous ·. We have established this so firmly that women themselves believe it. But it is only very few peoples in the world who, like us, prefer monogamy. In societies where women have both permission and the opportunity to be polygamous they would by no means appear to be reticent about it.

So when the women in Kinsey's · report declare that the sight of naked men does not excite them this is possibly an acquired taste; or when they say that naughty jokes · and pornographic · pictures have no effect on them.

But even though these may be acquired tastes, we must respect them as facts: these things do not have the same effect on the majority of women as they do on most men. On the other hand sentimental love films and music would appear to have a certain sensual influence on many women.

Nor must it be forgotten that there are a number of women who react like men — and in the same way a number of men who are not excited by things which the majority of men find stimulating. (See also Fantasies, sexual).

A woman is not abnormal because she becomes sexually stimulated by other things — and in a different way from men.

Physical titillation in the man

It is the tip of the penis in particular — the glans, or head of the penis as it is also called — that is sexually sensitive.

It may be the foreskin · being pulled backwards and forwards over the tip of the penis or it may be rhythmical pressure on the bared head of the penis that has the greater effect.

The sensitivity of the bared tip of the penis may in some men — especially in a dry state — be just as great as that of an eyeball. (See also Genital Organs, male).

Physical titillation in the woman

It is a disappointment for many men to find that many women are nowhere as interested in having their breasts fondled as men are interested in fondling them.

274

Men are also disappointed when they discover that a woman feels nowhere near the same way as a man about the presence of the penis in the vagina. But it happens to be the way most women are. The most important place for titillation in the woman is the clitoris. (See Genital Organs, female). The clitoris is situated between the smaller vaginal lips just above the entrance to the vagina and the end of the urine pipe.

It is really like a small penis, or the tip of a small penis. It is shaped more or less the same as a man's penis and can be filled with blood in the same way. It is very sensitive to the touch or to rhythmical pressure. As muscle fibres connect it to the smaller vaginal lips as well as to the muscles around the entrance to the vagina and the rectum, even pressure or influence brought to bear elsewhere can be transplanted to the titillatory organ itself, i.e. the clitoris.

The clitoris can — just as has been mentioned in the case of the penis — become extraordinarily sensitive in certain situations. On the other hand it should be borne in mind that very few women experience sufficient titillation of the clitoris through ordinary sexual intercourse·.

Throughout the ages many men and women have believed that a woman was not normal unless she had an orgasm as a result of ordinary intercourse. A vaginal orgasm has also been spoken of as opposed to a clitoral orgasm. It is desirable to clear up some of these misunderstandings: it is rare for a woman to have an orgasm as a result of ordinary sexual intercourse.

There are women who have orgasms through influence brought to bear on the muscles round the rectum and the vagina, by the tickling of the smaller vaginal lips and by direct tickling of the clitoris itself. And when the orgasm takes place a great deal happens in all these places — and in many other muscles too. But the centre of the influence is still the clitoris.

In the same way as it is possible to put on the lights all over a room by pressing a single switch, the influence brought to bear on a clitoris can release an orgasm all over the body. Many men and a few women regard it as a sort of declaration of defeat if titillation has to be centred on the clitoris. This is entirely wrong.

The clitoris is the centre of the erotic feelings in a woman in precisely the same way as the tip of the penis is the centre in a man.

This cannot be repeated too often.

Oceans of misunderstandings have arisen due to the superstition about vaginal orgasms.

It would therefore be reasonable if the man (and the woman) were to concentrate to a greater extent on the tickling of the clitoris. Here it is important for a man to realize that a woman's sensitivity can change without even the woman herself being aware of it. Sometimes she will want to have her clitoris tickled violently — at other times very gently. At one time she may prefer a slow rhythm — at others a shade faster. Her wishes regarding intensity and rhythm can vary during the act itself and from one occasion to another.

A woman should be allowed to complain without a man's becoming offended and giving up. He should also be able to accept it if the woman wants to take over the actual tickling herself.

Here, mutual confidence and trust can work wonders. The woman's dissatisfaction, her wish to change rhythm, intensity etc., are liable to diminish with the years.

The clitoris can be tickled in many different ways. It can be done directly with a finger, by means of cunnilinctio · or by the fact of the man's pubic bone — and in some instances the root of the penis — pressing against it during intercourse.

Furthermore there may be several different forms of indirect tickling, for instance by contracting the muscles round the larger vaginal lips, round the entrance to the vagina, in the vagina itself and at other points on the floor of the pelvis.

What method one selects depends on many things. As long as a woman is not certain of having an orgasm the more direct form of titillation will probably produce the best results — and in this way a foundation is laid upon which subsequent developments can be made.

Many women complain of not feeling anything inside their vagina. They think they are abnormal or even frigid ·. Others have believed that it was immature to prefer clitoral titillation.

On the contrary, however, direct tickling of the clitoris may be regarded as a normal point of departure, at any rate during the many initial years of a relationship.

The two first-mentioned methods have furthermore the advantage that they render the woman independent of the man's erection and powers of endurance.

This can be a relief for both parties. In some cases (but it may take several years) the ability to titillate the clitoris indirectly may become greater and greater. It is extremely rare, however, that a woman ever obtains an orgasm when the penis is introduced, for instance, from behind — i.e. unless the clitoris is directly tickled by either the woman's own or the man's finger. Nor is there any question of the orgasm becoming 'deeper' with time, in the sense that it should take place further inside the vagina. What is possible however, is that in some cases titillation of the clitoris can take place at an increasingly greater distance from the clitoris, i.e. more and more indirectly as larger and more areas become involved. *i. & s.h.*

Tongue, tongue-kiss: The use of the tongue in various forms of kissing and petting sometimes shocks the entirely inexperienced, for it is a strong stimulant. It is known in countless peoples all over the world and at all times, so there is nothing perverse or abnormal about it whatsoever.

Touch: See Petting, Erogenous zones; Fantasies, sexual; and Titillation, sexual.

Transgestism: The Latin term applied when homosexual men adopt the mannerisms, behaviour, way of walking, etc. of women. It is by no means all homosexual men that are feminine.

merely be a question of revulsion at the thought of being a man. This revulsion can be so violent and such a fixation that the person in question may seek permission, through his doctor and from the police and the Ministry of Justice (who are responsible for such matters in Denmark) to wear female clothing. Permission of this nature is occasionally given in Denmark, but there are probably no more than a couple of dozen men availing themselves of it at moment.

False transvestism can occur in instances where the sex of a hermaphrodite · has been mistaken at birth. In such cases they may wish to "change sex", in other words change from men's clothes to women's clothes because they really *are* women.   *s.h.*

Trial Marriage: By this is meant a couple who live together without being married in order to see how they get on — the idea being to make sure of what they are doing before sealing the more cumbersome legal or ecclesiastical bonds.

The present-day housing shortage · in Denmark makes solutions of this sort difficult.   *i. & s.h.*

Trial years, trial nights: The idea that two lovers might really like to know whether they actually suit each other — before they marry — is by no means new. The old-fashioned form of engagement (and other customs in our cultural sphere in Europe) was designed with the object of investigating whether young people would be able to stick each other in the long run after all.

Transvestism: The Latin term applied to the desire to dress up in the clothes of the other sex, i.e. the desire on the part of men to dress up as women, and that of women as men.

As women in general are allowed to wear men's clothes as much as they like, i.e. wear shorts, shirt-blouses, long pants and so forth, we find the extreme instances (in particular) in a few men who for one reason or another like to dress up as women.

This desire can naturally coincide with homosexuality ·, but there may also

women they worship and admire and wish to marry — and those whom they want sexually and whom they can go to bed with. It is a very unfortunate differentiation to make.

'Trouser-week': An old Finnish custom according to which a betrothed couple were allowed to sleep together during the last week before their wedding providing they kept their pants on. We know of other little games of this sort. We have no need to look so far. Here in Denmark a betrothed couple are allowed to go camping together, but woe betide them if they fail to keep their pants on. "Why weren't you careful!" ask the irresponsible people who failed to tell them how to be careful. (See Birth control). *s.h.*

Truth: Something we learn to admire. We learn to be honest and speak the truth. The seeking for truth and the recognition of truth are of fundamental importance to all science, but the fact has not always been recognized. Many have opposed scientific searching after truth in a fanatical manner because they believed it was dangerous and harmful.

A few still do. We had probably better differentiate between the scientific truths and those we go around telling each other every day.

The everyday truths can be unpleasant things — aggressiveness · — things that hurt, unnecessary things. The person who tells the truth is not always the finest and most honourable of persons. (See also Lie, Consideration, Simulate). *i.h.*

Troubadour love: A very spiritual kind of love in which one dreams about one's beloved, writes poems to one's beloved, worships her and, though doubtless wanting her physically, does not wish the yearning to be fulfilled.

It is not so very uncommon to find men who differentiate sharply between the

U, V & W

(For technical reasons "V" and "W" have been mixed.)

Undefiled: See Virgin.

Understanding: A word that causes many peoples to see red. Nevertheless, a more understanding attitude towards many aspects of our sex lives is to be recommended. We have attempted to understand the background to tolerance . and prejudices ·. We understand the man whom vanity drives to force his wife to have an orgasm ·. We understand the woman who believes that her revulsion ·, modesty ·, and lack of inventiveness are naturally inherited and that every cheerful suggestion on the part of the man is perverse · and abnormal ·. But understanding is not the same thing as resignation.

When we hear about a big boy who bullies, teases and generally makes life miserable for smaller boys at his school it is understandable that we should feel he should be punished.

C. C. Kragh-Müller, the well-known Danish educationalist, once told of a boy like this who was sent up to his headmaster because it was felt he should be expelled. While the boy was sullenly waiting for his interview to begin he examined a wall calendar with interest. Before the headmaster could start the boy exclaimed: "Is it the fourteenth today? Then it must have been my birthday yesterday!"

It is by no means always so easy to trace cause and effect. Psychologists · have a reputation for being so confoundedly understanding. But after all this does not mean we have to tolerate everything with mild indulgence. On the other hand one metes out punishment to a boy in a different way when one knows him to be a child whose birthday nobody can be bothered to celebrate. *i. & s.h.*

Unfaithful, unfaithfulness: If a person who is bound to another person has sexual intercourse · with a third person without the other person's knowledge or against the other person's wish we call it being unfaithful and the act unfaithfulness. (See also Faithfulness and Conquer).

We take unfaithfulness very seriously. We attach importance to being the fathers of our own children and regard a woman as our property. The woman, for her part, is slightly more generous, for we have persuaded her to think that men are more polygamous · — and then of course we do not come home pregnant.

Unfaithfulness is not the tragedy people so often like to make of it. We do not own another person, but of course we can enter into a gentleman's agreement. We can agree that we will both do our best to resist possible temptations.

The reason why we are so much against unfaithfulness is partly because we are a little afraid the other person may find somebody who is nicer than we are. As a rule we have no need to be so afraid, for we have a certain start.   *s.h.*

Uniform: Uniform plays a part in sexual relations in various ways. There are men who think all nurses are wonderful irrespective of the rest of their appearance. Stewardess uniforms can also be attractive. In a corresponding fashion there are women who find policemen, airmen and soldiers attractive — also irrespective of the rest of their appearance. This admiration of course has its effect on the profession itself, for it results in many young people wanting to become nurses and pilots, etc., on account of the much-admired uniform.

Finally we know that permanently homosexual · men can also prefer certain uniforms. The sailor's uniform would appear to be particularly attractive.

Furthermore, we should not forget that black brassieres, black panties, pink roll-ons, silk stockings, tight sweaters — or whatever one happens to find particularly exciting — are also a kind of uniform.

There is no question of perversity until we become entirely dependent upon this sort of thing. The fact that it seems to be the one and only thing in life for a limited period is naturally nothing to be alarmed at, but if the infatuation disappears entirely with the 'uniform' — well, that is when it is approaching a certain one-sided development.   *s.h.*

Unnatural: See Natural and Normal.

Unsensitiveness: Here we are thinking particularly of sexual unsensitiveness (see Frigidity). We speak very seldom about a man's sexual unsensitiveness, but more often about a woman's. However, in both women and men, unsensitiveness is not physical, but there may be a question of a mental barrier. (See Inhibition).

We also find people without appetite (see Refusal to eat) but this does not mean that they can live without food. The appetite, the sexual desire ·, can be impeded, but it is fairly improbable that the need, the actual sexual urge, should not be present. It is possible to be hungry without having any particular appetite.
                    i. & s.h.

Upbringing: The way in which we are brought up as children (and here is meant all influences brought to bear upon us during our childhood and youth) are of extremely great importance to the development of our subsequent personality.

When we start discussing whether hereditary traits and factors are of greater importance than those acquired after birth we should bear in mind that it is a discussion without end. We still have no idea exactly how great a part the two factors play in relation to one another, but one thing remains quite definite: we cannot alter hereditary factors. We can, on the other hand, alter the manner of upbringing. Furthermore we know that upbringing can play a considerable part.

We know that precisely the same people born into different human societies and at different times in history develop entirely differently. We do not believe that a little Chinese child adopted by two Danish parents in Denmark will suddenly begin to talk Chinese. Parents can admittedly do little themselves, for we parents are ourselves products of the upbringing we have received — and thus of the society in which we live.

We cannot bring up ideal children — for ideal children would not be happy in this society. All we can hope to do is slightly alter what already exists. Unfortunately the conscious influences form the lesser side of upbringing — but we can try to increase our tolerance. (See Intolerance).

Direct sexual instruction has naturally been playing its part in shaping the attitude to sex in recent years, but as we can see elsewhere (see Governess and Dippoldismus) punishments can also produce fatal consequences. And the child who has never seen an affectionate caress pass between his parents will find it a little difficult to accept the romantic description of sweet passion given him by grown-ups.

— — —

A little boy at a kindergarten had observed how one kid brother or kid sister after the next kept arriving. So he went to the nice young kindergarten mistress with his problem: "Well, you see," she explained to him, "when two people love each other terribly much, well, the Daddy plants a little seed in the Mummy's tummy ..." "Aw, shut up!" he interrupted her. "My parents are always fighting!" —   *s.h.*

Urolagnia: A refined way of expressing the pleasurable sensations connected with piddling — also called urination. The same thing applies to excretion — "doing big business" — namely that it is a lovely feeling. Whether one chooses to call a lovely feeling sexual, or say that erotic sensations are lovely, is a matter of definition.

Vaginal Orgasm: See Orgasm, vaginal.

Vaginism: A contraction of the vaginal muscles rendering intercourse · difficult or impossible. It is often due to anxiety · and can be treated with calmness and patience and possibly certain forms of petting ·, which can be an excellent form of introduction to a more comprehensive sex life. In serious cases one should go and see a doctor ·. Relaxation · can also help by making the person more conscious of the muscles on the floor of the pelvis. But the anxiety involved should not merely be overcome, but preferably treated too.   *s.h.*

Vanity: An exaggerated interest in whether one is making an impression.

Of course this is such an easy explanation, but when is such interest exaggerated? (See also Looking-glass). We all want to be a success. This is entirely reasonable and quite normal ·. (See also Exhibitionism). But on one score in particular vanity can become harmful, namely when a man insists on a woman's having an orgasm ·; because a good lover should be considerate · and not an egoist ·. In other words, to do so in reality is a coarse demand that she should satisfy his vanity, and the result is often that she merely pretends to have an orgasm instead, which is harmful to their relationship.

This sort of camouflaged egoism · and misplaced consideration · is unfortunately very widespread. As often as not it is not the person who lies who does anything wrong, but the person who cannot bear hearing the truth.

Of course we must be allowed to be vain, to go out of our way to make an impression on others; it is a human right. But it does not entitle us to ask others to leap for joy when they feel no inclination to do so. On the other hand there is no point, either, in a girl merely saying to herself: "Well, now he's got to satisfy me!" and then perhaps heaping scorn on him afterwards when she fails to have an orgasm ·. (See Unfaithfulness and Happiness). *i.h.*

Warped: When we consider the jungle of restrictions, demands, prejudices ·, taboos ·, and hushings-up through which we have to force our way in the course of our upbringing it is astonishing how we manage to become human beings at all by the time we are half or fully grown and have to step out into the light. It is hardly surprising that a number of people remain more or less stunted, unable to develop themselves to the full. In other words, become warped.

Sometimes we speak about having a warped sex life, but a person's whole mentality can become warped. (See also Personality, Morals and Shoes).

Fortunately, however, there is a majority amongst each generation in whom discipline never entirely gets the better of nature ·. Is this not encouraging? *s.h.*

Wedding day: The day a marriage is entered into is called a wedding day and the date — the anniversary — is marked in some way every year to show that a man and his wife still love each other — even in cases where sometimes they do not. As a rule it is the husband who gives his wife flowers or some other little gift — but there is no reason why it should not be a mutual gesture. (See also Modesty).   *i.h.*

Wedding depression: A sense of emptiness, sadness and disappointment that quite often comes over one or both newlyweds just after their wedding. We also recognize something called birth depression, which is what many mothers experience just after they have given birth; examination depression, which comes after an important examination; Christmas depression, and so forth. It is often in connection with something big and important to which one has been looking forward for some time — with great expectations; something other people speak of as being delightful and wonderful — and on the great day they ask: "Now you're happy, eh?!?" — and so on.

So many expectations mount up during the period of waiting that reality seldom lives up to them. Figuratively, one could put it this way: that if, on the great day, one's feelings are only 99.9% of what one — and other people — expected, the disappointment will be so great there is risk of a depression — of the kind one could kick oneself for, but which is none the less insuperable for all that. (See also Love thermometer).

Christmas depression is another example. Even grown-ups have an unconscious idea that at Christmas all wishes — even the biggest ones — will come true. It is for this reason Christmas can sometimes be a bit of an anti-climax. Even the loveliest presents cannot be or become as big, mysterious and exciting as the wonderful, boundless hopes one had — the unopened parcels whose bows are still intact . . .

It sometimes helps a little if one is prepared — and dampens down one's expectations a little accordingly. But it is hard to avoid these depressions completely.

It also applies to a very great extent to one's first experience of sexual intercourse. (See also Cinema).   *s.h.*

Wedding night impotency: In our times there are fortunately not so very many couples for whom their wedding night is their first experience of sexual intercourse. This first experience is often a great disappointment for both parties.

As mentioned in many places in this book, a happy sex life is something one must learn to have together. It often takes, not months, but years. Even though the wedding night is not one's first sexual experience it may very well be a disappointment for all that, amongst other reasons because we attach extraordinary expectations to this night — not that there is any real reason for doing so.

Thus it is not uncommon for a man to fail to have an erection · out of sheer scaredness of not being able to do so. An understanding and confident attitude on the part of the woman — combined with patience — as a rule will be able to 'cure' this kind of impotency ·, and others too. See likewise Wedding Depression, Orgasm.   *s.h.*

Venereal Diseases: There are ailments which are infectious in that the ailment can spread from one person to the next. We can catch a cold from the person we happen to be sitting next to in a bus. We may catch measles from a person with whom we shake hands. Children can catch German measles by playing with each other. All the germs or viruses carrying these diseases are fairly robust. They can survive happily on a hand and can tolerate being cooled off, warmed up or even being dessicated.

But there are other diseases whose germs are more delicate, germs that can only tolerate certain temperatures or a particular degree of humidity. Such ailments can only be transferred from one person to the next when the persons concerned are in very intimate contact with one another.

Sexual relationships bring us into about as intimate contact with one another as is humanly possible. Therefore diseases whose germs are so delicate they can only be transferred in the course of relationships of such intimacy are called venereal diseases.

An increase in the numbers of Danish youth (traceable to the increased birth rate during the war years) has produced a few problems in Denmark, among them the fact that these young people have begun to have sex lives now, and there is naturally a proportionate rise in venereal diseases amongst them too.

Elsewhere in this book we have mentioned crab-lice · and scabies . These might also in a way be called venereal afflictions seeing that they are most frequently transferred in the course of intimate relationships. But when we speak of venereal diseases we think principally of two: 1) *gonorrhea*, and 2) *syphilis*. Gonorrhea has been known in Europe since ancient times and is the most widely spread venereal disease. It can be dangerous if not treated and if allowed to develop into inflammations. As a rule it is quite easy to treat.

Syphilis made its first appearance in Europe in about 1500 in the form of a pest, killing almost a third of the population. Such was the power of superstition in those days that the disease · was believed to be punishment for sins committed (see Epicureans). Henry VIII was one of the victims.

As a point of interest can be mentioned that during the Middle Ages a lively form of sex life was practised in the public bathing establishments — which was a thorn in the Church's eye. When syphilis came to Europe at about the time of the discovery of America, it was via the bathing establishments in particular that it spread. The Church thereupon started a violent campaign to have the bath-houses closed, and, apart from distant countries such as Finland, succeeded in getting people to stop washing themselves completely. It caused the perfume, wig and snuff industries to flourish.

There are between 5,000 and 10,000 cases of gonorrhea in Denmark a year, but only between 100 and 500 of syphilis.

Gonorrhea : If one has had sexual intercourse and caught gonorrhea, the first symptoms may appear two days later, a few days later or not until a week or so later. The first sign — symptom — of the disease is usually an itch and later a searing pain in the urine pipe (see Genital organs) especially when pee'ing.

It means the gonococci — gonorrhea germs — have attacked the mucous membrane in the urine pipe. The inflammation thus caused may result in yellowish or greyish matter coming out of the urine pipe. The symptoms are fairly clear in men, but in women they may sometimes be a little difficult to distinguish from other minor troubles. But in the event of the slightest doubt it is better to go and see a doctor straight away before the disease spreads to the rest of the genital organs.

— — —

You can go to your doctor ', who may examine you himself (see Gynaecological Examination) or may send you to a specialist. You can also go to one of the public venereal disease clinics. The addresses of these clinics and the times at which they are open can be found on the poster pillars erected in various parts of Copenhagen. You can also look up under *Læge* (doctors) in the red telephone directory and find a specialist in skin diseases or venereal diseases. It is better to visit a doctor once too often and hear there is nothing the matter with you than go to one too late and hear him say you should have come a long time ago.

Syphilis : The symptoms do not appear so soon after infection — the first signs appear from between a week or so to a month after intercourse.

As a rule a sore appears on the place where the syphilis bacilli have entered the skin, i.e. as a rule on the sexual organs.

The sore is of a rather special type as it feels hard but not painful. In the case of a man it is usually on the penis, while in women it comes inside either the smaller or the larger vaginal lips (see Genital Organs, female) and therefore a little more difficult to detect.

Here again of course, it is better to go and see a doctor once too often rather than too late. (See above under *Gonorrhea* concerning doctors, clinics and specialists).

The doctor takes a sample of the mucous membrane in the urine pipe with the help of a piece of cotton wool on a stick, or from the actual sore, and has it examined under a microscope. It can be a little unpleasant but does not hurt very much. A slightly older syphilis infection can also be detected by means of a blood test (Wassermann).

In the olden days it was difficult, but nowadays cure is comparatively easy and quick. Both gonorrhea and syphilis can be cured by injections in the muscles (e.g. in the buttock). Gonorrhea can often be cured after merely a few treatments, but syphilis takes a little longer. In both cases the sooner one goes to see a doctor, the faster the cure can be effected. And one can be completely cured.

A man can guard against catching venereal diseases — at least to a certain extent. (See Prevention). A woman cannot. Incidentally, it is possible to catch venereal diseases without having had sexual intercourse — and it is also possible to catch a venereal disease on other parts of the body, i.e. not only on the sexual organs; but it is fairly rare.

According to Danish law, anybody who has reason to believe he or she has been infected with a venereal disease *must* go and see a doctor about it.

The trouble is that there are ignorant people who do not, and people who are afraid, or shy ·.

If you are shy of going to your own doctor, go to any other doctor at all. He (or she) can then either treat you himself or send you to the proper place for treatment. *s.h.*

Wet dreams: See Emissions, nocturnal.

Whore, to whore, whorehouse: If a married person had sexual intercourse with a person other than his or her marital partner, the practice was known in old Danish legal terminology as *whoring*.

In the Old Testament it had a more specific meaning, namely that if a man had sexual intercourse with another man's wife it constituted an infringement of the other man's proprietary rights, for he *owned* his wife. Thus the commandment: "Thou shalt not covet thy neighbour's wife." But married men were welcome to go to bed with all the unmarried girls they liked and who were willing, including their neighbour's daughter.

Whorehouse is an old term for brothel ·. Nowadays to go whoring means more or less the same as having indiscriminate sexual intercourse and is usually used in a condemnatory sense. *s.h.*

Wife exchange: The practice of offering one's guest one's wife as a bedfellow is known amongst many peoples, including the Eskimoes. It sounds so strange and festive in our ears, but originated in an extremely practical and sober outlook on life.

Women were not a man's property in the same way and her virtue was not such a great problem. Furthermore it was reckoned that the guest would have brought his sexual urges along with him on his long journey. One naturally hoped that he and his wife would be just as understanding the next time one happened to pay *them* a visit. *s.h.*

Virgin: The term applies to a woman who has never had a penis · up inside her vagina. It has also merely meant unmarried — in other words corresponding to Miss. (See also Maidenhead). The interest in virgins and virginity has varied with the centuries. It is when a woman is owned by her husband like a cow or a sheep that we can observe interest in virginity flourishing. As far as is known approximately 5% of Danish women are virgins on their wedding day. In present-day USA there is a variety of virgin-worship that is somewhat grotesque, the technical virgin, or *demi-vierge*, who has tried all the forms of sexual fun with the sole exception of the one that deflowers her hymen. *i.h.*

Virginity: See Maidenhead.

Witch Trials: An incredible number of witch trials were carried out by the Church (The Inquisition) in Europe during the Middle Ages. They were an offshoot of the strict suppression of sex life common at the time.

These trials, which were nearly always accompanied by refined forms of torture, moreover had a particular purpose, namely that of forcing the accused to give a *fully detailed* account of sexual excesses, perversities · and other activities invented by the ecclesiastical prosecutors. The imagination displayed was so incredible that it actually reveals more about what occupied the minds of the ecclesiastical authorities than what the victims had done in reality. (See also Personality).

The poor creatures were tortured until they confessed the most dreadful things — all of which were suggested by the judges at the trial in question. Both men and women were accused, their ages ranging between five and eighty-five. Some 900 people were burnt to death at the stake in Bamberg (Bavaria) alone in the course of twenty-four years. In one particular bishopric at least 30,000 witches were burnt over a period of 150 years. A Spanish fanatic succeeded in sending over 100,000 persons to their death as witches. During the course of 200 years the population of Spain was reduced from 20 million to 6 million as a result of witch trials. (See Incubus).

Witch trials took place from approximately 1200 to 1800.   *s.h.*

Words, naughty: As mentioned in the articles on Taboo and Superstition, it is not only ignorant natives who believe in the supernatural. We also have a large number of spheres in which we believe in magic.

We believe in the magic of *words*. There exists a long list of words we are afraid of. For that reason they are a little exciting, but none the less forbidden.

They are words most people know but pretend they have never heard. Even nice respectable old ladies must have heard them somewhere or other and had them explained. They are what we call naughty words. Some people even believe that such words are ugly in themselves. Some believe that even a Chinese would be able to hear that the Danish words *gaa afsides* (meaning to 'step aside', i.e. 'be excused a moment') sound nicer than *tisse* (meaning to piddle).

We have placed our emotions in these words (see Projection). But whether "namow" or "nam" mean something pompous or horribly vulgar in Bandar is more than you or I can hear.

A little girl once said to her Granny: "Look, there's some dog-shit!" Granny flew up: "Sssh! You mustn't say such things!" There was a pause, and then the little girl asked, cautiously: "May one say 'Hey, diddle-diddle!'?"

Perhaps, by printing a selection of the known and lesser known naughty words we might be able to deprive them of some of their magical powers. But we shall print them upside down, so that only those who want to need read them.

John Thomas, cock, prick, prong, wank, rootle, do, turd, fart, cunt, sod, bugger, fuck, screw, lay, shit, knob, piss, squeeze the lizard, toss off, arsehole, etc., etc.

You will doubtless admit — if you have read them — that these words look pretty dreadful in print — but only the words you knew beforehand; *they* seem shocking, even though some of them are possibly words we use in everyday life.

We have a taboo against seeing these words in print despite the fact that they are, after all, merely chance combinations of letters. The words are not naughty in themselves, but we have learnt that they are if we use them. We can establish that it is not the naughty words in themselves, but the feelings they arouse in us, that are of importance.

'Latrine' is more respectable than 'lat' or 'the lats', and both are better than 'bog' or 'bogs'. But latrine — from the fine old Latin word *latrina* (for *lavatrina*, in turn from *lavare*, to wash) now has a crudely institutional (army, prison, school, outdoor privy) ring to it and is not fine enough, and even the nicer 'lavatory' has had to be polished up and sophisticated into 'WC' and even 'toilet', because, so it is asserted, the old words have been worn into crudity through protracted use. If the theory of wear on words is correct it is probably high time we substituted old words like 'eat' and 'drink' and 'sleep' with the brand-new, never-before-used *crink, crongle* and *crunge*.   *i. & s.h.*

Voyeur: See Peeping Tom.

Y & Z

Yohimbin: Is the extract obtained from the bark of an African tree. It has been used a great deal as an erotic stimulant. Just as in the case of a number of other aphrodisiacs, the effect of yohimbin is extremely dubious. Everything that makes a person healthier and stronger will presumably strengthen the sexual interests as well, but it is unlikely that special powders or pills have any effect. Even that of hormones is problematical.

Zeal: Defined in the dictionary as "hearty and persistent endeavour".
Our sexual abilities develop sluggishly. Things alternate between encouragement and defeat, between progress, standstills and reversals. And nobody ever achieves absolute perfection — but then we would probably be as well not to hope for it.
The sign of a good marital relationship is that it can always get better — and it goes on getting better.   *i. & s.h.*